The Essential Shankly

The Essential Shankly

Revealing the Kop Legend
Who Launched a Thousand Quips

John Keith

WITH A TRIBUTE FROM SIR TOM FINNEY

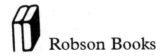

Robson Books

First published in Great Britain in 2001 by
Robson Books, 10 Blenheim Court,
Brewery Road, London N7 9NY

A member of the Chrysalis Group plc

British Library Cataloguing in Publication Data
A catalogue record for this title is available from the
British Library.

ISBN 1 86105 465 3

Typeset in Plantin by FiSH Books, London WC1.
Printed and bound in Great Britain by
Creative Print & Design (Wales), Ebbw Vale

Contents

*Dedicated to Nessie Shankly, a wonderful lady,
who said of her husband...*

'When I married Bill I married a man to whom football was
a fierce passion. When he came to Liverpool in December
1959 I knew it was a big challenge to him and he threw
himself into the job determined that the club would be
successful. I think everyone will agree he succeeded in that.

In Liverpool, with its traditional love for football, Bill
found kindred spirits who shared his enthusiasm for the
game.

I tried never to bother him when he came home with some
football topic occupying his mind. If he didn't want to talk
about it I didn't interfere. But if and when he brought the
subject up I hope I gave him a little bit of sound advice, at
least now and then.

I went to Wembley for all three FA Cup Finals when Bill
was manager and the first time, in 1965, was unforgettable.
Liverpool had never won the Cup before and the emotion
was incredible. When we travelled home on the Sunday and
got off the train at Lime Street the sight of the massive crowd
that greeted us took my breath away, it was too much...I
was in tears.

Whenever Liverpool lost a game – and that doesn't happen
very often – Bill would come home, go into the kitchen and
clean the oven again and again until it was spotless. It was one
of his ways of working out his disappointment. Another way
was mowing the lawn.

People have said to me that we must have had a clean oven.
But because Liverpool didn't lose many matches I suppose
you could say it was in need of a clean more often than not!'

Preface

Bill Shankly is the most unforgettable character football has ever known. There have been more successful managers. They include his own Liverpool successor Bob Paisley, who lifted the European Cup three times among an amazing haul of trophies, and Sir Alex Ferguson, who has amassed a fantastic collection of silverware at Manchester United and Aberdeen. But it was another managerial luminary, Brian Clough, who once observed: 'Greatness is measured in passion as well as prizes.' And there has never been anyone quite like Shankly.

He was outrageous, inspirational, funny, ironic, obsessed, driven...the extrovert of extroverts. Yet he possessed remarkable human warmth and unselfishness.

This book sets out to present the many qualities of Shankly. A torrent of words has been written about him since his death in 1981, much of it by people who never knew him or maybe never even met him.

I was one of a small batch of journalists who were close to him and I was privileged to be asked by Shankly to produce the match programme for his Anfield testimonial game in 1975.

To compile this book I have delved into my own written and recorded conversations with Shankly and other archive material to present his thoughts and opinions on a host of topics, his reflections on his career as a player and manager, and the ultimate collection of the comic Shankly stories.

I hope it offers a definitive insight into Bill Shankly, the manager, the man, the legend.

John Keith

A Tribute from
Sir Tom Finney

'Bill was the most unforgettable character I've ever met in football, a unique man. He will always be a god in the eyes of Liverpool supporters and rightly so for what he achieved at the club. His legend will live on and on into the new millennium.'

So says Sir Tom Finney, the player whose skills Bill Shankly drooled over and hailed as the greatest he had ever seen. This is role reversal at its most dramatic for it was always Shankly bombarding the media and any publicity outlet at his disposal with his views on Tom Finney, the majestic forward who was his Deepdale colleague in the latter phase of Bill's playing career.

Many share Scotland international Shankly's passionately held conviction that Finney was the greatest player of them all, even surpassing his fellow knight and England winger Sir Stanley Matthews because of his sheer versatility and scoring output.

But Sir Tom, who could have been forgiven for blushing when Shankly so frequently and so fervently hailed his talents, needed no coaxing to delve into the memories of a lifetime to salute and offer a special insight into the man who was appointed Liverpool manager in December 1959.

Sir Tom takes us back a further 22 years, to when he first

met Bill Shankly, and reveals that even then there were clear signs that within his resolute, stocky frame was the stuff of managerial greatness:

> I was an apprentice plumber and joined Preston as a 15-year-old in 1937. Bill was then in his twenties and an established player at the club. He was a good one, too and went on to play for Scotland soon after I joined the club.
>
> Like so many professional players of that era the war took six years out of Bill's career when he was at his peak, with the Football League programme being suspended from 1939 until 1946. But he was a fine wing half, as we called them in those days. As a young boy I looked on him as one of the stalwarts of Preston.
>
> He just lived for the game. He was a fitness fanatic. He really looked after himself and didn't have a lot of time for players who didn't keep themselves in absolutely prime condition.
>
> These were traits he was to take into management. He had no time for anybody drinking or smoking or anything like that. He just lived for football. His conversation was nothing but football. He talked of nothing else. It wasn't that he couldn't. He just didn't want to!
>
> He would come to watch the club's junior teams play and at the end he would always come and have a word and say you'd had a good game. Bill liked offering encouragement to up and coming players.
>
> Even after we'd finished training in the morning Bill would always be keen to do an extra session in the afternoon. He'd look for people to come back with him and I used to do the afternoon stints which might be practising ball control or bouts of head tennis. He was so keen it was unbelievable.
>
> He was certainly a big influence on my career. Not only could he win the ball but he was a good passer. He

could distribute it when he'd won it. It was a great help to someone like me to have a player like Bill keeping the supply lines going. All wingers need service and Bill provided it, all right.

I first played in front of Bill in the wartime competitions. That included a game at Wembley, when I was just 19, in the Wartime Cup Final against Arsenal, which we drew 1–1 before winning the replay 2–1 at Ewood Park.

Bill was then serving in the RAF and, just like he'd done after junior games, he kept encouraging me before and during matches. His enthusiasm knew no bounds. It was unquenchable. He was such a great character in the dressing room. He relaxed everybody and it was just tremendous fun being with him. He made us laugh. He would even tell a few tall stories to put a smile on our faces. There was never any question of Bill being bothered or worried about who he was going to be playing against. That was the last thing on his mind.

It made a lasting impression on me that while he would discuss the strengths and weaknesses of the opposition it never bothered him in the slightest going out on the field, even if he had to face people like Raich Carter or Peter Doherty, two of the finest inside forwards of their era. As far as Bill was concerned he was every bit as good as the other fellow.

He never stopped talking during games and, regardless of the score, with Bill you never lost a game until the 90 minutes were up. He was never beaten until the final whistle went.

These were all qualities he took with him into management, the ability to motivate his players and get the best out of them. After the war I always felt he would stay in the game as a coach because coaching was becoming a big thing at the time. In fact, Preston were one of the pioneers in this field, ahead of most others. I know Bill learned a lot about training and tactics from the staff at the club, going right back to the days when he first arrived at Deepdale in 1933.

We were one of the first to start five- and six-a-side games in training and that's something Bill took with him right through his managerial career.

At Preston we were also alive to short corners and practised throw-ins and free kicks. Things like that were foreign to English football at the time. Generally, a throw-in was a throw-in. But we tried to work something from them with the aim of giving us maximum benefit. We were very much a thinking club and Bill took it all on board.

But after hanging up his boots in 1949 Bill went the hard way. He went straight into management with Carlisle followed by periods in charge at two other Third Division clubs, Grimsby and Workington.

I think, though, that it was a great learning process for him. They were stepping stones and gave him invaluable experience. His next job was as assistant to his former Preston team-mate and fellow Scot, Andy Beattie, at Huddersfield, who were then in the old Second Division.

Bill eventually succeeded Andy as manager there and developed players such as Denis Law and Ray Wilson before Liverpool came in for him to be their manager.

He was tailor made for them, really. Liverpool were a sleeping giant waiting for someone to wake them up. They drew big crowds but just couldn't get out of the old Second Division.

Bill's judgement was spot on and the success he had was incredible. Not only did he sign some tremendous players, such as Ian St John, Ron Yeats, Gordon Milne and Peter Thompson, but when he arrived he kept the entire backroom staff, which just doesn't happen nowadays.

People like Bob Paisley and Joe Fagan were at Anfield

when Bill arrived but he'd weighed up what great assets these men were. Even though he hadn't worked with them previously he kept them together like a family, which became a great strength of the club.

It was the hallmark of Liverpool's success under Bill and the continuation of it after he'd left, with Bob Paisley going on to win a fantastic number of trophies, more than any other manager.

Sir Tom, nicknamed 'The Preston Plumber', hung up his boots in 1960 after scoring 187 goals in 433 League appearances for his hometown club and 30 in 76 England outings. His retirement came at the end of Shankly's first half season in charge at Anfield and Sir Tom added:

After I'd finished I joined the *News of the World* and was sent to Liverpool games quite frequently. I used to go and have a chat with Bill before the match and although he was always pleased to see you he'd never discuss anything to do with Liverpool.

I suppose it was because I was with a newspaper . But that was a quality he always had. He told people only what he felt they should know or what he wanted them to know. He was very clever at things like that.

In common with millions of others, Sir Tom, then running his plumbing business, remembers the day in July 1974 that Bill Shankly stunned the nation and beyond by announcing his resignation as Liverpool manager:

It was an absolute bombshell. People were ringing me up and asking had I heard the news. They were gabsmacked. I got calls from business contacts in Liverpool who were terribly upset. They were flabbergasted. As indeed I was. You just couldn't believe it because Bill just lived for the game.

After the initial shock my first reaction was: What on earth is Bill going to do now? There is still a mystery over why he really did leave.

The nation was stunned for a second time in September 1981 when Bill Shankly died. An unforgetable man, to those privileged to have known him, had passed on. Sir Tom Finney, a legend himself, is certain of Bill's enduring place in history:

I used to joke with Bill that because of all the nice things he used to say about me he should have been my agent! He was a unique person. I've never met anyone like him and I've absolutely no doubt that the memories of Bill Shankly will never die.

1

The Road To a
Red Revolution

The most significant decision in the entire colourful and colossal history of Liverpool Football Club was made in the dying weeks of the 1950s. That was when the directors appointed Bill Shankly as their new manager, thereby placing Anfield in the path of a tornado, the power of which neither they nor the public had bargained for.

Shankly's transformation of Liverpool, from a club marooned in mediocrity into a major power, is globally recognised. But there was much more to the man than his innate football knowledge, germinated at Preston North End in the 1930s and cultivated playing for Scotland and during management spells at Carlisle, Grimsby, Workington and Huddersfield.

There was more to him, also, than a fiery passion honed in his spartan Ayrshire home village of Glenbuck where he would sell jam jars to raise a few pence and where the spirit of camaraderie, which he would later imbue into Liverpool, was instilled into him.

The quality that separated Bill Shankly from almost every other manager was his humour. In another life he might have been a comedian, or even an actor, because I believe that deep inside he had the stirrings of a frustrated thespian.

Every day was an act for Bill. Not in a false way but in the sense that he always had an audience and he always gave something of himself. Front stage was where he liked to be and the fact that it was a football stage did not detract from his qualities of showmanship. He had a sense of comic timing that would have done credit to Bob Hope or Jack Benny. And he had a burning zeal and drive that could have moved mountains.

When he crossed the Pennines from Huddersfield to take charge of Liverpool in December 1959 he was laying the first brick in building a new empire – a football dynasty that was to enjoy success at home and abroad unprecedented in English football.

Some have said that the union between Shankly and Liverpool was pre-ordained by the gods. Certainly it was a marriage that was to propel a club struggling to escape from the old Second Division, and with a ground that had seen better days, onto the glittering peaks of our national game and to acquire the resources to transform Anfield into the superb, modern stadium it now is.

Above all, Shankly was a leader, a man of vision. His qualities moved Kevin Keegan, one of Shankly's most inspired signings, to declare:

> He was a tremendous motivator. . . he would have made a great politician. He would have made a great leader in wartime. He was like a Winston Churchill figure for me. If he'd said something people would have got up and followed him.

Given the scale of Liverpool's massive success in domestic and European football it is jolting to reflect that when Shankly arived at Anfield the club had never won the FA Cup.

Their last trophy had come in 1947 when they won the League title in the first official season after the war, when the team included Shankly's fellow-Scot, Billy Liddell, and a certain Bob Paisley, the man who was to succeed Shankly so brilliantly.

But the first task for Shankly after taking over the reins was to restore Liverpool to the top flight. They had been languishing in the Second Division since relegation in 1954.

Like Paisley and Sir Matt Busby, the inspiration of Manchester United, Shankly's roots were in a mining community. He was born in the coal-mining village of Glenbuck in Ayrshire and when William Shankly entered the world on 2 September 1913 its population had waned to less than one thousand.

Bill was one of 10 children, with four brothers and five sisters, and he was the second youngest child. His mother, Barbara, was a popular woman in the close-knit, religious community, and his father, John, became a well-respected tailor after working for some time as a postman.

Life was not a bed of roses but it was certainly character-forming for Shankly who vividly recalled his childhood:

> I don't think I was in a bath until I was 15 years old. I used to use a tub to wash myself But out of poverty with a lot of people living in the same house, you get humour.
>
> I was one of 10 children. That was the fashion then. You had families of 14. I was one of five boys and five girls. We lived with my mother and father in a small house and our village of Glenbuck possibly resembled Outer Mongolia. You'd have a hard job finding it even though it's only about 10 miles off the A74 to Glasgow.
>
> It was a very difficult upbringing. My mother and father must have been marvellous people to pull us through. It was cold in the winter and the snow lay for four months at a time. I don't know how they fed us and kept us going, to tell you the truth.
>
> Possibly we stole more turnips than anyone else! We used to boil them and eat them with salt and pepper on them. Everywhere we went we had to walk. We had to walk four miles to the cinema and four miles back. So it was running and walking, running and walking all the time.

So I think our childhood was unbelievable because my parents were so successful looking after us despite all the problems.

Clearly football was in the Shankly blood. His mother's brothers were both in the game. Robert played for Rangers and Portsmouth, where he became chairman, while William played for Preston and Carlisle, where he became a director.

Those two clubs were to loom large in Bill's career...and, like him, all his four brothers went into professional football. Alec with Ayr United and Clyde; James with Portsmouth, Carlisle United, Southend United and Barrow; John with Portsmouth, Blackpool and Alloa; and Bob with Alloa and Falkirk, whom he later managed, along with Dundee and Hibernian, before becoming general manager of Stirling Albion.

But, contrary to popular myth, Bill did not play for the exotically named 'Glenbuck Cherrypickers' who played in the Ayrshire League. They did offer him a trial at the age of 16, decided he was too young and the club then folded within a year. So the young Shankly played his junior football for Cronberry, about 12 miles from Glenbuck.

He was 17 when a local scout, Peter Carruthers, recommended him to Carlisle United. He went to Brunton Park for a month's trial. Despite being on the wrong end of a 6–0 score-line against Middlesbrough Reserves in his first game, Carlisle saw enough to sign him on. He became a full professional in July 1932 and made his debut the following December against Rochdale.

It meant that Shankly had achieved his first ambition:

In Scotland your main aim, first and foremost, is to play football as a professional. And the second is to play for Scotland. If you don't have that ambition then there's nothing for you.

I was about seventeen and a half when I went to play for

Cronberry, a junior team which was semi-professional. One of the things which was very good and lucky for me was that I knew my position. Sometimes boys don't know and people will look at a youngster and wonder whether he's a defender, a midfield player or a forward.

But I knew right away where I wanted to play when I went for a trial with the junior club. 'I want to play right half, I'm number four,' I told them. That's what you'd call now a midfield player, defending and attacking and maybe getting an odd goal or two. But 70 per cent defence.

From that day on with Cronberry I never looked back. I was so lucky to find my own position.

I signed for Carlisle as an 18-year-old in July 1932 and I was very fortunate that the trainer there was a man called Tommy Curry, who had played for Newcastle United. He later became trainer at Manchester United and perished in the Munich disaster.

He lived near Carlisle's ground, as I did. I was staying in digs close to Brunton Park. Tommy was one of the greatest men in my life. He gave me a beginning in English football. He knew the game.

On my first Sunday at Carlisle I played in a match and had cramp all night because I hadn't done the strenuous training. Next morning I went to the ground for a bath and all the players, including a lot of old stagers, were there.

They brought out the cards and started playing brag. Where I came from the two games you played were brag and pontoon. So I joined in with the players and lost all the money I had.

So there I was, on my first weekend in Carlisle, without a penny! Skinned! But Tommy Curry gave me a couple of bob and looked after me. And from then on, every Thursday night he'd take me and few others to his house for a meal and a game of cards.

So Tommy was one of the key men in my early career. It's the beginning that counts. If you get on the right road you've a chance. If you get on the wrong road there's nothing for you.

There was no doubt that Shankly was in football's fast lane. He made just 16 League appearances for Carlisle in Division Three North before being transferred by the Cumbrian club to Preston North End for a £500 fee in July 1933, just a year after his arrival from Scotland.

Preston, one of the Football League's founder members and the first ever English champions, when they achieved the League and FA Cup double in 1888–89 without losing a game, were in the old Second Division when they signed Shankly. But in his first season at Deepdale he helped them to win promotion, playing in 24 of their 42 games as they finished second to Grimsby. Shankly quickly won a glowing reputation for his brilliant wing half play in Preston's number four shirt, and soon his country would beckon.

Shankly's move south into English football coincided with the era of some illustrious attacking players, including the goalscoring legend of Everton, William Ralph Dean.

When I came to England the great Dixie Dean was the star at Everton. At the end of my one season at Carlisle he led Everton to Wembley and helped them win the FA Cup by beating Manchester City.

Dean was an amazing player and Everton were a famous club. I watched him play and saw some of the fantastic goals he scored. Then, after I moved to Preston, I played against him.

There were a lot of great players then. As well as Dixie there was Hughie Gallacher, and Alex James, who were just finishing when I was starting. But just to be on the same field as those three was really something.

Many years later I sat next to Dixie at a lunch on the

day he died. The function was at a Liverpool hotel on the day of a Mersey derby at Goodison in 1980 and I was asked to stand and pay tribute to Bill.

I said: 'He belongs in the company of the supremely great, like Beethoven, Rembrandt and Shakespeare.' Little did I know that he would die at the game a few hours later. I'm glad he heard me say it.

Joining Preston provided Shankly with the foundation for his football creed, one he would shape nd hone all the way to Liverpool.

Shankly was indeed thankful that fate had led him to the Lancashire club despite his initial reluctance to leave Carlisle. He had been earning four pounds ten shillings a week at Carlisle at a time when the maximum wage in English football was eight pounds.

Preston offered him only 10 shillings a week more than he was receiving at Brunton Park and, despite a 10 per cent slice of the £500 transfer and a £10 signing-on fee, Shankly dithered about leaving Carlisle.

He was persuaded to move by his brother Alec who pointed out that it was the opportunity Preston offered rather than the money that was the crucial factor in his decision.

'It was wonderful advice,' Shankly recalled.

Just as I was lucky at Carlisle to have Tommy Curry as trainer so I was fortunate to go to Preston where I learned so much. They were years ahead of their time.

They used to have tactical talks even then and the coaching and training was brlliant. They had two Tynesiders there called Bill Scott and Jim Metcalfe who had a training system that would be modern now.

It was all tabulated in my mind and I picked up so much from the training there. Preston would take something out of each game and use it as a movement in the training session. So everything we did was real. They talked sense.

The second of Shankly's great ambitions was realised on 9 April 1938 when his country made their first call on his wing half talents. He collected his first Scotland cap in a 1–0 win over England at Wembley, watched by a crowd of 93,267.

He was one of four Preston players in the team that achieved Scotland's first ever Wembley clean sheet against the old enemy, thanks largely to goalkeeper Dave Cumming who, ironically, won his only peacetime cap.

It was the sweetest of debuts for Shankly, a player raised to idolise Rabbie Burns, Robert Bruce and William Wallace – and with a tartan pride to match.

Shankly recalled his feelings at wearing the Scotland jersey:

> *It's fantastic. You look at your dark blue shirt, the wee lion looks up at you and says* 'Get out after those English bastards!' *No, we'd better say* 'Let's get stuck in!'

He played 12 times for his country, winning five official caps and making a further seven appearances in wartime and victory internationals. But he had no doubt about his worst Scotland experience. It came in a rain-lashed game against England at Hampden Park on 15 April 1939. This is how Shankly remembered it:

> Tommy Lawton headed in from a Stan Matthews centre a few minutes from the end to give England a 2–1 win. It was their first victory in Scotland since 1927. It was pelting down and as the ball went in like a bullet I could hear the 'swish', then the ripple of water coming off the net. 'Pick that one out,' Lawton shouted. And I felt as if I'd been hit in the stomach by a bag of cement. It was a terrible feeling.

Three weeks after Shankly's Scotland debut he was appearing before another 93,000-plus Wembley crowd to pick up an FA Cup winners medal in Preston's 1–0 win over Huddersfield Town, a club he would later manage.

The Cup was won thanks to a dramatic penalty just 30 seconds from the end of extra time. George Mutch was adjudged to have been brought down inside the area by Huddersfield captain and centre half Alf Young.

Photographic evidence challenged referee A.J. Jewell's decision and showed that Young's tackle had taken place just outside the box. Mutch was dazed by Young's tackle and, if he had not recovered sufficiently, Shankly would have taken on the spot kick responsibility – despite once missing a penalty at Anfield – and at the Kop end to boot! Eight of his 13 League goals for Preston came from penalties and he managed to score against Liverpool at Anfield in a 2–2 draw on 2 February 1938.

But Mutch, still dazed that day at Wembley, stepped up to take the penalty and his shot crossed the line off the underside of the bar. The Cup was bound for Lancashire and Bill Shankly proudly collected his winner's medal from King George the Sixth.

The penalty award was cruel on Young, who had given a superb display in the Huddersfield defence, and he disputed the penalty long after he hung up his boots. But for Shankly and Preston victory was a welcome reversal of fortunes after their 3–1 defeat by Sunderland in the previous year's final. Mutch recalled:

> After going down to Young's tackle in the penalty area, when I came round I was concious that my body was one mass of aches. I was groggy.
>
> I didn't even understand that a penalty had been awarded. They handed me the ball. I placed it automatically, thinking that it was funny they'd given it to me, an injured man.
>
> As I took my run-up I wondered what I was doing and why. I don't remember aiming at the goal.

But Mutch's historic kick became the first penalty to decide a Wembley final following the first period of extra time played at the stadium. It was Preston's first FA Cup triumph since that great double by their team of 'Invincibles' almost half a century earlier.

Shankly retained a special place in his affections for the FA Cup, enthusing:

> The greatest thrill and elation is when the final whistle blows at Wembley and you've won the Cup. You thank God – that's the first thing you do! I played in three Cup finals – 1937, 1938 and 1941. There was only one good player on the field. That was me!

But, removing his tongue from his cheek, Shankly added:

> There's nothing in the world to compare with walking out of that Wembley tunnel just before kick-off. It's what you've been waiting for . . . the game you've been looking forward to, the crowd greeting you, the pomp, and the king or the queen shaking hands with you.
>
> As a manager you'd wear your best suit but it really doesn't make any difference what you wear. If you win the Cup you can wear the oldest thing you've got and somebody will say you look well dressed!
>
> Before the war I met the King twice at Wembley, in 1937 and 1938. That was a great thing . . . it was awesome.

A year before Shankly's international call-up and those two stirring Wembley victories over England and Huddersfield respectively, a youngster signed for Preston who was to become Shankly's benchmark of excellence. His name was Tom Finney, who vies with Stanley Matthews as the greatest winger England ever produced. Matthews was knighted in 1965 but Finney's long overdue knighthood did not come until the 1998 New Year Honours List . . . a richly earned reward that would have delighted Shankly.

Finney joined his home town club as a 15-year-old shortly after leaving school in 1937 and turned professional in 1940. In Shankly's eyes there was no argument about Finney's talents. The player who began his working life as an apprentice plumber was rated by Shankly as 'the finest ever', a claim enhanced by Finney's ability to perform brilliantly in almost any position. Said Shankly:

Stan Matthews was an individualist who was a fantastically fit player. His father had been a boxer who influenced him. Matthews was a brilliant man. He could run away and leave you standing. He could twist you and turn you and deceive you. And he could do it right upfront facing you. He was a rarity in the game.

Then, younger than Matthews, was Tommy Finney. He played as a teenager in the same Preston team as me in a wartime Cup final at Wembley in 1941 and gave an exhibition against Arsenal. Tommy was at his peak after the war had ended. He was the greatest player I've ever seen.

He was five feet seven and a half and 11 stone. He didn't have a big frame but he had sturdy legs with strong calves. It meant that he could leap off the floor and was good in the air. He was a natural left-footed player and his control of the ball was unbelievable, especially his close control.

He could attack you from the front, facing you, and run past you. You saw him . . . then he had gone! A lot of players can play with their back to goal, or sideways, and get away with it.

But he could turn round and face you, go up to you and deceive you, which is a difficult thing to do. Very few players can do it. But Tommy's control was closer than anyone else's. He never lost possession. The ball was always his.

And he was crafty. He knew where you were and he

always had the ball the furthest away from his opponent. If you were on the left-hand side Tommy would have the ball on the right-hand side. So you had to follow him to get at it. And he was always ready to switch it about.

All the great players also had a great awareness, not only of their own ability but also of their opponents'. So Tommy would deal with them the way he thought they should be dealt with.

He was quick, he was elusive, and he would reach the by-line countless times to cut the ball back. Raich Carter once said to me: 'If I played in the same team as Tom goodness knows how many goals I'd score in a season. All I'd need to do was leather them into the net!'

And Carter, by the way, could leather them! He and Finney in the same club team would have filled the net. Carter might have scored 100 goals in a season playing in the same side as Tommy.

Tommy had all the attributes, but above all, if he got inside the 18-yard box and you touched him it was a penalty. He had the ability to beat you inside or outside the box.

As you approach the goal the pitch gets narrower. In the 18-yard box it's smaller again, hence the congestion. But he could beat you inside there. No disrespect to all the other great players like George Best and Stan Matthews, who was a fantastic player with pace and everything else but Tommy Finney had more control of the ball than them. It was his. And when he was carrying the ball, it was still his. Some players carry the ball – but it's not theirs.

Johann Cruyff could play too, but in a different way. Tommy was a player who could puncture the opposition down the flanks and get to the by-line. When you get there the whole game changes.

Cruyff and players of his like didn't get to the by-line. They weren't flank men. They weren't wide players like

Finney and Matthews. Raymond Kopa and Francisco Gento of Real Madrid could both get to the by-line. They were clever but they were in a bigger hurry than Tommy Finney. They were showy and flashy whereas Tommy was more composed.

If Tommy had been playing when I was a manager I'd have paid however many millions it took to sign him. Without doubt. No danger.

Before the outbreak of World War Two, Shankly added a further four Scotland caps to his collection with another outing against England, and games against Wales, Northern Ireland and Hungary.

During hostilities Shankly was a corporal in the RAF, based at Bishopbriggs, outside Glasgow. As well as doing his bit for the war effort, Shankly was a keen participant on several sporting fronts. He won a cup as a middleweight boxer and in May 1943 appeared in a fund-raising baseball match organised by the borough of Hitchin and the local United States Air Force base as part of their Wings For Victory Week, aimed at raising £210,000 to buy eight Mosquito and 10 Spitfire aircraft.

He kept in trim football-wise by making three guest appearances for Norwich in 1943, under the name of 'Newman'. He also guested for Arsenal, Luton Town, Bolton, East Fife, Cardiff, Northampton and Partick Thistle. And, as fate would have it, one outing for Liverpool – against Everton!

He wore the number four jersey at Anfield on 30 May 1942 and helped Liverpool to a 4–1 win against the club who were to become his arch rivals. The Liverpool manager was George Kay and Shanks had a vivid memory of his team selection technique:

I played for Liverpool against Everton during the war in the Liverpool Senior Cup, as a guest from Preston. All the players were in the passageway including Billy

Liddell and myself. But George Kay, the Liverpool manager, didn't speak. He just went round touching people on the shoulder. If he touche you then you were playing!

During the war Shankly managed 23 outings for his own club Preston and he and Matt Busby, who had captained Liverpool up to the outbreak of war and was still on Anfield's books, played together for Falkirk against Rangers in the final of the 1943 Scottish Cup. A 1–1 draw meant the outcome was decided on corners... Rangers winning 11–3.

Shankly played another seven times for Scotland during the war and when peace returned he was a married man. He met Agnes, or 'Nessie' as she was known, when she was in the WRAF stationed at Bill's camp. She had never heard of 'Bill Shankly the footballer' – but she was very impressed with Bill Shankly the man.

They were married in her home city of Glasgow in 1944. They spent a week's leave together but didn't go away on honeymoon. After all, the football season was due to open! But the war had taken its toll in sport as in every other walk of life. Shankly recounted:

The war cost me and everyone else six years of our careers. When the war started I was only in my mid-twenties. I'd just got into the Scottish team and played five successive matches. I was an international regular.

The war changed all our lives. For instance, I was single when war broke out but when it ended I was married. In 1939 I'd no intentions of getting married. It was the furthest thing from my mind. I was married to the game.

But the war changed people's minds as well as their lives. I got married and I never had any regrets. So, for me, something positive did come out of the terrible thing that war is.

Before the war they didn't have all the names for players that they have now... sweepers and strikers, and playmakers and all kinds of crap to confuse you. The game also changed after the war because the ball and the boots were a bit lighter and the style of the kit altered.

But the game is played only according to the players. If you've got a team of Tom Finneys and Peter Dohertys and George Bests and Bobby Charltons you don't need tactics. Just send them out on to the field and they'll win you the game.

But with so many great players having lost six years of their careers to the war there was a lull after it because there was a shortage of talent. It was 8, 9, 10 years before the game got back to normality.

After the war Manchester United had the brains to keep all their older players and go and buy more old players like Jimmy Delaney and Johnny Carey. Some clubs dumped and discarded their old players but United didn't. They collected them and won things. Age doesn't really matter. It's how fit you are that counts. United realised that and they built a team, a ground and a great club.

Peacetime signalled the resumption of Shankly's Preston career. He played in 41 games, scoring five goals, in 1946–47 and made 32 First Division appearances, netting six goals the following season. It was during these years that Finney stamped his skills profoundly on the English game and another Preston player emerged as a hard-tackling wing half in the combative tradition of Shankly himself

His name was Tommy Docherty and Shankly provided an immortal line when Docherty, set for a controversial career that was to include managing Manchester United, was about to take over the number four Preston shirt. 'Don't worry, son,' said Shankly, 'This jersey knows its own way around!'

Shankly was delighted at Docherty being the man to

succeed him at Deepdale and recalled:

> Tommy went to Preston and played right half like me.
> He joined later in the year I left. [Shankly left in March
> 1949 and Docherty arrived in November 1949.]
>
> He was the same type of player as me. He came in and
> did very well at Preston, a very good buy at £4,000 from
> Celtic. A good player and a hard-man.
>
> I'd love Tommy Docherty in my team. I once said to
> him: 'If I had five Bill Shanklys and five Tommy
> Dochertys, plus a goalkeeper, we'd beat the world!' He
> said 'Listen, if there were five Bill Shanklys and five
> Tommy Dochertys we wouldn't need a goalkeeper!'

Shankly believed that laughter played an important pre-
match role.

> It's good to have some humour in the dressing room
> before a game and, as a player, I provided it by telling
> exaggerated stories. In the mining village of Glenbuck,
> where I was brought up, the old men who worked in the
> pit told exaggerated stories.
>
> One of them used to tell a tale of how he was so strong
> that he pushed a ton of coal for a mile before he realised
> the truck was off the rails! I used to sit in the dressing
> room at Preston and somebody would ask me what was
> my best season. I'd reply: 'That season I scored 15 hat
> tricks!' It was just a laugh to lift the tension. If you're
> tense anything makes you laugh.

Shankly achieved the third of his trio of football ambitions in
1949. He had climbed the professional ladder and
represented his country as a player and now hung up his
boots to step onto the new rung of management.

In March that year he retired as a Preston player, after
making 297 League appearances and a record 43 consecutive

FA Cup outings for the Lancashire club during his 16 years at Deepdale, and returned to Carlisle United as manager. His first game in charge was on 9 April 1949 and of the club's remaining seven matches that season they won one, drew four and lost two under his command to finish 15th in Division Three North.

Shankly's return as manager to his first professional club was significant for his relationship with the Brunton Park fans. It revealed the passionate rapport he had with supporters and the powerful oratory that was to prompt one observer, later in his career, to comment, 'If Bill told the Liverpool crowd to march through the Mersey Tunnel and storm Birkenhead, they would do it!' With a style and passion many politicians would have died for, Shankly's 'granite' burr would pour from Carlisle's public address system always – starting with the words 'This is your manager speaking...'

As he recalled his early days in management Shankly enthused:

> I spoke at Carlisle to the people before the game and the people loved it. I used to tell them if I'd dropped a player out of the team, or left them out and I told them why. I told them about the game the week before. And this was a real 'riot' thing. Everybody was there early at Carlisle.

Shankly also made a memorable impression on Ivor Broadis, the inside forward who played 14 times for England. Broadis had moved from Carlisle to Sunderland but Shankly gave him permission to train at Brunton Park during the week to save him travelling. Broadis, who later played for Manchester City and Newcastle, recalled:

> I was very appreciative of Bill allowing me to train at Carlisle. So I said to him one day: 'Bill, why don't you and your wife come to my house for a meal one night?

You're very welcome.' I'd only just got home that evening when there was a knock at the door and there was Shanks and Nessie on the step. 'We've come for our dinner, Ivor!' Shanks announced. That was Bill. Just incorrigible and absolutely unforgettable.

In his full season in charge Carlisle finished ninth and in 1950–51 they were third. But that summer Shankly was on the move . . . and it might have been to Anfield some eight years early! Shankly revealed:

> Liverpool sent for me and offered me the manager's job. But the only snag was that the manager didn't pick the team. The directors did that. So I didn't take it. I said to them: 'If I don't pick the team what am I manager of?' I went back to Exchange Station and got the train home. When I did go to Liverpool I was the first manager to pick the team.

So instead of Anfield and the First Division it was to Grimsby Town that Shankly went. They, like Carlisle, were in the Third Division North and in his first season in charge he guided them to runners-up spot, three points behind Lincoln. However, since only the champions were then promoted Grimsby just missed out. The following season they finished fifth and on 2 January 1954 Shankly resigned to take over another Third Division North club, Workington.

It was a shock move by Shankly because Workington were struggling to survive. The Borough Park club ended the season in 20th place. However, the Shankly factor had a major impact the following year when they shot up to eighth. His resurrection of the club, who finally lost their league status to Wimbledon in 1977, brought many admirers.

In December 1955, he accepted an invitation from Andy Beattie to become his assistant at Huddersfield in the old First Division. But Huddersfield went down at the end of that season, finishing next-to-bottom over Sheffield United. When Beattie resigned Shankly succeeded him as manager on 5 November 1956. He was now in the same division as Liverpool and, like the Anfield club, found promotion back to the top flight an elusive target.

But Bill Shankly's period at Huddersfield was another major step on the road to the 'kingdom' he was to inherit and revitalise at Liverpool. He reflected:

> After finishing playing at Preston I went back to Carlisle to start in management and from there to Grimsby, Workington and Huddersfield and all the time I was adding to my training store. My training system was completed during my time at Huddersfield.
>
> Being at Huddersfield was one of the greatest things that happened to me because Andy Beattie was manager prior to me. He laid down the laws and the directors were all for the manager. That is how it should be, of course, providing the manager's good enough. If he isn't then they've got to sack him.

During his time at Leeds Road, then the home of Huddersfield, he oversaw the rise of two players who were to reach stardom for club and country. Shankly brought a certain Denis Law into the reserve team and then blooded him in League football, the platform for his remarkable success with Manchester United and Scotland. Having initially been transferred from Huddersfield to Manchester City and then onto Torino he returned to England and Old Trafford glory, his moves costing a then fantastic £280,000.

Shankly was also the catalyst in the career of Ray Wilson, who had just been demobbed from the Army when Shankly arrived at Huddersfield. He was playing in the reserves at wing half and Shankly converted him to left back. Wilson graduated into one of the finest players in that position the world has ever seen and after joining Everton was one of

England's World Cup-winning heroes in 1966.

Shankly remembered the day he delivered some wonderful news to Wilson in the spring of 1960: 'I went to his house to tell him that he'd won his first England cap in the team to play Scotland at Hampden Park.'

Wilson's international debut, on 9 April, was a painful one. He broke his nose after only two minutes but gave an assured performance in a contest that ended in a 1–1 draw.

The game, which brought him the first of 63 England caps, was also notable for an impressive display by Motherwell centre forward Ian St John who would later face Wilson in Mersey derby combat as Liverpool and Everton players respectively. Enthused Shankly:

Wilson was a first teamer at Huddersfield before Denis but it was really something when they faced each other in our five-a-sides. You could have charged people to watch them pit their wits against each other.

Law was only a young boy when I arrived at Huddersfield. He'd joined the club as a ground staff apprentice in April 1955 and didn't become a full professional until almost two years later.

I gave him steak and milk to buid him up physically. But Law had strength of character. Although he didn't look the strongest of boys he was strong willed. He fought with the heart. And the head, of course.

Law was easy to teach. He didn't argue with the referee or linesmen. He conversed with them in a different manner. In other words he flannelled them. He did it naturally but I think I helped him, too. If a decision was given against him he'd cotton onto a linesman and have a little conversation with him. And maybe the next decision went his way.

He did the same with referees. He spoke to them nicely and they must have thought: 'He's a nice lad.' He didn't show dissent. He was a very good actor. Instead of rushing over and telling them what to do he'd say: 'Yes, you're right, ref.'

I did exactly the same when I was a player after advice from my brother Alec and through my own experience. I realised very early on that you couldn't win by arguing with referees. So I used to side with them when decisions went against us! We've even had goals disallowed and other players were going mad, going frantic. But not me. I used to say to the referee: 'You're right. It's a good decision.'

It's not that I'm the most patient of people. I'm what you'd call an impatient patient man. But I'd still tell the referee he was right. As years passed the referees got to know me and maybe I got away with some things that were beneficial to me! This is all part of psychology.

It's the people who make the fewest mistakes in life who are the most successful. So if you eliminate your mistakes you can't go very far wrong. It's even more important to try to teach people not to do the wrong things than teaching them to do the right ones.

My brother Alec told me when I was just a little boy not to argue with the referee. He said to me: 'Don't show dissent because you can't win. It won't change his mind just because you argue with him. If you do you can be sent off. Now fancy being sent off for talking! You won't upset him. He's only blowing the whistle. He doesn't score goals or stop goals.' Referees are human beings and while they don't set out to make mistakes it's easy to do so. Refereeing's a very difficult job.

It's very difficult to change a boy's nature. He might be a natural moaner. Dissent might be his middle name. You've got to preach to him repetitively. Drum it into him every day. That could be monotonous. But not if it's the truth. I helped Denis not to show dissent.

I was in a lift in New York and as it approached each floor a recorded message warned: 'Mind the steps, mind the steps.' It was repetitive, yes. But it was a good thing. So eventually even the biggest dissenter in the world can be changed by making him realise he's battering his head against a brick wall and only upsetting himself.

I'm often asked why so many schoolboys with great potential don't come through and make it. It's a burning question. At Huddersfield we got our fair share of Scottish schoolboys including Denis.

But I know clubs who have had dozens of schoolboy internationals through their books over the last 20 years. Some of them might even have totalled 100. Yet very few have made the grade. So there's something wrong somewhere.

I had three years with Law and I organised his training. He went into general training sessions and was then taken out to do stints on his own. He did a lot of ball work and three-a-sides and five-a-sides. He wasn't overburdened. He was a young boy and we were giving him special food for energy. He did training sessions that he liked and on Saturdays in matches he'd give you everything he had.

He'd run himself into the ground. So you couldn't ask him to do it on the field and off it at his size and weight. If youngsters get over-trained when they're young it can finish them for all time as players. We had the experience in our family of my brother John who was one of five of us who played football.

He went to a club at an early age and they strained one of his heart muscles. That was bad for my brother. If something happens that's tragic and affects people you can learn lessons from it.

There was a lesson for me that when you're looking after young boys there's an art in bringing them up and developing them for football. It's not the easiest thing in the world. I was very careful.

The influence of Shankly had a profound effect on Law, whose distinguished playing career ended in 1974. He said:

> The first day I met Bill Shankly I couldn't believe there could be a man so involved with football 24 hours a day, every day. It was his whole life. There will never be a man like him ever again in football. I've never met anyone before or since with the same passion and love of the game.
>
> He was obsessed with fitness, he absolutely hated players being injured even to the point of ignoring those who were! But above all he gave you a confidence and made you feel cocky. He was an unforgettable man.

At the end of Shankly's first half-season in charge at Huddersfield they finished 12th and improved to ninth position the following year. They ended the 1958–59 term in 14th place and Shankly knew that they needed new players. But they did not have the money to buy them. So in the November of the following season, his ambitions unfulfilled, and with no Huddersfield contract, he took up an invitation from Tom Williams, then Liverpool chairman, to take charge at Anfield.

Shankly remembered the momet that changed his life, Liverpool's future, and which proved to be a watershed for the football world.

'Mr Williams said: "How would you like to manage the best club in the country?" "Why?" I asked, "is Matt Busby packing up?"'

It was a typical Shankly response. Yet he knew that the Merseyside club, a giant that had fallen on hard times and which was flirting with promotion, offered the challenge he wanted. He was made for them. They were made for him.

The red half of the city was yearning for Liverpool to return to the top flight from which they had been notably absent since the stigma of relegation in 1954 . . . a fate even harder to swallow because of Everton's promotion from the

Second Division the same year.

And Shankly recalled with passion and pride his invitation to take command of Liverpool: 'When Liverpool wanted me as manager they walked into Huddersfield Town's ground. On my own doorstep they invited me to go to Anfield. So when they wanted me they came for me.'

Shankly, having rebuffed Liverpool when he had been approached eight years earlier, this time grasped the opportunity presented by former manager Phil Taylor's departure, amicably agreed between Taylor and the board at a meeting on the night of 17 November.

Shankly recalled:

I met Mr Williams one night some years before I joined Liverpool when I was Huddersfield manager. Everton had made a bid for Denis Law and I thought there may have been some Everton players I could sign as part of a deal.

So I went to Anfield where Liverpool were playing Everton in the Liverpool Senior Cup. It was a big competition in those days because with the clubs being in different divisions these games provided the opportunity for them to play each other.

There was a big crowd but despite that there was something drab about the Anfield atmosphere. Liverpool were in the Second Division . . . and it looked like it.

As I walked into the directors' box I jokingly remarked: 'When are they going to turn the lights on!' They were so poor. Mr Williams heard me and turned round. We exchanged a few words but all in good humour, I must add.

Some months later Liverpool came to Huddersfield and we trounced them 5–0. Law and Ramon (Ray) Wilson ripped them to shreds. Wilson collected one ball, ran the length of the field and scored. Liverpool looked rubbish that day.

But I think it was because of the way Liverpool played that convinced Mr Williams that I was a manager who could create a team. The following season I met him again . . . on the slope leading to the Huddersfield dressing rooms when he walked up to me and offered me the Liverpool job.

I'll never forget it. I was impressed by his forthright way of speaking. I was impressed at the way he had gone about asking me to be the Liverool manager.

I always called Mr Williams 'De Gaulle'. He was a tall man and I thought he looked and moved like him. I can see him now, striding around in front of a group of people who trailed around him like coolies.

He had great power in the Liverpool boardroom – and used it. He ran the board. We had a partnership. We didn't always see eye to eye but the partnership worked, as the record books prove.

Great teams were created, the training ground which he had acquired for the club years earlier was modernised and training tactics revitalised. And the stadium itself was modernised and developed.

Shankly's last match as Huddersfield manager was, ironically, a 1–0 home win over Liverpool on 28 November 1959. Two days later he was appointed by Liverpool and took over officially on Monday 14 December at the age of 46 and with an annual salary of £2,500.

His first match in charge came five days later, but it was not an auspicious start as Liverpool crashed 4–0 at Anfield against Cardiff City with a team that lined up like this: Bert Slater; Alan Jones (making his debut in place of injured John Molyneux), Ronnie Moran; Johnny Wheeler, Dick White, Bobby Campbell; Fred Morris, Roger Hunt, Dave Hickson, Jimmy Melia, Alan A'Court.

Shankly had not picked the team for that match. He had left the job with a selection committee of directors and executive staff, saying: 'I didn't feel it would be right to interfere so soon after arriving. I wanted to have a look first.'

He even found something positive to snatch from the heavy reverse in his inaugural game as manager. 'You can often learn more from defeat than from victory,' said Shankly. 'So we've got plenty to think about.'

The new boss did pick the team for the next match. But Liverpool lost that, too, going down 3–0 at Charlton on Boxing Day.

But Liverpool won 2–0 in the return with the London club at Anfield two days later. The Shankly phenomenon was born and the challenge of transforming Liverpool was one he took on with gusto even though there were massive problems to overcome on and off the field:

My idea was to build Liverpool into a bastion of invincibility. Napoleon had that idea. He wanted to conquer the bloody world. I wanted Liverpool to be untouchable. My idea was to build Liverpool up and up until eventually everyone would have to submit, give in.

But when I arrived at Anfield it was the biggest slum in Liverpool. You should have seen the place. We had to bring in water from Oakfield Road at a cost of £3,000 to flush the toilets and the ground was dilapidated.

My priority when I arrived was to get to know the staff at the club, the people I'd be working with, the players I had on the books, the ones I felt were good enough and those I felt weren't good enough.

It was a question of assessing the whole place, which meant assessing the directors as well. Then there was the question of money to buy players. A manager has to treat all the directors differently.

They are human beings with different personalities. You've got to handle them all differently. You don't speak to one director the same as you'd speak to another. I had to try to instil into them that the potential at Liverpool was as great as anywhere in the world which, of course, has been proven.

Huddersfield were also in the Second Division and not too long before I joined Liverpool we beat them 5–0 with 10 men. That saddened me even though everyone at Huddersfield was rejoicing. It saddened me because I'd been to Anfield and I knew what was possible there.

The training ground was big but it wasn't good enough. Anfield was big but it needed renovating. And so did the team. All there was when I came was potential.

And, really and truly, that's all you can ask for because if you can build a team you know the crowd is there to support you. This has been proven over the years as Liverpool have made football history.

It wasn't long before I found out the Liverpool people are unique. But they do have similarities to the Glasgow people. They can be wild and demonstrative but they'll give you their last penny.

They're good souls... they're good hearted. They'd open the door and invite you in for a cup of tea. They'd give you money if you needed it. And they're football mad.

It's well known that Liverpool's crowd is the most enthusiastic in the game. This is a deep-down enthusiasm, deep rooted, genuine and spontaneous. They are also the fairest crowd in the game. But not only are the Liverpool fans great supporters they've also got a great sense of humour.

The only reason I left Huddersfield and came to Liverpool was because the potential was tremendous. In football you fight on the field to win but a manager has battles to fight on the inside... political battles. So I went to Liverpool to try to prove something to the directors and make them think along the same lines as me about the vast potential of the club.

Candidly, it was a shambles of a place when I came.

The team wasn't a very good one and the ground was run down, largely due to the war. It just wasn't good enough for Liverpool or for the people of Merseyside.

My conception of a successful football combination is a manager, the players and the crowd. The manager and the players can work together and if they're successful they win games and the crowds will come in. So that the manager and the players and the crowd are the most important people at a football ground.

And I felt more for the people here that paid, because actually the people, the crowd pay to get in – and the players get paid. They get paid for going in to the ground, and the crowd have to pay to do that. It's the crowd who pay their wages really. So the people who watch are very important. And, of course, if the players are giving them what they want then the players are really the heroes.

I knew before I joined Liverpool that the Kop was the Kop. It's expanded and grown world famous since then. But they've always made a noise on the Kop. I remember going to Anfield with Huddersfield. Liverpool won a corner kick at the Kop end and I recall turning to a director and saying: 'Wait until you hear the noise this crowd makes.' It was a fantastic noise.

So I knew the crowd right away. I knew how passionate they were and that they would turn out in fantastic numbers if we gave them what they wanted. I proved that because in my 14 seasons as manager we averaged 45,000 attendances.

But when I joined Liverpool the big club in the city was Everton. When I started in management I knew that one day I would be the manager of the best team in the game whether it was Liverpool or Sheffield Wednesday or Arsenal. Whoever it was.

Right from the very beginning, when I was a boy wanting to be a footballer, I knew my destiny. My first job at Liverpool was to assess the players, the staff and the directors. I had to find out who could play and who couldn't.

Above all, I had to get the training staff together. Normally when a manager goes to a new club he takes his own men with him to safeguard himself. I could have done the same. After all, Huddersfield beat Liverpool in my last game as manager there.

But I didn't turf out any of the Liverpool backroom staff. I already knew Bob Paisley, Reuben Bennett and Joe Fagan. Joe was a player at Manchester City and I tried to sign him when I was manager at Grimsby. So the first thing I did at Liverpool was to call a meeting of the training staff.

I told them: 'I'm not going to kick anyone out as new managers often do. I'll lay down our plans, we'll all work in harmony and then, maybe, one day we'll get the players we need and that will be it.'

Gerry Byrne was transfer listed when I arrived at Liverpool. I soon took him off the list. I found out he could play. He became one of the most amazing players in the game.

While we started building the team I also had to get the training ground ready. It was big and spacious but in a mess and it took two and a half years to get it all ready and usable.

Having given a genuine vote of confidence to his backroom staff and launched the transformation of the club's training ground, Shankly addressed the task of overhauling his playing staff.

There was no pussyfooting around, as he emphasised:

If I've got players on my books I search into them to see what they are and what they're made of. I can tell within a month what a player is, whether he needs to get bollocked or be encouraged. Or whether he needs to be shifted altogether.

Liverpool finished the 1959–60 season in third place, again just missing out on promotion, although they did trail second-placed Cardiff, who went up with Aston Villa, by eight points.

In 1960–61, they were third agin – but Shankly was busy building the basis for the subsequent re-emergence of the Anfield club. Although he dispensed with 24 players his decision to keep faith with the backroom staff he had inherited was to prove a bedrock for Liverpool's future. Said Shankly:

> After I'd decided on the players who were going to be any good to me I had to sell the others or let them go for nothing. I was looking for a spine . . . a goalkeeper, a centre half and somebody up the front.
>
> But when I arrived at Liverpool they had no money whatsoever to buy players. But after about 18 months a man came onto the board called Eric Sawyer, an accountancy man from the Littlewoods organisation with a big job in their mail order division. He was an ambitious man.

In the summer of 1961 Shankly made two signings that were to be hugely significant in the rise and rise of the club – and they were both players he had wanted to recruit for Huddersfield.

Their names were Ian St John and Ron Yeats, centre forward and centre half respectively, in the spine of the new Liverpool that would later be completed by Tommy Lawrence, who was already graduating through the ranks at Anfield when Shankly arrived. Said Shankly:

> I read in the Scottish *Sunday Post* that Ian St John of Motherwell had been put on the market. I went to a board meeting and there was a discussion about players.

I said that St John was up for sale. One of our directors said: 'We can't afford to sign him.' But Mr Sawyer said: 'We can't afford not to sign him.'

We went to Motherwell the following week, saw St John playing in a match then brought him down to Liverpool the next day and signed him. That man Mr Sawyer was really and truly the beginning of Liverpool. Here was somebody who was willing to spend money. He said to me: 'If you can get the players I'll get the money.'

St John set the place on fire. He scored three goals in the Liverpool Senior Cup at Everton where we lost 4–3. That was in the May of 1961.

St John cost £37,500 from Motherwell and his debut hat trick in the Liverpool Senior Cup, a competition used in those days to bring together Merseyside's arch rivals, who were still in different divisions, was achieved against no less an opponent than Brian Labone, the formidable Everton centre half who would go on to captain his club and win 26 England caps.

And even though Liverpool lost by the odd goal in seven it was one of those rare occasions when the Anfield fans in the crowd of 51,000 didn't care about losing to the old enemy. They had seen a new red star born in the crew-cut, darting, ebullient centre forward with a touch of cockiness called St John. His name was chanted by supporters who, later that summer, had another reason to be happy with the arrival of his fellow-Scot, Yeats, from Dundee United for £30,000. Said Shankly:

I'd seen St John play in a match against Ron Yeats and we were after him, too. We went up to Dundee United but didn't get any joy. But the next day they rang and said: 'You can have Yeats for £30,000.' I said: 'Right... we'll meet you in Edinburgh tomorrow.' We did and we signed Ron.

Yeats, later to manage Tranmere before becoming Liverpool's chief scout, vividly recounted that first meeting with Shankly:

> I'd been put on the transfer list at Dundee United because I asked for a two pound rise! At the time I played for the British Army team and our colonel was a friend of the Liverpool chairman T.V. Williams.
>
> Liverpool were looking for a centre half and the colonel phoned T.V. Williams telling him I was on the list at Dundee United. The result was that I received a telegram where I was stationed at Aldershot. The message said that a club wanted to sign me and I was to go to the Station Hotel in Edinburgh.
>
> The telegram hadn't said which club were interested in me but as I walked into the hotel foyer I could see our manager and directors with some other people who, unknown to me, were Bill Shankly and the Liverpool directors.
>
> I didn't really know who to speak to first. But it didn't matter because Shanks came marching out of the crowd, looked up at me and said: 'Bloody hell, you're a big lad. You must be seven feet tall!'
>
> I said: 'No, I'm six feet two.' Shanks replied: 'That's near enough seven feet for me, son!' I was taken aback by him. Then I asked the worst question I ever asked him.
>
> I said: 'Where's Liverpool?' I meant whereabout in the country was it. But it was like a red rag to a bull. He came right up to me and said: 'What do you mean ... where's Liverpool? We're in the First Division in England.'
>
> He replied: 'I thought you were in the Second Division.' And Shanks said: 'We are at the moment ... but when we sign you we'll be in the First Division next year!'
>
> So, of course, I signed for Liverpool. How can you refuse to sign for anybody who has so much faith in you as Shanks had?

The arrival of Yeats at Anfield provided one of the classic Shankly stories. 'I've signed a colossus!' Shankly proudly told reporters. 'Come in and walk around him!' Standing 6ft 2ins and weighing 14 stone, Yeats was an imposing figure. He immediately became Shankly's captain, leading the new Liverpool to promotion in his first season, as Second Division champions, eight points clear of runners-up Leyton Orient.

One of Shankly's early signings, Gordon Milne, who had cost £12,000 from Preston, was a regular in the team along with Gerry Byrne, Roger Hunt and Ian Callaghan, who broke into the side on a regular basis in November 1961 after making his debut in April 1960. Shankly enthused:

> Yeats and St John were the most vital signings for Liverpool. Just as Mr Sawyer laid the foundations in the boardroom, those two were the beginning of Liverpool on the pitch. We got Liverpool out of the doldrums and into the big league. We won things and it all went from strength to strength.
>
> Yeats could have played in the Second Division on his own, with no other defenders with him, and still helped us win the title. A fantastic man . . . six foot two, strong as an ox and the quickest thing on two feet.
>
> All right, he didn't have Peter Thompson's trickery. But as a defender there were very few in the game in the same class. And St John up front was scoring goals and making chances. He also helped to bring on Roger Hunt, who was also a great player.
>
> So we just walked out of the Second Division. We won 10 and drew one of our first 11 matches that 1961–62 season.

The year was doubly memorable for the Shankly family with Bill's brother Bob guiding Dundee to their first ever Scottish League championship, finishing three points ahead of Rangers with Celtic in third place, eight points adrift. To mark this outstanding brotherly feat *Charles Buchan's Football Monthly* got the two men on opposite ends of a telephone line for an article by Pat Collins in which Bill was quaintly referred to as 'Willie'.

Bill told his brother of his feeling of elation on the day Liverpool clinched promotion with a 2–0 home win over Southampton on 21 April when Kevin Lewis scored both goals. 'Nothing was more satisfying than that ... what a day!' Bill exclaimed to Bob. 'The players were up to their knees in mud but as far as I was concerned the sun was out and shining strongly.

The following season, Liverpool's first back in the top flight, was one of consolidation in the League, in which they finished a respectable eighth. And in the FA Cup they reached the semi-final, missing out on Wembley through an agonising 1–0 defeat by Leicester in a match Liverpool dominated. It was the season of the 'big freeze', when the weather played havoc with fixtures, but one game that had a red-hot atmosphere was the first League meeting of Liverpool and Everton in 11 years, staged at Goodison in September 1962.

It drew a crowd of no fewer than 73,000, astonishing in today's terms, who saw the contest end with honours even in a 2–2 deadlock. Kevin Lewis, stand-in for the injured St John, and Roger Hunt scored for Liverpool in reply to goals from Roy Vernon and Johnny Morrissey. The return at Anfield in April also ended all-square in a goalless draw and Everton went on to win the championship under Harry Catterick's management, which sparked off an intriguing era of rivalry with Shankly.

'I think I could make more excuses than Harry,' Shankly quipped. But it was no laughing matter for the losing team and supporters in derby combat, which reached a new intensity during the Shankly era as he admitted:

If we got beaten I just wanted something to do when I went home. If we lost to Everton it was even worse. After one derby game we lost I went home and I washed all the back kitchen that Saturday night.

Yet Shankly needed Everton. He needed a target for his outrageous comments... the 'enemies' from three quarters of a mile away at Goodison Park gave him something to bounce off. He reflected:

If you have two teams in one city like there is in Liverpool there will always be conflict, if that's what you want to call it. At one time it was very tense and exciting when Everton had great players like Alan Ball and Howard Kendall.

When they had a good team which was the equivalent of Liverpool, or better than Liverpool, the games were tense. The rivalry is like it is for Celtic and Rangers but without the bigotry.

I've seen supporters on Merseyside going to the ground together, one wearing red and white and the other blue and white, which is unusual elsewhere. You get families in Liverpool in which half support Liverpool and the other half Everton.

They support rival teams but they have the same temperament and they know each other. They are unique in the sense that their rivalry is so great but there is no real aggro between them. This is quite amazing.

I am not saying they love each other. Oh, no. Football is not a matter of life or death... it's much more important than that. And it's more important to them than that. But I've never seen a fight at a derby game. Shouting and bawling, yes. But they don't fight each other. And that says a lot for them.

If I had a business and needed a work force to be successful I would take my work force from Merseyside. And we would wipe the floor with everybody. They've got hearts of gold... and they can work. All they need is to be handled like human beings, not bullied and pushed around.

So I'd pick my work force from Merseyside and anybody else can pick theirs from anywhere else and we'd have a go with them. And I'd win. We'd be successful.

Merseyside is a distressed area with a lot of unemployment. People have a hard time. But they've got a big spirit. I think deep down they've got a spirit that when they're on your side and all working together they take a bit of beating.

During the 1962–63 season the Liverpool boss added another cog to his machine with the acquisition of wing half Willie Stevenson, who cost a bargain £7,000 from Glasgow Rangers. Stevenson had been languishing in the reserves at Ibrox but became a fixture for Shankly's Liverpool.

By the start of the following season another star had arrived. Talented winger Peter Thompson was recruited from Preston for £40,000. With Callaghan on the right and Thompson on the left they formed a wing pair that the legendary Everton centre forward, Dixie Dean, said he would love to have played between. By now, Lawrence had taken over from Jim Furnell as goalkeeper and Liverpool swept to the 1963–64 championship with a regular team of: Lawrence; Byrne, Moran; Milne, Yeats, Stevenson; Callaghan, Hunt, St John, Melia or Arrowsmith, and Thompson. Shankly recalled:

Ian St John could have been possibly the best midfield player of all time if he'd been used there regularly. We withdrew him to a slightly deeper role in 1963–64, brought in Alf Arrowsmith up front and won the League. Everton had been champions the year before us and I remember a newspaper cartoon showing me going across to Goodison to take the trophy!

Liverpool won the title despite losing their first three home games. The championship was clinched, with three games to spare, on a sun-kissed April day in a carnival Anfield atmosphere when Arsenal were demolished 5–0. In those days of two points for a win Liverpool finished with 57 points, four ahead of runners-up Manchester United with Everton in third place a further point adrift.

Shankly's strike force was simply rampant. Hunt, who had been recruited from Lancashire junior club Stockton Heath after being spotted by former Liverpool and England defender Bill Jones, built on the form that had seen him set a club record of 41 League goals in Liverpool's rise from the Second Division two seasons earlier.

He contributed 31 of Liverpool's 92 championship goals with his attack partner St John scoring 21 and Arrowsmith netting 15. Wolves, Stoke City, Sheffield United and Ipswich were all hit for six at Anfield while Aston Villa had five put past them.

Shankly had answered the Kop's prayers. He had become their football messiah by establishing Liverpool as the best team in the country and also launching a European odyssey that was to shatter all records for an English club. It was a massive triumph for Liverpool's system of play and the training methods Shankly had laid down, a creed he had honed and fashioned during his managerial learning curve at Carlisle, Grimsby, Workington and Huddersfield. Shankly expounded on his playing and training philosophy thus:

> Improvisation...that word covers the whole affair. If you've got players who can improvise, who can adjust immediately to what happens on the field, then you've got something. So instead of breaking down the flank they're on they can switch it across to the other flank and break through there.
>
> It also has something to do with conserving energy because Liverpool play 50, 60, even 70 games a season.

To do that you can't really run flat out all the time. Our system's designed to nullify and confuse the opposition. It's designed to win matches. And it's economical.

Everybody at Liverpool does his share. They are all part of the pattern. It might be your turn to go for the final pass... it may be somebody else's. Above all the main aim is that everyone can control a ball and do the basic things in football. It's control and pass... control and pass... all the time.

At the back you're looking for someone who can control the ball instantly and give a forward pass. It gives them more space and time to breathe. If you delay, the opposition have all run back behind the ball. It's a very simplified affair and, of course, very economical.

At Liverpool we don't have anyone running into no man's land, running from their own half with the ball into the opposition half. That's not encouraged at all. That's nonsense. If you get a ball in the Liverpool team you want options, you want choices... you want at least two people to pass to, maybe three, maybe more.

But in some teams if you get the ball nobody wants it off you. The rest of them go away and leave you! They turn their back on you. But at Liverpool there's someone to help you.

That's why Kenny Dalglish was such an instant success in English football because he came to a club that when he got the ball he was getting help. He had choices. And he's the kind of player who thrives on that.

So it's all so simple. Get the ball, give an early pass, then it goes from me to somebody else and it switches around again. You might not be getting very far but the pattern of the opposition is changing. Finally, somebody will sneak in.

Running into no man's land is a terrible thing, a terrible waste of energy. We play a pass instead of running with the ball. And when you deliver a pass at Liverpool you've only started. You've got to provide back-up and be ready to take another one from somebody else. After another couple of passes you might be back in the game again . . . you, who started the movement.

It's all give and take . . . it's options . . . it's improvisation. That's the big word. You don't have to run the length of the pitch and try to score goals. At Liverpool it's like a relay race. People like Gordon Milne were in the relay by getting the ball and giving it to someone else.

This collective playing system at Liverpool has helped to prevent injuries. No player is asked to do more than another. Everyone shares the load.

We've also managed to avoid a lot of injuries because we've been very cautious in the initial, pre-season training period which takes about five and a half weeks. In other words the club doesn't tear players to pieces in three or four days by sending them running up sandhills or doing road work.

They train on the grass where they play. Then they rest. I've never seen a game played on a road yet! If you saw them training in the early stages of pre-season you'd say they were lazy. That's what I want people to say . . . that they're not doing very much.

There's a gradual build-up. We don't ask players to stretch their legs out until they're ready. A lot of injuries can be caused by the initial training being wrong. A man can break down two months into the season and it can be caused by something wrong in the pre-season work. It has to be a patient process of building up.

We once learned something from Ray Clemence who pulled a muscle kicking a dead ball. It's hard work kicking from the floor and he injured his leg doing it one pre-season. It affected him so much he missed a couple of games. In fact, his absence cost us the League that season.

So we had to curtail him. We had to stop him kicking dead balls in his initial, pre-season training. So all these things are taken into consideration . . . not to kick a dead ball too early, not to sprint too soon, not to exert yourself too much. They train hard, yes. But only when they're ready.

Shankly was a fervent advocate of the Liverpool practice of the players reporting each morning to Anfield to change into their training kit before travelling on the team coach to the club's Melwood training ground, returning at lunchtime the same way. His successors Bob Paisley, Joe Fagan and Kenny Dalglish carried it on but it was discontinued in October 1992 during Graeme Souness's period in charge. Now, apart from rare exceptions, the Liverpool players visit Anfield only on match days.

These were Shankly's thoughts on his tried and tested routine:

Preparation is everything. Players sweat and if it's a cold day you've got to wear a sweater in training to cover your kidneys. And if you've not worn it you have to put it on afterwards to keep you warm.

Our system is that the players arrive at Anfield in the morning, strip there and then go to our Melwood training ground on the team bus. They train for an hour and a half but that's not to say they'll work for all that time. Some players might be demonstrating a function to others before it's their turn. It's not how long you train . . . it's how much you put into it that counts.

If you train properly maybe 35 minutes a day would do you. So Liverpool training is really based on exhaustion and recovery and little areas of two-a-side and three-a-side and five-a-side. And you have to work hard like a boxer . . . shadow boxing, skipping and moving.

You work hard twisting and turning – which the game's

all about – and exhausting yourself before recovery, which becomes gradually quicker. The foundation of the training is basic skills, control, passing, vision, awareness, exhaustion and recovery. If you're fit you've got a tremendous advantage over everybody else.

After training the players relax and have a cup of tea. If you perspire heavily, which happens in summer with a sweater and track suit on, and then go into the bath within five or 10 minutes of finishing training, you'll sweat all day because your pores haven't closed.

So that was stopped. After a cup of tea they might even have a walk round before sauntering back onto the bus for the 20-minute journey back to Anfield. By the time they get back there their pores will have closed and they'll be ready for a bath, probably 40 or 50 minutes after finishing training.

They'll also be ready to eat something. We call this the 'warming down' period and this is one of the reasons why Liverpool are fitter than other teams whose players train and shower at the one place then sweat all day. That doesn't sound very much but to me it's a very, very important factor. It may sound silly. But nothing Liverpool have done is silly.

Liverpool have training boards at Melwood which you can play the ball against. When you put the ball in a net it doesn't come back out. But with the boards at our training ground the ball comes straight back and the player has to control it.

I saw Tom Finney doing this very thing round the back of the stand at Preston. From four yards' range he'd hit the ball against the stand and take it in his stride with his left foot, control it, shield it, dribble with it a little bit then play it against the stand again. When it came back he'd control it with his right foot and carry it a little bit.

He was the star of stars but he was practising basics because he wanted to be even better at particular skills.

That's very important because opponents can come in on the blind side and take the ball off you if you can't control and shield it. Being able to take in your stride a short pass straight at you is not an easy thing to do, or a natural thing to do. But it's a key skill in football and Finney used to practise it.

Geoff Strong and Tony Hateley, who came to Liverpool from other First Division clubs, Arsenal and Chelsea respectively, found our training hard. It wasn't that it was harder than they were used to...it was different because we trained to play football. We had little two-minute spells of torture, with half a minute breathing space, then torture again. They weren't used to that.

If you're a half miler and someone tells you to run a marathon you'd find it hard because it's a different race. We are talking of exhaustion and recovery. We had a killer of an exercise with the big boards at Melwood. We put Strong and Hateley in there with a player acting as goalkeeper at each end, who was really only a feeder of the ball.

It was a tough exercise. It was 50 yards long inside those boards and 45 yards wide. Just two men would be involved in the function. And Strong and Hateley succumbed. They went down sick when they first joined Liverpool.

It would have made anyone gasp. It was control, dribble, shoot, sprint...control, dribble, shoot, sprint... oh, dear God, it was a killer! Both Strong and Hateley were ill through it. So we had to change it and instead of putting them in there for two minutes we reduced it to a minute.

Eventually we increased it to a minute and a half and then back to two minutes when they'd got used to it. By then it meant nothing to them and I said to them: 'Now you're ready to play!' They got to the stage where they could do as long as 20 minutes in there.

It was non-stop. It was continuity. We didn't want them to have breathers in there. They had breathers in other functions. It was the same in the three-a-side games. If anyone kicked the ball away so they could have a rest one of the training staff would throw another ball on.

So, after our training, playing football was the easiest thing in the world. Liverpool players went out ultra fit, ready to play, with their lungs and legs exercised. We knew when they went through this barrier that they were ready. We had our yardstick.

Football is about stopping and starting and twisting and turning. So that's how you train for it, with a little breather now and then when you stop, even though it's only temporary. It might be for only a split second. But you stop. If you're running a mile race or a marathon you don't get the chance to stop and get a breather.

So we trained them to play fotball and sometimes we just gave them breathing exercises...jumping up and then breathing, sprinting then breathing and so on.

Shankly's forthright views on coaching were also central to the football evangelism he brought to Liverpool. FA coaching courses were never top of his popularity parade and in the early days of his managerial reign not a single member of the Anfield backroom staff held an FA coaching badge! Shankly had his own standards, the product of his career as player and manager, which he forcefully proclaimed:

When people ask me my credentials for being a manager or a coach I have one answer...Bill Shankly. They're my qualifications, the way I was born. And that's all the qualifications anyone needs in the game I'm in.

I didn't think it was necessary to take an FA coaching course. I didn't think it was going to make me any better. If I took a course am I going to be a better man six days later because I've got a piece of paper?

That's nonsense. Chamberlain came back from Germany with a piece of paper . . . the worst f—— piece of paper we've ever had!

I've been to Lilleshall, yes. I've been there umpteen times. I wanted to go there and listen to people to see what I could pick up. There's always something you can pick up, even from the most stupid people. Sometimes you can learn something. You can see when someone is doing something wrong so you learn to do the opposite.

I think my yardstick would have been too high for some of these FA coaches to pass. They've got coaching badges but I'd have liked them to pass my school. What is a coach? He's a man who knows something about the game and who is able to convey his ability to other people to make them better at their job.

Maybe if you paraded a lot of FA coaches in front of me I'd turn them all down. I'd like to vet some of them and see if I thought they were qualified to be coaches. I'm quite certain I've seen a lot who have coaching badges where I might have said to them: 'I'm taking that badge off you.'

As manager of Liverpool I got two FA Cup winner's medals, three championships and a Second Division championship, one UEFA Cup, three Charity Shields and six Central League winner's medals . . . that's 16 in 15 seasons. So I'd like them to come to my coaching school! I'd have probably failed some of them.

Peter Doherty, Raich Carter and I went to the coaching school and got a schoolteacher trying to teach us to f—— play! One day while I was there one of these teachers toe-poked the ball. I said to him: 'Hold your horses . . . wait a minute . . . Jesus Christ! You've just toe-ended the f—— ball. I'll show you how to kick the ball . . . how do you want it! Do you want it stabbed, or hit, a follow through or the Mashie Niblick! I think I'd better take this school over.'

I told him where to go! In coaching the practical thing is the main thing, demonstrating how it should be done. If a boxing coach is teaching you how to hit a punch ball and Jack Dempsey comes along and shows you the professional way you won't look at the other fellow. It's Dempsey you'll follow.

Five of us from Liverpool went to Lilleshall, staying at a hotel in Wolverhampton and going to the school each morning. There was Bob Paisley, Joe Fagan, Reuben Bennett, Ronnie Moran and I and the place was a riot.

Wherever you looked one of us was taking a class... Joe there, Bob here, me over there and Ronnie and Reuben somewhere else. The coaches were just sitting in the background. We took over.

The care and development of young players was also close to Shankly's heart:

Not enough schoolboys make the grade. Every year England throws up 12, 14, 20 schoolboy internationals. So do Scotland, Wales and Ireland and there are many more on the fringe. It's a difficult job to pick the best boys. They may be in Middlesbrough, they may be in Portsmouth. Who knows?

It's a longstanding mystery. Where do they go? What happened to them? Over the years hundreds of schoolboys who can play football leave school and not enough of them make the grade when they go straight in as professional players.

A lot of boys are picked up from junior and lower division teams. But I'm talking about the schoolboy internationals who look brilliant players and go straight to big clubs on leaving school. But within two or three years you don't hear any more of them. Where have they gone?

They can be trained and coached out of the game. If

I'm going to speak to players, whether they're schoolboys, youth team players or full time professionals, I'm going to speak to them in a language they all understand, not a language that only a few understand. That's what's wrong.

You get politicians who stand up and speak in a language that very few people can understand. They should simplify and clarify the meaning of what they're going to say. You have to get through to people. Then they know what you're talking about.

So maybe the boys get confused by all the jargon and the coaching. Maybe they're over-coached or badly coached. They've got to be trained according to their physique. I'm not saying all coaches are bad coaches.

But in our training we had men like Bob Paisley, Joe Fagan, Reuben Bennett and Ronnie Moran who had allocated jobs for the day and I was around watching all of them as a manager has to do. Ant if it was a reserve team player I wanted to know about I'd go to Joe and he'd tell me.

Ian Callaghan was only a little boy of about 5ft 6in and eight and a half stone when he came to Liverpool. He went on to play a record 855 games for the club and holds the all-time record of 88 FA Cup appearances, more than any player in the history of English football. If that little boy, who worked like a slave on a Saturday, had been hammered during the week in training there might not have been any Ian Callaghan in Liverpool's team.

When Phil Thompson came to Liverpool he didn't look like an athlete or a player at all. He was so thin and his legs were like matchsticks. I said: 'He tossed up for his legs with a sparrow...and lost!' But I knew, of course, that he could play. I knew right from the start that he had the ability. But he's another one who had to be helped and not over-trained.

So I think that all the talk about extra ball-work,

additional sessions and twice daily training could be damaging youngsters. I do not believe in training twice a day... even for full time professional players. It's all rubbish.

But they're bringing young boys back and giving them two training sessions. And in the middle of the second session they're bored and they're tired. They're making them sick of the game. So they're doing them no good at all.

If they're natural football players – and they should be able to play if they're signed on as professionals – they've got skill inside them. Now if you can get them as fit as that individual can be then he'll do things that he would not do if he was over-trained or bored. He would lose that little bit of balance and not do things as quickly as he could. So keeping them perfectly fit is the important thing.

There comes a time even in Liverpool's initial pre-season training that we stop training twice a day. I don't believe in it. No way. If you train twice a day then you have to curtail your sessions and the first one has to be an easy one. If it's a hard one by the time they get to the second stint the players will be tired and bored after 20 minutes.

Never mind people saying that's all that players do in a day. Football's a game that doesn't last for a week. If you box you train for six months for one fight. In football you play every week and train every day and you hardly have any close season. To go on year after year for 10 to 12 years as some players do you can't be training twice a day.

The year after Shankly had brought the championship to Anfield for the first time since 1947 he achieved a feat that had proved beyond all his managerial predecessors and one that Liverpool supporters feared they would never see. He

led them to their first FA Cup triumph, 73 years after
Liverpool's formation following a rent squabble within the
Everton club who split and moved to Goodison Park.

When Wembley referee Bill Clements blew the final
whistle to signal Liverpool's 2–1 extra time conquest of
Leeds United on 1 May 1965 it satisfied a yearning to lift
the Cup that had become agonising for the club and its
fans. And Liverpool enjoyed a swashbuckling baptism in
Europe, marching all the way to an epic Champions Cup
semi final against world club champions Internazionale of
Milan.

With the emergence of local products Tommy Smith and
Chris Lawler, versatile defenders who would both play for
England, and the £40,000 signing of Geoff Strong from
Arsenal, the team that became synonymous with Shankly in
the Sixties was in place. It lined up: Tommy Lawrence;
Chris Lawler, Gerry Byrne; Gordon Milne or Geoff Strong,
Ron Yeats, Willie Stevenson; Ian Callaghan, Roger Hunt,
Ian St John, Tommy Smith, Peter Thompson.

Liverpool's amazing re-emergence as a football power
coincided with a Merseyside showbiz explosion. The
Beatles led a musical outpouring that embraced a host of
groups including the Searchers, Billy J. Kramer and the
Dakotas, The Swinging Blue Jeans as well as solo artiste
Cilla Black, while the likes of Ken Dodd and Jimmy
Tarbuck beefed up the nation's laughter supply.

Another group borrowed a classic from the Rodgers and
Hammerstein musical *Carousel* to make a record that not
only topped the charts but became the Liverpool FC
anthem. When Gerry Marsden and his Pacemakers cut
'You'll Never Walk Alone' they had no idea that it would
become immortalised as the Kop's special song, a hymn for
all seasons and all occasions be they solemn or triumphant.

But the glitter of the Mersey pop stars and comedians
during the mid-sixties was matched by Shankly's players,
appraised by their manager like this:

Tommy Lawrence in goal did well for us. We were looking for a bigger keeper than Tommy. He was thickset and we wanted somebody tailer. But Tommy's contribution was a great one and he could anticipate and play like a defender. Joe Mercer called him the first 'sweeper keeper'.

Chris Lawler was a cool customer. Very quiet. But he could play. We were playing five-a-side one day at our training ground. Chris at that time was in the first team while Tommy Smith, who was a little bit younger, wasn't. Tommy was always knocking at my door saying: 'When am I going to be in the team?' I'd reply: 'Well, I can't play 12 players, Tommy, or there'll be an objection!'

In this particular five-a-side game Tommy slid into Chris in a tackle and accidentally caught him with the sole of his boot on the ankle. Chris was really sore. Before Chris had got up off the ground his ankle was all blown up. But, to show the thinking of Tommy, as we were coming off towards the changing pavilion he came up to me and said: 'Will I be in the team on Saturday?' He was so keen to be in the team he wanted to take Chris's place. Tommy, by the way, was in the team on the Saturday.

Gerry Byrne at left back was a fantastic player. Amazing to think he was on the transfer list when I arrived at Liverpool! He achieved the impossible by playing almost the whole of our FA Cup final plus extra time against Leeds with a split collar bone. I was once asked to choose my favourite Merseyside player and I picked Gerry.

At the heart of our defence was Ron Yeats, the man I called a colossus, the middle of our central spine. He was inspirational as a player and as captain.

Gordon Milne was a fetcher and carrier of messages in midfield. He took the ball off the opposition defence and played it forward while Willie Stevenson had his special characteristics. He could drive a ball 50 yards and pinpoint it. There was elegance about his play.

When we bought Geoff Strong from Arsenal he was a front man. But we didn't buy him as an attacker or anything specific at all. We signed him as a footballer, like they used to do in the old days. Geoff could play in the middle of the field, at the back or up front and he became a great sweeper. I was very disappointed Geoff didn't play for England and win a lot of caps.

He was a very unlucky man. Circumstances were against him. We bought him as Tommy Smith was just starting. Tommy was very young and to keep him down would have been criminal. But Geoff played some fantastic games for us. If we'd signed him five years earlier he'd have been an even greater player. He could have become one of the finest sweepers of all time. He was as cool as a cucumber with a brilliant brain. He could have played in any team in the world.

Ian Callaghan had a crucial role to play, starting in a 4–2–4 formation. If you'd played 4–4–2 in the early days you'd probably have been booed off the pitch. But Ian made a 4–2–4 into 4–3–3 because he had so much industry. He covered the back and if we played against someone like Bobby Charlton he would drop back and cut his service a bit. Instead of getting four passes Charlton might only have got two.

Callaghan had the stamina to do that so he was a crucial man in our set-up. We left Roger Hunt upfield to conserve his strength, like Jimmy Greaves. He was a brilliant player. He could leather the ball into the net. He didn't slip his goals in the net quietly... he battered them in.

His attack partner St John was a strong, sturdy, cunning player who needed no motivation. He was one of the key players who could be withdrawn into midfield. If he'd played there regularly he could have been the best midfield player in the game. He could tackle, he was good in the air, he had brains and he had craft.

Peter Thompson did more damage, indirectly, than anybody else by running past opponents. And he entertained the public. I know one supporter who went to Anfield and told me that after he'd seen Peter doing his tricks in the warm-up, flicking the ball onto his shoulder and his head, he wasn't concerned about the match because he'd got his money's worth even before the kick-off. Peter was strong, 11st 9lb of bone and muscle. A great player

Ten of those 12 players were capped by their country, the two cruelly unlucky ones being Strong and Stevenson who were snubbed by England and Scotland respectively.

The squad had been stripped of the scoring instincts of Arrowsmith, whose invaluable 15 goals in the previous year's title success had come from only 20 appearances. His touchline tussle with the great Bobby Moore in the Charity Shield duel with West Ham at Anfield in August 1964 left him with knee damage that, effectively, prematurely ended a richly promising career. But the team Shankly built was imbued with his spirit, passion and pride, captured pithily when he announced:

You feel that there's never a cause that's lost. And if anyone is in a position where they feel that causes are lost and they are pessimistically thinking then there's nothing for them. That has been the gospel we've preached at Liverpool.

Liverpool finished only seventh in the First Division that 1964–65 season and suffered the shock and indignity of losing 4–0 to Everton in the Anfield derby in September. Shankly's kitchen got a good cleaning that Saturday night! Everton rubbed salt in the wound by completing a double over their neighbours with a 2–1 Goodison win the following April, and Liverpool would not finish as low in the top flight for almost 20 years when they were eighth in 1993–4, a season that began with Graeme Souness in charge and ended with Roy Evans in command.

The glory for Liverpool in 1964–65 came in cup combat at home and in their new playground of Europe. They began their FA Cup campaign with a 2–1 third round win at West Bromwich Albion but there was unexpected drama at the next hurdle. Liverpool were paired with Stockport County, who were then propping up the old Fourth Division. Even with memories of Second Division Swansea's amazing 2–1 sixth round win in front of the Kop the previous season Stockport were considered mere cannon fodder for the reigning English champions.

Shankly even missed the game – his only first team match absence in 15 years at Anfield – to make a Continental trip to watch Liverpool's European Cup opponents, Cologne of West Germany. On his way back he asked a porter at London's Euston Station if there had been any shock results. 'Yes,' replied the porter, 'Peterborough beat Arsenal.' Then Shankly caught sight of a newspaper and saw the result... Liverpool 1 Stockport County 1. He held it up to the porter and roared: 'What do you call that if it's not a shock!'

Liverpool duly restored equilibrium to football's form book by winning 2–0 in a fog-shrouded Edgeley Park replay, won 1–0 at Bolton through a rare headed goal from Callaghan, then disposed of Leicester City 1–0 at Anfield to book a semi final collision with Chelsea.

But three days prior to that Villa Park encounter with Tommy Docherty's highly rated young title contenders Liverpool had the strength-sapping engagement of a European Cup quarter final play-off with Cologne after their home and away meetings had ended in deadlock without a goal being scored. Liverpool had made an impressive march on their first season in Europe, a new experience for Shankly

as well as the club and something for which he swiftly
realised 'you had to have your wits about you'. Shankly
reflected:

> Entering Europe was something new for us and you
> encounter different things...different climates,
> languages, food. And it takes a long time to get yourself
> stabilised in Europe.
>
> The Europeans are devious. They tell you 'Liverpool
> are too good, too strong...' And this is to soften you up
> and simmer you down to try to beat you. We were lucky
> in that the first team we were drawn against were
> Reykjavik of Iceland who were not the strongest team in
> the world.

Liverpool saw off their part-time Icelandic foes on an 11–1
aggregate, but not before the Kop had heralded Anfield's first
ever European game with some antics of their own. Feeling
somewhat sympathetic to the visitors they cheered every time
Reykjavik had the ball and booed whenever Liverpool were
in possession!

This reduced many Liverpool players to laughter and
contrived to present Reykjavik with their only goal of the tie,
scored by Felixson. But a more daunting task lay ahead, as
Shankly admitted:

> We were paired with Anderlecht and seven of their
> players had been in the Belgium team that had just
> drawn 2–2 with England at Wembley. I thought they
> outclassed England who were lucky not to get beaten.
>
> I met the Anderlecht secretary in London and he was
> very helpful. His club had played a lot of European
> football and he gave me a foolscap page of hints and
> advice on playing in Europe.
>
> Our game against Anderlecht at Anfield was a night of
> milestones. We wore the all red strip for the first time.

Christ, the players looked like giants. And we played like giants.

We used to play in white shorts with red stripes, white stockings with red tops and white piping on the jerseys. But we switched to all red and it was fantastic.

The introduction of the all scarlet strip had a huge psychological effect.

I went home that night and I said to Ness: 'You know something... tonight I went out onto Anfield and for the first time there was a glow like a fire was burning.'

The atmosphere you could have cut with a knife. It was just unbelievable. The next time it was anything like that was when Celtic came in the Cup Winners Cup. I said to Ness: 'That's it... we're going to play in all red from now on.' Now the whole bloody world's copied us!

But it was a fantastic night. We won 3–0 and it was the beginning of Tommy Smith. We sent him out to sweep up with No. 10 on his back and players like Paul Van Himst and Jeff Jurion hardly got a kick.

Tommy Smith was a brilliant, fantastic player. He was a man at 16 and ready for the big team at 17. Not only was he a hard man but he could play. Because he wore No. 10 on his back somebody said to me: 'Your inside left doesn't score many goals!' But, of course, that was only a number. He was our sweeper up at the back.

By this stage Shankly and the Kop had formed a mutual admiration society.

Football, above all, is a working class game and the Kop is a special place. I identified myself with the Kop. One Saturday at twenty-five past two I went onto the Kop. And a little bloke said to me: 'Stand here, Bill. You'll get a better view.'

I identified myself with the people because at the end

of the day the game belongs to the people. And if you don't have the people on your side then you've got nothing. I was a working class boy. I was part of them. I wouldn't let anyone say anything against the Kop.

One night we were playing in a fog against Walsall in a Cup tie and we scored a goal at the Anfield Road end of the ground. The Kop couldn't see that far so they made up a song and chanted: 'Annie Road, Annie Road, Who Scored The Goal?' And they sang back: 'Tony Hateley Scored The Goal.'

At my testimonial match in April 1975, the year after I'd retired as manager, I kept a promise I made to a Kopite that I would go on to the Kop again. And I enjoyed it. I didn't go in for bravado or anything like that. I went in amongst them because I worked for the supporters . . . I was their man.

The Kop is a unique place. But I didn't just go on the Kop. I went into Anfield Road, the paddock, the stands . . . in fact, the whole of Anfield.

Liverpool is not only a club. It's an institution. And my aim was to bring the people close to the club and the team and for them to be accepted as a part of it. The effect was that wives brought their late husband's ashes to Anfield and scattered them on the pitch after saying a little prayer.

That's how close the people have come to this club. When they wanted to scatter the ashes of their loved ones, who wanted to be part of the club when they were dead, I said to them: 'In you come, you're welcome.' And they trooped in by the dozen.

One young boy got killed at his work and a bus load of 50 people came to Anfield one Sunday to scatter his ashes at the Kop end. It was very, very sad. Another family came with a man's ashes when the ground was frost-bound. So the groundsman had the difficult job of digging a hole in the pitch inside the Kop net.

He dug it a foot down at the right-hand side of the post facing the Kop and a casket containing the man's ashes was placed in it. So people not only support Liverpool when they're alive. They support them when they are dead. This is the true story of Liverpool. This is possibly why Liverpool are so great. There is no hypocrisy about it. It is sheer honesty.

Laughingly I have said, when a ball has been headed out of that particular corner of the net: 'That's the bloke in there again! He's having a blinder today!' But I wasn't trying to be funny, really. I don't think we lost a goal at that end for years after the man's ashes were placed there.

Liverpool completed their demolition job on Anderlecht with a 1–0 win in the Brussels return through a last minute Hunt goal which gave them a 4–0 aggregate triumph. The two goalless meetings with their next opponents Cologne, who had to make two trips to Merseyside after the first one had seen the game wiped out by a blizzard, set up a dramatic decider in neutral Rotterdam.

Liverpool smashed the stalemate by sweeping into a two-goal lead through St John and Hunt only to be pegged back by Cologne. At the end of extra time the teams were still level at 2–2. And at that time that meant the team to go through to the semi final would be decided on the spin of a disc. If it came down red Liverpool would progress. If it fell on the white side Cologne would go through. The referee hurled it into the air and down it came . . . only to stick on its side in the mud!

The tension was almost unbearable for Shankly and his players. When the disc was spun a second time the leap of joy from skipper Ron Yeats told its own story . . . Liverpool were in the semi final. It was a cruel on Cologne and ironic for Yeats. He had lost the toss at the start of the match and at the start of extra time!

Shankly's team shrugged off the mental and physical demands of that muscle-pounding, nerve-jangling evening in

Holland to jet back to England and topple a fancied Chelsea side in the FA Cup semi final at Villa Park three days later. A goal from Peter Thompson and a Willie Stevenson penalty gave Liverpool a 2–0 win and set up a Wembley duel with Don Revie's Leeds United. Shankly and his players were now one game away from filling that yawning gap in Liverpool's roll of honour.

And what an amazing climax to the season awaited them . . . the FA Cup final on 1 May followed three days later by a European Cup semi final first leg against master tactician Helenio Herrera's Inter Milan! The way the Wembley day began and ended was music to Liverpool's ears, as Shankly recalled:

> I was on *Desert Island Discs* which was on the radio while we were travelling to Wembley on the coach. Ian St John was listening to all the Scottish tunes I'd asked for!
>
> I had Cup final tickets in my hand and as we were going up Wembley Way I went to the front of the bus, opened the door and handed them to two Liverpool supporters. I said: 'Pay me next season.' But I didn't want paying. Money doesn't come into it with me. Not at all. I was at Wembley for them.
>
> I've seen boys sitting in tee-shirts soaking wet at FA Cup games drinking Oxo. They might not do that for League games. But the FA Cup is another story. Everyone wants a Cup final ticket.
>
> Tension's a big thing. Liverpool had never won the Cup and neither had Leeds. We were coming out of the Wembley tunnel and I was alongside Leeds manager Don Revie. I turned round and said to Bobby Collins, the Leeds captain: 'How are you, Bobby?' He said: 'I feel awful.'
>
> The tension was difficult for both teams as it always is at Wembley. But we decided on a plan of relaxation, of enjoyment of the game. That was our approach. It's a

holding turf and we decided to play it simple and for nobody to do any extra running with the ball and, therefore, save our strength.

It will never be recalled as one of the great finals. Ninety minutes elapsed without a goal being scored. But it did produce one of Wembley's greatest examples of personal heroics, which made Shankly swell with pride when he recounted it.

I don't like picking out one Liverpool player ahead of another because they all gave me everything they had. They worked for me and I worked for them.

But you don't hear many people talking about Gerry Byrne yet he did what nobody else in the world could have done that day at Wembley. He played for almost two hours with a broken collar bone. He was injured in a challenge by Bobby Collins just five minutes after the game had started. But he played right through the match and the half hour extra time. It was a fantastic feat by a fantastic player.

But we didn't give our hand away. Bob Paisley came back after attending to Gerry and said: 'His collar bone's gone.' So we just left him in the left back position, holding his arm. Nobody except Bob and I knew until half time when the rest of our players were told. But Leeds had no idea. Nobody outside our dressing room knew until after the match.

Byrne recalled: 'When Bob Paisley came on I told him my leg was hurt. It was only when I got to my feet that I knew my shoulder was damaged. I could feel the bone.'

Shankly revealed:

I had personal experience of a similar situation when I was playing for Preston at Blackpool just after the war. Andy Beattie said at half time that he'd strained a leg. I said: 'Well, stay on Andy and see what happens. You mightn't have much to do. We'll take a chance.'

He was playing right back and I was at right half. There wasn't much pressure on him, we fiddled through and he got away with it. If he'd have gone to another position he'd have given the game away that he was injured.

There were no substitutes then and there were none at Wembley in 1965. At half time we could see Gerry's collar bone was split. The pieces were grinding together. Our doctor tried to freeze Gerry's shoulder but couldn't.

But we kept it a secret from Leeds. If we'd stuck Gerry at outside left and taken him out of the road Leeds would have realised there was something seriously wrong. But we never disclosed it.

It was another example of psychology and it helped us win the Cup for the first time in the club's history. Gerry Byrne should have got all the medals for the game. He was the hero and he was one of the great players.

Byrne's massive contribution was not restricted to his personal courage. He also helped set up the first goal of the game by turning the ball into the goalmouth for Hunt to score with a gentle, stooping header just three minutes into the extra period.

Was the FA Cup bound for Anfield at last? Not before that tireless, talented competitor Billy Bremner had done his bit to try to wreck the Kop dream with a volleyed equaliser. But the jangling nerves of Liverpool and their followers were transformed into whoops of delight when, with nine minutes left, Callaghan crossed and St John leaped to send a bullet header into the Leeds net.

'I saw that Cally was going to cross it and I presumed it would be short,' said St John. 'The ball came to me perfectly, straight to my head, and that was it. I couldn't miss. The goal yawned at me as big as the Mersey Tunnel.

'But when I saw it nestling in the back of the net I was overcome with emotion. I almost couldn't believe it. But when the lads mobbed me I knew it was true. The Cup was ours!'

The Anfield fans were equally ecstatic. 'Ee aye addio... the Queen's wearing red!' they chanted, thrilled by the visiting monarch's choice of colour. And as Ron Yeats became the first Liverpool captain in history to hold aloft the FA Cup, Shankly walked the hallowed Wembley turf and took a salute worthy of any emperor.

Winning the FA Cup for the first time in the club's history, ending a 73 year wait, was a great relief, I can tell you. It was a terrible thing for the club to have gone that long without winning it. It was a terrible thing to bear. There were all sorts of stories that if Liverpool did win it the Liver Birds would leave the Pier Head!

Liverpool used to get taunted that they'd never won it. And rightly so. I think the FA Cup is the hardest cup in the world to win. Never mind the European Cup. That's not sudden death in one game like the FA Cup. You've not got home and away ties in the FA Cup. There's no second chance unless you force a replay.

That FA Cup win was the most emotional day for Liverpool in their entire history. Winning the European Cup was also a great achievement. But that was relatively new. The FA Cup had been in existence since football began. And people had lived and died without seeing Liverpool win it.

After an incredible Sunday homecoming, when an estimated half a million people turned out onto the streets of Liverpool to see Shankly and his players parade with the trophy on an open-top bus, he took his squad to Blackpool for a short breather before they embarked on their challenging Italian job against Inter in the European Cup semi final first leg two days later.

Shankly had first discovered Blackpool during his playing

days at Preston North End. 'I as at Preston for 16 years and we used to go to Blackpool for special training I find it a very bracing place, just right to train and relax,' said Shankly. 'In fact I even go on holiday there. I did go to Las Palmas once. But Nessie doesn't like flying and I don't like to be too far away especially as I travel right through the football season. So Blackpool is an ideal place. It's also just a short distance away. So even if the car got a puncture I could always walk home!'

Gordon Milne had missed the FA Cup final through injury and he and Byrne, the two casualties, almost raised the roof at Anfield when they walked around the ground with the newly captured Cup before the kick off against Inter. Ronnie Moran, playing the penultimate game of his long career, came in for Byrne and Strong continued at number four in the absence of Milne.

The Anfield gates had been closed hours before kick-off, a fact which prompted skipper Yeats to ask as the team bus drew into the stadium car park: 'Where is everybody?'

'They're in the ground already... it's a 54,000 full house,' came the reply from a steward.

The Inter side carried an awesome reputation and had world class players including the Spanish pair Luis Suarez and Joaquin Peiro, those great Italians Giacinto Facchetti, Sandro Mazzola and Mario Corso, and Brazilian winger Jair. And they were managed by celebrated coach and tactical maestro Herrera, the Argentinian who had devised the break-away, defensive system of *catenaccio*.

The Anfield atmosphere was electric and the Kop sang 'Go Back To Italy' to the tune of 'Santa Lucia', as the world and European champions wondered what had hit them. Only four minutes had gone when Callaghan seized on a Strong pass, sped down the right flank and crossed for Hunt to volley past goalkeeper Sarti. Mazzola briefly punctured the Anfield hysteria with an equaliser but a clever Liverpool free kick routine allowed Callaghan to put them ahead again after 34 minutes.

Five minutes before half time Lawler, who had walked

down the aisle to get married the previous day, moved upfield
on one of the attacking sorties that were to bring him 61
Liverpool goals. His shot from outside the box flew into the net
only for Austrian referee Karl Kainer to disallow it for offside
against Strong, who seemed clearly onside when Lawler shot.

St John did make it 3–1 after 75 minutes and, but for a
header from the Scot that flashed narrowly wide and Sarti's
save from a Hunt shot, Liverpool's win would have been even
more emphatic. But it was sufficient to send Liverpool to
Milan confident of reaching the final in their quest to
become the first British club to win the European Cup. And
that May night at Anfield remained a marvellous memory for
Shankly as he 'replayed' some of the great matches he had
witnessed during his life:

> I've been asked what was the greatest game I've ever
> seen. I could say the 1960 European Cup Final between
> Real Madrid and Eintracht Frankfurt at Hampden Park.
> I'm not too sure if it was the greatest game I've seen
> because it was very one sided . . . Real won 7–3. But the
> goals certainly made it the greatest spectacle. I think
> Real Madrid were the greatest professional team who
> ever played, the greatest of all, and not only for their
> display in beating Eintracht.
>
> I think the toughest, most tense game I've seen was
> Manchester United against Real Madrid in the
> European Cup semi final second leg in 1957. United
> lost the first leg in Madrid 3–1 and the return was the
> first European game played under the Old Trafford
> floodlights, watched by a crowd of 65,000.
>
> United went 2–0 down in 10 minutes. But they fought
> back and goals from Tommy Taylor and Bobby Charlton
> gave them a 2–2 draw on the night. I was also at Old
> Trafford when Real came back to play what was called a
> friendly. But there were no friendlies when you played
> them!

United marked man for man but Real beat them 5–1. Real showed all their tricks, all their skills. But it wasn't just Gento, Kopa, Puskas and Di Stefano who were magnificent players for Real. They also had great players you don't hear talked about.

The centre half from Uruguay called Jose Santamaria jumped the height of the crossbar. And there was a brilliant player called Jose Rial, an inside forward. He was the man who caused all the damage at Old Trafford. Di Stefano and company took the markers out of the way and Rial cut United to pieces.

Players like Kopa and Gento could slice the opposition apart with pace and cleverness. They'd have a 4–4–2 formation to contend with in modern football ... if there's any such thing as modern football. I don't think there is. Things change and adjust, sometimes there's no wingers, then there's a dearth of strikers or centre backs. There's always a shortage of a certain player.

But as a professional team Real were magnificent, both individually and collectively. They could play it round in little rings all day long if they wanted to. Now the talk is of building from the back. But Real could do that at the front. They could have a little game just outside the box then have a shot at goal. They were the best team I've ever seen and Brazil, with Pelé, were next.

As far as Liverpool games are concerned the greatest night was at Anfield in May 1965 when we played Internazionale of Milan in the European Cup semi final first leg, three days after we had won the FA Cup for the first time by beating Leeds United. Inter had not only won the European Cup, they were club champions of the world, having beaten the South American champions Independiente of Buenos Aires. They were managed by the great Helenio Herrera and had players whose names rolled off the tongue.

We won 3–1 and could have won by more. We had a

Chris Lawler 'goal' disallowed for offside. The FA Cup was paraded around Anfield by Gordon Milne and Gerry Byrne before kick-off and I've never known an atmosphere like it.

All told, it was the greatest game I've seen. Real against Eintracht was a procession. No way our game against Inter was a procession. We were pitting our wits against the elite. It had atmosphere, excitement and superb football on a ground that was dry and bumpy, more like a Continental pitch.

But Liverpool raised their standard that night to a tremendous height. Roger Hunt scored a goal with a shot three feet high. He scooped it. And Herrera said: 'That's not an English goal. That's a Continental goal.' Which it was. And it was all down to the training boards at Melwood. He got a few goals like that.

Herrera admitted afterwards: 'We have been beaten before but tonight we were defeated.' And they were. We ran them off their feet. They hadn't met a team like Liverpool.

Ian Callaghan recalled: 'That was an amazing night and a fantastic atmosphere with Gerry Byrne and Gordon Milne walking round the running track with the FA Cup. We were lucky to have the Cup because on the Saturday night in London, Ian St John wanted to take it down to Trafalgar Square to show the supporters.

'If he'd taken that out of our hotel we'd never have seen it again! Fortunately, Colin Wood of the *Daily Mail* persuaded him not to! For the European game on the Tuesday I remember the Inter players going out onto the pitch and doing a strenuous training stint before kick off. I don't think Shanks had ever seen players work so hard before a match.

'We could see them sweating as they came down the passageway and Shanks told us: "They'll be tired before they start." At that time, Inter were rated the best team in the world but Shanks played it right down, as he always did. It was only when we came in at the end that he told us what a great result and performance we'd given to beat them.'

Yet a passage to the final – ultimately won by Inter at their own San Siro Stadium with a 1–0 victory over Benfica – proved beyond Shankly's side. Perhaps they never had a chance of making it, given the evidence of corruption uncovered by the *Sunday Times* and Shankly's allegation that Spanish referee Ortiz de Mendibil had been bribed.

Liverpool's pre-match hotel base was at Lake Como and even then the alarm bells were ringing. Or, rather, church bells. Shankly was so concerned that the volume of the local church bells would disturb his players that he and Bob Paisley went to see the monsignor in charge. Said Shankly:

> I asked him if he could stop them ringing just for the night so my players could sleep. He said he was sorry and he could understand our concern but he couldn't do that.
>
> So I then asked him if Bob could climb up and muffle the bells with bandages and cotton wool! Bob just collapsed in laughter, the monsignor said that would not be possible either and we just had to put up with the noise.

But when it came to noise the San Siro sound effects almost burst the eardrums when Liverpool walked out for the second leg on 12 May. An off-field hate campaign had been waged against Liverpool, accusing the players of taking drugs and the fans of being drunk, and as smoke bombs rained down from the 90,000 crowd the atmosphere in the stadium was vicious and poisonous.

Corso reduced the aggregate deficit by scoring directly from a free kick that swerved past Tommy Lawrence. But Shankly, Paisley and the players were adamant that referee Mendibil had signalled an indirect free kick. 'It was definitely indirect and the ball didn't touch anyone on the way in,' said skipper Ron Yeats.

Then Peiro levelled the two-leg score after kicking the ball away as Lawrence was bouncing it. 'At that time it was a foul if you went near a goalkeeper in Continental football so we were amazed when that one was allowed to stand,' said Roger Hunt.

Inter secured their place in the final with a superb goal from Facchetti to climax a fine move started by Corso and Suarez. Liverpool were out. But the odour of corruption remained and Shankly revealed:

I was told before the game in Milan that whatever happened we would not go through to the final. I had the feeling that something was wrong politically and I believe there were some investigations later about Inter and Liverpool.

We can't really prove anything but I remember being told that we would not win. It was just like a war that night. Two of the Inter goals weren't legal and I think the atmosphere affected them as well as us.

I'm not saying that if the decisions on the pitch had been right we wouldn't have lost. Perhaps we would have done. But of all the people I've seen and met that referee is the one man who haunts me. But we went close to winning the European Cup at a time when no British club had won it. Celtic became the first two years later.

I was delighted for Jock Stein when they did it and there are no sour grapes from me when I say that the Inter team they beat couldn't compare with the one we played. Nor was the Benfica side beaten by Manchester United at Wembley in 1968 nearly as good as the Benfica team Inter defeated after they played us in 1965.

It had been an eventful first season in Europe for Liverpool and Ian St John believes it had valuable ramifications for the future. 'To lose like we did was heartbreaking but at least we learned things,' he said. 'We learned about travel, the waiting around and all the little things that can go wrong like bad roads and poor training pitches. These were lessons absorbed by the club which later helped Liverpool win things in Europe.'

The following season, 1965–66, was another championship year for Liverpool to complete a three-year run of League title, FA Cup and League title again. The 1966 success was record-breaking for the fact that Liverpool used only 14 players! It was the fewest ever to be called on by any club in a championship winning season. Aston Villa equalled Liverpool's feat when they won the title in 1980–81.

In addition to the familiar Liverpool 12, Alf Arrowsmith made only five appearances and Bobby Graham just one. Consistency had become a Liverpool trademark, establishing them as a power at home and abroad, a triumph for Shankly's methods and football philosophy:

People have asked me what motivation is. It's geeing people up, preparing them mentally for the game, maybe saying something to take a little bit of weight off their mind. There's a bit of psychology involved.

But Liverpool really didn't need to motivate players because deep down each one was responsible for the performance of the team. And we weren't expecting a player on his own to win a game by himself so we shared out the worries, we shared the play...we shared everything.

We didn't need motivation at Liverpool because they were all paid the same and were always trying to win something. They were always in a high bracket. Their status kept them going. We really didn't need to motivate or joust them, apart from one or two.

We had a boy called Alec Lindsay who was full of skill. A real class player. He'd been at Bury a long time and Alec needed a bit of a needle occasionally, especially in training because he found the training hard.

It's a manager's job to find out the temperament and characteristics of all his players...what makes them tick, what boosts them up and what knocks them down. Then he's got to treat them accordingly. It's as simple as that. So after a while you know all your players inside out. If you can't do that then you're not a manager. There's nothing for you.

There are some players you can't help. Their temperament's just not right. So you've got to forget them. But the majority can be helped. One of the things my brother Alec talked about concerned the things you should do as a player and things you shouldn't.

Eliminate the bad habits and concentrate on the good habits. To live the life of an athlete is very important. No over indulgence and everything in moderation. Food, or a drink of beer, in moderation won't do you any harm. Overdone, yes. But at least with beer you can sweat it out. If you lose some strength you can't pump it back in. Since I went to Liverpool I've given boys steak and milk to help build them up. I'm talking about promising boys who maybe needed a little extra strength.

There are players with skill who promise a lot but never fulfil it. Maybe they don't have the appetite. Perhaps playing every week is too much for them. They might do better if they played once a month.

I'll tell you who makes players. It's not coaches...it's the mothers and fathers. Yes, you can develop players and improve them, as we've done at Liverpool. A good player can play better in a good team than he can in a bad team.

The day before matches, I gave the players a team talk in a room which has a table top football pitch. We talked about the opposition who had been watched by one of our staff, usually Reuben Bennett. And all we were looking for was the formation they played, 4–4–2 or 4–3–3, and whether there was an individual with some characteristic we might be able to stifle.

I'd never discuss at length the strengths of the opposition. If we were playing Manchester United, for instance, I'd never talk about George Best, Denis Law or Bobby Charlton. If we did we'd frighten ourselves to death. I overheard one of our players come out of one of my tactical talks before a game against United and say to whoever was next to him: 'Are Best, Law and Charlton not playing?' That was music to my ears. We are only concerned with us . . . not how great the opposition were.

I'd have a joke during the tactical talk. We were serious about ourselves but not the opposition. We didn't want to degrade them. We just didn't want to talk about them. I can make a joke by retorting. I'd drop bombs in the form of jokes.

Just like the Continentals do, we started going away to a suitably quiet hotel for every match including home games, leaving about half past eight or nine o'clock on a Friday night for our hideout after the players had eaten at home. The squad stayed together and we were the first club in England to do that.

We'd get to our hotel for about 10 o'clock before home games and the players would have tea and toast, with a little honey, and go to bed. On the morning of the match they'd have breakfast and toast for lunch. If they'd had no breakfast they'd have a poached or scrambled egg for lunch.

For a long time our results in London were not what they should have been so I delved into it. We used to go on the two o'clock train and have afternoon tea and then have a dinner in London at half past seven. They were going down the card from soup through several courses. We were over-eating. So we stopped that and went, instead, on the 5.40 train and had our meal on board.

We'd get to the ground, home or away, about an hour before kick-off and sometimes I'd say to the guy at the door: 'Here's a box of toilet rolls, Charlie. Give them to the opposition when they arrive.' Something always happens that you can make a joke of and men like Bob Paisley and Joe Fagan are aware of what's going on.

The players knew it was a team effort. They'd been brought up not to worry too much as individuals because they know we aren't expecting them to win the game on their own. We wanted them to share the worries as well as share the ball. We've never expected Roger Hunt or Kevin Keegan or whoever it is to win the game by himself.

We tried to give everyone a touch of the ball as soon as possible after kick-off That was the main aim. If all of the players have touched the ball early on and done it right they've all started on the right footing. Whereas if you try to do something clever and it breaks down it can take the confidence out of you.

If a player hasn't had a kick for 20 minutes he'll wonder when he's going to get into the game. We wanted to keep doing the simple things and to be patient even if we hadn't scored early. Ninety minues is a long time. Patience is the key. And the number of goals we scored in the last five minutes over a period of many years was unbelievable.

If we lost a game – and we didn't lose many – we'd have an inquest. You can always learn more from losing a game than winning one. So if we lost one we'd have a free-for-all discussion in the big lounge at Anfield on the Monday with everyone, staff and players, having their say. We'd even have full scale discussions when we won.

We wanted players to be confident but not over-confident. Over-confidence is a form of ignorance. That's nonsense. It means you're talking too much. But football can bring you down to earth quickly. With a crash. There's a happy medium. We wantcd sensible confidence.

If you have a team playing as a team who know each other, know each other's pattern of play and know what to do in given situations then it's the simplest thing in the world to play. But there are some teams, possibly, who don't know what they're trying to do or what the plan is.

If you want a tap fixed you get a plumber, if you want the lights sorted out you send for an electrician. We also had specialist places for players to play in a particular area. Gordon Milne for instance. We didn't complicate things. We gave them a job to do, one which was easy to understand.

When I go to see a team I want to be able to identify them. I want to be able to say: 'They can play. They've got a system.' And that's what Liverpool had. A system that could be identified.

Tommy Docherty had it. I could tell a Chelsea player from his panache, his control and his kicking of the ball. I say to myself: 'That's a Tommy Docherty player' because he'd given them a bit of style and class. I'm looking for a team to be identifiable, to know what they're doing, what each other's doing and what they should be doing. This is what football is all about. It's really a simple game.

But I've seen teams and I don't know what the hell they're trying to do. I can't identify them. I don't know what their method is. They look like total strangers. I can't identify with many teams but there are one or two trying to emulate Liverpool. It's a compliment to Liverpool that others are trying to copy them.

The method at Liverpool is preparation and adjustment, by that I mean adjustment on the day. I went to Madrid to see Nottingham Forest and Hamburg play in the European Cup Final at the Opera House of Football ... the Bernabeau Stadium. Oh, God. What a place, even without Caruso! But Cloughie made an adjustment to Forest on the day and won the European Cup.

But you can only do that if you've got the players. And

I think the main player in that Forest game was John Robertson. He can make 4–4–2 into 4–3–3 with his skill, his coolness and his brainbox. He's one of the best players in the game.

Liverpool's 1965–66 European journey took them all the way to the Cup Winners Cup final with another extraordinary Anfield evening en route. They collided with Celtic in the semi final second leg after losing 1–0 at Parkhead. In the return a fire scare turned out to be steam rising from the fans in the 54,000-plus crowd and Geoff Strong, limping and bandaged suffering from cartilage trouble, proved the Liverpool hero with a 67th minute goal following an earlier strike by Tommy Smith.

But Shankly's side lost 2–1 after extra time in the final at Hampden Park to West Germany's Borussia Dortmund, a game preceded by another characteristic story concerning the Liverpool manager.

The night before the match was memorable for the fact that Shankly sent the Press to bed – a feat surely unique in the annals of soccer!

It was almost midnight at Liverpool's hotel in Largs and the only occupants of the lounge were four sportswriters in a card school. Dave Horridge, then of the *Daily Mirror*, recounts the story.

A voice we all knew suddenly rasped: 'Hello, boys.' Together we replied: 'Hello, Bill.' We carried on playing, Bill carried on waiting. But waiting for what?

We soon knew the answer. He pounced on the assistant manager as he entered the foyer and a tirade ensued. What had happened, apparently, was that a group of miners staying at the hotel had made a lot of noise the previous night.

It was news to us but we said nothing. Bill boomed at his quarry: 'The miners might regard this as a holiday but the players and these Press lads are here to work.'

Then he turned to us and said: 'You couldn't sleep last night, either, could you boys?'

Nobody said anything above an inaudible mutter but Shanks was not to be deterred. 'There you see,' he told the assistant manager. 'Make sure it doesn't happen again. Good night – let's go to bed boys.'

He stood aside with his arms outstretched indicating very clearly that our card game was over and we were all going upstairs. We did exactly that. He is the only manager who would try and the only manager who could succeed in sending the Press to bed.

Borussia had accounted for West Ham in the semi final – winning 2–1 at Upton Park and 3–1 in Dortmund – and Liverpool found themselves facing a well-organised side, sound and solid in defence and menacing in breakaways.

Although Liverpool were in the driving seat for virtually the whole game they were defied by the goalkeeping of Hans Tilkowski and it was Borussia who took the lead through Sigi Held after he had been put clear by a magnificent pass from Lothar Emmerich, whose four goals in the two legs had destroyed West Ham.

Hunt prodded in an equaliser for a disjointed and jaded Liverpool but an extra time goal sent the trophy Borussia's way.

Emmerich and Held started the move which ended when Libuda floated the ball towards the Liverpool net. The towering Yeats attempted to head clear but could only help the ball on and under the bar.

So once more Liverpool had tasted frustration when in sight of a European prize.

But on 13 August 1966 Shankly's side and Everton met in the Charity Shield at Goodison Park, which was preceded by a unique lap of honour. Rival captains Ron Yeats and Brian Labone carried the League championship trophy and the FA

Cup, won by their respective clubs, while Roger Hunt and Ray Wilson, England team-mates that year, proudly displayed the newly won World Cup. A Roger Hunt goal was the only one of the game to take the Shield to Anfield.

Watching from the Liverpool bench, having been given a ticket by Shankly, was an absorbed 15-year-old called Kenny Dalglish, who was on a trial with the Anfield club and played one game for their B team against Southport .

But homesickness and a promise to go to West Ham for a similar trial meant that it would be another 11 years before the magical Scot signed for Liverpool from Celtic to become a legend in his own right.

The Charity Shield win was a high water mark for Shankly because Liverpool were to miss out on more trophies for the next six seasons although their consistently high League positions meant that they were campaigning in Europe every single year! This run would stretch all the way to 1985, when it was ended by the Heysel tragedy.

But on their second venture into the European Cup, in 1966–67, they were sent reeling out of the competition by the then emergent force of Ajax of Amsterdam. They encountered the Dutch side and a young, unknown forward called Johann Cruyff after disposing of Petrolul Ploesti, the team from the Rumanian oil fields, with considerable difficulty.

Callaghan and St John gave Liverpool a 2–0 lead from the Anfield first leg to take with them for the return when the lights went out on them in the dressing room and very nearly on the field! Petrolul won 3–1 – the goal that kept Liverpool alive coming from Hunt – and the tie went to a Brussels play off when goals from St John and Peter Thompson finally beat the stubborn Iron Curtain unknowns.

Liverpool then walked into a football blitz in the next round – crashing 5–1 to Ajax on a night when fog descended on Amsterdam like a blanket. Shankly – he revealed to me years later – even ran onto the pitch unnoticed in the fog and shouted to Willie Stevenson: 'Don't worry about attacking –

we've got a second leg to come yet!'

Cruyff claimed one of Ajax's nap hand – Lawler scoring a consolation goal – and the incorrigible Shankly announced afterwards that the task of pulling back the leeway was not beyond his side.

As the shock waves of the result hit Merseyside, Everton fans could not contain their glee, one of them telephoning the sports desk of the *Daily Express* to declare: 'Now we know for sure Ajax does kill 99 per cent of all germs!' Shankly recalled:

> There were a lot of very good teams in the European Cup and I said: 'If I had a pick of who to play I'd pick Ajax.' Sure enough, we were drawn against them. And we went over there and they belted the life out of us in the fog. From where we were sitting I couldn't see the game. When we were down 2–0 I ran onto the pitch. I said to Willie Stevenson and Geoff Strong, who were up the pitch trying to score goals: 'Listen boys, we've got another game to play in Liverpool. It's not even half-time yet.' We got beaten 5–1 and it was mainly through haphazard play, although in the tiny parts of the game we saw they were better than us.

In the return game a Peter Thompson shot hit the woodwork early in the match but two goals from Cruyff, giving a bewitching performance and making it a hard night's work for Yeats and his defenders, and two from Roger Hunt produced a 2–2 draw – and Liverpool went out on a 7–3 aggregate.

Three consecutive seasons in the Fairs Cup brought little joy to Liverpool as they strived for a European trophy. In 1967–68 they were beaten on a 2–0 aggregate by Zoltan Varga-inspired Ferencvaros of Hungary after beating Swedish side Malmo (4–1 aggregate) and Munich 1860, whom they disposed of 8–0 at home before sliding to a 2–1 away defeat.

It was in Budapest for the away leg with Ferencvaros that

Shankly proffered one of his immortal lines. Upset about the service for the team in the hotel dining room he barked at the waiters: 'What's the trouble here? Don't you understand... are you all foreigners?!'

Bilbao knocked Liverpool out in the first round of the 1968–69 competition by virtue of the spin of a disc after each side had won their home legs 2–1 ... Liverpool experiencing the other side of the coin following their lucky toss-up against Cologne five seasons earlier.

A 14–0 aggregate romp against Republic of Ireland side Dundalk in the 1969–70 Fairs Cup – memorable for Shankly's glowing praise of Dundalk steak which he described as the best in the world – was followed by defeat against Vitoria Setubal of Portugal on the away goals rule.

Some claimed that Shankly's loyalty to the older players, who had brought the club their collection of silverware, was too strong and that he should have injected new blood at an earlier stage. Whatever the merits of that argument, the watershed came at Vicarage Road on 21 February 1970 when rank Second Division outsiders Watford knocked Liverpool's ageing team out of the FA cup with a 1–0 sixth round victory. It was time for change at last, as Shankly recounted:

We had a great team in the Sixties. But if we'd had Ray Clemence in goal then we'd have won the European Cup and all the cups under the sun. I say that because I think Ray Clemence was one of the greaest goalkeepers of all time. If he'd have been in that 1960s team I don't think anybody could possibly have beaten us.

We won the League, the FA cup and the League again in 1964, 65 and 66. We reached the Cup Winners Cup final in 1966 but lost.

My best spell as a player was from when I was 28 until I was 33. If you've looked after yourself and behaved yourself I believed that by the time you were 28 you'd learned the game and you're a tradesman. I'd bargained for all these players going on until they were 30, at least. Well, they didn't do that. Some of them waned a little bit.

One day in 1970 we went to Watford in the sixth round of the FA Cup. We were without Peter Thompson, who was one of the greatest players of all time, and Tommy Smith, who was one of the best players who's played in England since the war. Never mind about being a hard man. That's trash. Tommy Smith could play.

But maybe it was a godsend that neither of them could play at Watford, who were in the Second Division. If those two had played they could have beaten Watford on their own. But we lost the game 1–0 and I decided after the match that that was it. I had to break the team up and start again.

We'd already dipped into the lower divisions to buy Alec Lindsay, Larry Lloyd and Ray Clemence. We couldn't go and pay £100,000 for a player and put him in the reserve team. So we went into the lower leagues to pay maybe £30,000 or £40,000.

We had to say goodbye to players who had been great players. But the team had to change and we dipped into the lower divisions for new blood. The changeover wasn't easy because it meant losing men who had been great servants, who had won the FA Cup for Liverpool for the first time and put them on the map.

But the changes had to be made. Ray Clemence had been at the club a few years and had collected a couple of medals by helping the reserve team win the Central League 10 times in 12 seasons, which takes a bit of doing.

But it helped the players get into the habit of winning, which is the best habit of all to have. So after our game the first result I wanted to know was how our reserve team had got on. Our motto was: 'Win, Win, Win.'

Sometimes it didn't matter how we won but as time went on and you got results you gained more confidence and you changed the pattern. You played better and you entertained as well as winning.

Clemence, signed from Scunthorpe for £18,000 almost three years earlier, replaced Lawrence. Out went Yeats and St John as Shankly reshufled his resources which had been fortified since their last trophy win by the acquisition of Emlyn 'Crazy Horse' Hughes from Blackpool, who cost £65,000 as a 19-year-old in February 1967. He was a player right in the Shankly mould:

> I tried to sign Emlyn after his first game for Blackpool in their last match of the 1965–66 season at Blackburn, who had already been relegated. We'd won the championship and a couple of months later England won the World Cup.
>
> Matt Busby and Jimmy Murphy from Manchester United were also at Ewood Park that night. They were looking at Mike England who they were keen on signing, although that didn't materialise.
>
> But the Blackpool manager Ronnie Suart told me there was an 18-year-old from Barrow making his first team debut. His name was Emlyn Hughes. He played against Bryan Douglas, who was one of the all-time greats, in the Finney class. But the boy had a very impressive game, even though an end-of-season game with nothing at stake was the wrong time to judge him.
>
> But Emlyn made it a cup tie. He even got a player sent off for retaliating against him. So I tried to buy him at the end of the match . . . after he'd played just that one game. But Blackpool wouldn't part at that time and it was February of the following year before I signed him, for a fee of £65,000.
>
> I knew after seeing him just once that he was a winner. There are some players you go to watch who you think can play but you're not quite sure. Others you see, like

Yeats and St John, who you know are no risk. I could have risked my life on them.

I'd have bought them with my own money if I'd had it and as long as there was a bit of interest if they were successful. The same applied to Emlyn Hughes. I knew he was no risk, either.

Hughes, who went on to captain Liverpool and England as one of Anfield's all-time greats, will never forget his first encounter with Shankly:

Shanks came to my digs in Blackpool and signed me for Liverpool. Within a quarter of an hour of signing me he'd smashed his car, blamed the other person he'd bumped into and, when a policeman came on the scene, gave him a bollicking for not recognising me.

I was a raw 19-year-old who had played only a handful of First Division games. Yet he told off a policeman for not knowing who I was! Only Shanks could do that. He was unbelievable.

Shankly was thrilled by the arrival of Hughes and enthused:

Emlyn came in and took Gordon Milne's place. In the first pre-season he was at Liverpool we played a friendly against Cologne in Germany and Hughes was up against the great Wolfgang Overath, who was one of the best players in Europe. At half time Roger Hunt came in singing the praises of Hughes who never gave Overath a kick.

But again we employed our special system, something we did on only a handful of occasions. Overath was a special player so he had to get special attention. We adjusted. Hughes marked him closely. When we had the ball Hughes played. When we lost it he picked up Overath.

Ian Ross did a similar job for us when we played Bayern Munich in the Fairs Cup in 1971. We beat them 3–0 at home in the first leg and when we went to Germany for the return game I put Ross in as a destructive centre half against Franz Beckenbauer.

Not only did he keep Beckenbauer out of the game, he scored our goal in a 1–1 draw and was unlucky not to get a hat trick. The German manager admitted afterwards: 'Beckenbauer not play too good.' That was because Ross stopped him playing.

I also gave Ross a job shadowing Alan Ball in a derby game against Everton at Goodison. You don't always like to do that but Ball, like Beckenbauer, was one of the greatest players in the world. But we didn't make it too negative. When we had the ball we wanted to play. But when we lost it the man marker picked up.

I'd have liked to have signed Ball. He was my type of player, a special player. Just like Billy Bremner, Dave Mackay, Norman Hunter and, before them, Bobby Collins of Celtic, Everton and Leeds. What a player he was!

A trio of other players were on Shankly's wanted list – England's great goalkeeper Gordon Banks who was then with Leicester, defensive giant Mike England of Tottenham and Wales and that gifted Chelsea and England raider, Peter Osgood. For various reasons he missed out on all three.

Another who eluded Shankly's net, in 1966, was full back Bob McNab, who was on the verge of leaving Shankly's former club, Huddersfield Town and was destined to play for England.

'We agreed a deal for McNab and when we met him for talks Bill told him that he was the best player in the world,' revealed Peter Robinson, former Liverpool chief executive and vice chairman who was then club secretary.

'Later McNab told us that he would be signing for Arsenal. Bill told him he was making the biggest mistake of his life. Then he told him he wasn't good enough to play for Liverpool anyway! This was a player who was the best in the world a couple of days earlier!

'We also spoke to Leicester about Banks but we never got as far as serious negotiations and, instead, we signed Ray Clemence who went on to become a great goalkeeper. Bill also wanted England and Osgood but, like the Banks situation, nothing developed.'

Shankly's buys did include Alun Evans, who became the first £100,000 teenager when he was signed from Wolves as an 18-year-old in September 1968, and Larry Lloyd, recruited from Bristol Rovers for £50,000 in April 1969. But Shankly frustratingly missed out on two other transfer targets, as he explained:

> We wanted to sign Frank Worthington but we had to call off the transfer on medical grounds. It was nothing to do with me. I wanted to buy him but the specialist who examined our players told me to turn him down. I was ready to pay £150,000 for him. Frank was a good player. But the decision was out of our hands.
>
> Freddie Hill at Bolton was a great player and he was also turned down by our medical people when we wanted to sign him. I thought he was the best player in England then.
>
> I saw him play for Bolton against West Ham one night and Freddie tore them to pieces with sheer cleverness and deception. I said: 'He's for me. I'll have him.' But when he came to Anfield the specialist said we couldn't sign him. I was sorry about that because at £45,000 he would have been the steal of the century.
>
> Both Workington and Hill were clever players. Abilitywise nobody could turn them down. They had all the stuff.

Shankly's hopes for Tony Hateley were never fulfilled despite an impressive scoring output by the big striker whose most potent weapon was his outstanding aerial ability. He cost Shankly the considerable sum in those days of £96,000 from Chelsea in July 1967 and in his one full season at Liverpool he bagged 27 goals in 52 appearances, linking up with St John and Hunt.

Hateley, father of England international Mark, had a bitter-sweet launch to his brief Anfield career. After celebrating a hat trick in a 6–0 rout of Newcastle on his third appearance he went to Arsenal 48 hours later and sent a magnificent header past his own goalkeeper Tommy Lawrence as Liverpool crashed to a 2–0 defeat.

'It must have been the best own goal seen at Highbury,' said Arsenal's John Radford. 'Tony went up with George Graham and myself to meet a corner driven in hard by George Armstrong. He got there first and the ball flew into the top corner like a bullet. When we got another corner the crowd shouted for Tony to drop back. But he stayed in the centre circle!'

His spectacular own goal prompted the joke on Merseyside that when Hateley hailed a taxi that night the cabbie said: 'Which way are yer headin' tonight, Tony?'

But Hateley, who changed clubs six times in the Sixties for fees totalling £400,000, and also played for Tommy Docherty, Stan Cullis and Joe Mercer, insisted: 'Those top managers said I was worth the money they paid for me. I averaged 25 goals a season and more than half were scored with my head. At Liverpool I reckon I helped Roger Hunt score a lot of goals in my one full season there but I had injury problems and you know you've got to be 100 per cent fit with Bill Shankly.'

Hateley left Liverpool 14 months after arriving, joining Coventry for £80,000 in September 1968, and Shankly reflected:

If we'd had Tony when he was a boy we'd have made a

better player of him. But we gave him a job to do. He was one of the greatest headers of all time and scored some fantastic goals.

He was brilliant in the air and so we utilised that because we had Callaghan and Thompson who could go down the flanks and cross the ball. That's always dangerous. It's an elementary way of playing but highly effective if you've got someone who can head a ball like Hateley, Tommy Lawton or Dixie Dean.

Liverpool finished the 1969–70 campaign in fifth spot and Bill Shankly's second successful Liverpool side was taking shape. The following season a pair of university graduates, Steve Heighway and Brian Hall, emerged as exciting new players, earning the nicknames 'Big Bamber' and 'Little Bamber', soubriquets inspired by TV personality Bamber Gascoigne who presented *University Challenge*.

When Hall, standing 5ft 2in, joined the club, it prompted Tommy Smith to quip: 'Oh, look, Shanks has signed Jimmy Clitheroe!' Hall, a B.Sc., graduated at football via Liverpool reserves. In his early days at Anfield he worked as a bus conductor to supplement his income while studying, and used to arrive for training in his uniform. He was given a changing room peg next to Shankly who said to him one day: 'Do y'need a degree to be a clippie these days, son?'

But he became a valuable figure in Shankly's new-look team in a scenario of changing Anfield personnel which saw the departures of heroic Kop figures such as Hunt, St John and Yeats. Hall scored the decisive goal against Everton in the 1971 FA Cup semi final at Old Trafford and is now Liverpool's public relations executive.

Heighway, a B.A., is also still at Liverpool as director of youth and in charge of the club's new soccer academy. He was recruited by Shankly from non-League Skelmersdale United and the Dublin-born forward played for the Republic of Ireland before he had made his first League start for Liverpool.

His fast, high-stepping flank raiding complemented the industrious, terrier-like attacking qualities of Hall as important elements in Shankly's burgeoning side:

Steve Heighway was a great signing for us. He was at Warwick University and played for Skelmersdale. I went to see him at his university base at Coventry. There were a lot of clubs after him and one club phoned him the night I was there with him.

He was approaching his 23rd birthday then and about to graduate as a B.A. He qualified, came out and he was a revelation for us, a breath of fresh air. He had electric speed and was a clever player. We were lucky to get him when we did because Peter thompson had been slowed down by one or two injuries.

We couldn't keep Steve out of the team. That was the truth. We had to play him. It would have been terrible if we hadn't. He had pace, the ability to beat men and a good attitude to the game. He made an immediate impact.

Alec Lindsay was another Shankly recruit. He had been bought from Bury in March 1969 as a wing half or inside forward – in modern parlance, a midfield player. But Shankly and the Anfield 'Boot Room', the football brains trust that developed in a cramped, windowless room off the stadium corridor where Shankly, Bob Paisley, Joe Fagan, Ronnie Moran and the rest of the training staff would chew the football fat, saw Lindsay in another role . . . as a left back. He made a successful switch that was eventually blessed by England recognition.

In November 1970 Shankly made another landmark decision in the club's history. He paid Cardiff City £110,000 for John Toshack. Toshack was to form Shankly's new attacking spearhead with a bubbling youngster who would follow him to Anfield six months later, a combination that was a fitting successor to the bountiful partnership of Hunt and St John.

Despite all the upheaval Liverpool again finished a creditable fifth in the League in 1970–71 and lost to great rivals Leeds on a 1–0 aggregate in the Fairs Cup semi-final. But in the FA Cup they marched all the way to the final against Arsenal.

The team was not the only thing undergoing massive change. So was Anfield itself. Just a few days before Wembley a young player sat on a dustbin amidst all the rebuilding and reconstruction waiting to put pen to paper to complete a £35,000 transfer from Scunthorpe United. His name... Kevin Keegan.

The new boy was merely a spectator at the Cup final when Arsenal hit back after Heighway had put Liverpool ahead. The Gunners took the Cup in extra time to complete the Double having clinched the League five days earlier. The Liverpool team that lost so dramatically at Wembley lined up like this: Ray Clemence, Chris Lawler, Alec Lindsay, Tommy Smith, Larry Lloyd, Emlyn Hughes, Ian Callaghan, Alun Evans (substituted by Peter Thompson), Steve Heighway, John Toshack, Brian Hall.

Keegan, bought with the intention of replacing veteran Ian Callaghan as a midfield raider, made his debut up front, alongside Toshack, against Nottingham Forest in the opening game of the next season, 1971–72. A new era was under way and with evergreen Callaghan still a major part of it.

Yorkshire-born Keegan became the new sensation of English football, helping to inspire Liverpool triumphs at home and abroad and captaining his country, before his departure six years later for Hamburg with whom he won two European Player of the Year awards to add to a similar honour in England. For Shankly it was one of the greatest transfer coups of all time, ironically after his Everton counterpart Harry Catterick had dismissed Keegan as 'just another busy midfield player'. It was, Shankly revealed, a tip from an old friend and colleague that first set him on Keegan's trail:

I first found out about Kevin Keegan from Andy

Beattie. I was his assistant when he was manager of Huddersfield Town and after he left I took over. Andy lived in Nottingham and he was scouting for another club when he told me about Keegan. He'd been watching him for nine months.

Andy talked about Keegan incessantly. And Peter Doherty, who was scouting for Preston North End, raved about him, too. I thought, Christ, they can't both be wrong. So we concentrated on Keegan and Andy Beattie came to work for me at Liverpool.

Preston offered as much as they could for the boy. They were managed then by Alan Ball's father, Alan Ball senior. But because of Andy we got him.

Kevin Keegan was one of the most honest boys of all time. He was a working class boy. His father was a miner and I'd worked at the pit myself as a youngster. It was the kind of background I had. I was brought up in a mining village.

He was a little shy when he came from Scunthorpe. He didn't get a lot of money and when he came I didn't pay him that much either. But I told him: 'Listen, son. It's not what you get now. It's what you're going to get by joining Liverpool.'

I remember I didn't want to move to Preston from Carlisle. But my brother Alec said: 'Listen, it's not what you're getting now... it's the chance Preston are giving you for the future.' So I went.

Kevin was arguing over a fiver. So I told him what my brother Alec had told me. Kevin signed and then, of course, his wages were doubled and doubled and doubled.

Kevin started an initial period of training with us and he was first in everything. He was a fantastic little feller. We had to simmer him down in training. I said to him: 'No son. You don't train like that in the first two or three days.'

Here was a boy ready to go out and play a game on

the first day, to go out over the hurdles and be in front in every race. He wanted to be first in everything. I said to him: 'Take it easy, son. Put the brakes on. You're only preparing to train now. You're only getting ready to train. It's only the shadow boxing you're doing now.'

We didn't start the real training until three weeks before the season started. I've never seen such enthusiasm as Keegan showed when he joined us. You could tell from the start he was out to prove a point because of his humble background and hard upbringing. Keegan did so much in a short space of time that far from training him before a game it might have been better if he'd jumped out of bed to play!

Right from the start Keegan didn't want to lose. He was a winner. He looked a little bit sad sometimes. He seemed a bit out of place, sneaking into the corner. But he isn't that kind of boy at all. He's a good speaker. He's not only blossomed into a player but he can talk as well. I think he'll maybe get one of those jobs on television. Maybe he'll improve television if he does. Or perhaps he'll be Prime Minister. Who knows?

I saw Keegan first in an FA Cup replay for Scunthorpe against Tranmere in November 1970 at Goodison Park. But the first time I really concentrated on watching him was after he'd come to Liverpool. He played in a final practice match, between the first team and reserves, which was crucial to us, just before the start of the 1971–72 season.

They were usually tough, hard, close matches. But Keegan switched it all round. He played in the big team and helped them score seven goals. After that practice game on the Tuesday I said to him on the Thursday: 'Do you want to play in the big team on Saturday against Nottingham Forest?' He jumped at the chance.

We'd signed Kevin the previous May, just a few days before we played in the FA Cup final against Arsenal in our last game of the season. So after signing from the Fourth Division he played in the First Division at the start of the next season in the first match for which he was eligible.

That's how much he impressed me with his attitude to everything. And he transformed that practice match, when a player called Ian Ross, who played some very good games for us, was facing Keegan. Ian had played against fellers like Alan Ball and Beckenbauer and more than held his own against them. And he was a sensible lad.

I said to Ian: 'What about this boy, Keegan?' He replied: 'I couldn't get near him. I couldn't tag him down. He's too quick.' So that was it. Keegan went in against Nottingham Forest in the first match of the season and scored a goal.

Kevin went on to become European Footballer of the Year in two successive seasons, bracketed as one of the greatest players of all time. And he is. His exploits will never be forgotten. Nor will his guts. He went into the unknown by leaving Liverpool for Hamburg. He did it himself I'll tell you...he's some man. It makes you proud to know him.

I think his display in the 1977 European Cup Final in Rome, his last for Liverpool before joining Hamburg, was one of the greatest performances of all time in Europe. Berti Vogts, who was one of the best markers in the game, stuck to him like a leech from start to finish. But Kevin ran Berti off the pitch and eventually forced him to concede a penalty. It was a fantastic display. He gave you everything he had...all the time.

Shankly had a profound effect on Keegan, whose career after Hamburg embraced playing spells with Southampton and Newcastle before stepping into management at St James's Park, followed by a move to Fulham as chief operations officer. Said Keegan:

I could devote a book to talking about Shanks. But I would say his main asset was that he pumped you with confidence and inspired you. He was a great man, a great psychologist and a great manager in every sense of the word.

He made a point of knowing a person's character and personality and he knew the right way of dealing with them, which is crucial for a manager. He studied people so that he would know which players he had to cuddle along and nurse and those who needed a dressing down. It was all geared to making Liverpool a better team and it worked with amazing success.

One of the great stories that sums up Shanks happened shortly before he left Liverpool. He said he wanted to ensure that all the players got the right kind of financial rewards for their work for Liverpool Football Club.

He told us all to go to see him and ask for what we wanted. He said: 'If it's fair and I think you're worth it I'll give it to you.' I can remember all the players queueing up outside his office then going in one by one.

Some were in 10 minutes, some were in 15 and one player was in almost half an hour. I went in about sixth in line and shut the door. No sooner had I shut it than I was opening it again to come out.

The other lads asked me what had happened. Had I fallen out with Shanks? 'No,' I said. 'I'm very happy. I walked in, the boss said I'd done well and that he was going to double my wages. And I was only going to ask for a £15 to £20 rise!'

That's the sort of manager Bill Shankly was. He didn't need a chairman to ask if he could give a player a rise. He didn't have to go to someone else. He was his own man.

Keegan's partnership with the rangy Toshack was a Little and Large duo of prolific scoring output. The Welsh international, with whom I worked on a book of his poems entitled *Gosh it's*

Tosh, was moved to salute his attack partner in rhyme:

> He arrived on the scene like a breath of fresh air
> Displaying those qualities ever so rare
> Courage, ability coupled with speed
> Keegan, a boy who was born to succeed
>
> The scourge of defenders all over the land
> He relied upon me to lend him a hand
> We worked together a perfect pair
> Down to the ground and up in the air
> Though we play entirely opposite roles
> Six seasons together brought 200 goals.

The first season of the Keegan-Toshack alliance took Liverpool to third in the First Division in 1971–72, level on 57 points with runners-up Leeds and only one point behind champions Derby County. An offside verdict against a Toshack strike from a Keegan pass in Liverpool's final game at Arsenal cost Liverpool the title in a season when they went out of Europe to Bayern Munich in the second round of the Cup Winners Cup. But fate was with Shankly and his players the following season when they achieved a glorious double with triumph at home and abroad.

Shankly bolstered his squad before the campaign began by signing Scottish international Peter Cormack from Nottingham Forest for £110,000. Cormack was a player of craft and stealth and perfect in Shankly's eye to complete his team rebuilding:

> He was a good buy and a good lad. To a certain degree he was similar to Ian St John in his defensive work. We felt he was capable of filling a role in midfield and he did it well.
>
> There was a comparison between this team and the 1960s side. The players in the earlier team were capped by their countries by playing collectively. The seventies

team did the same. They played for each other and the international calls came.

His team swept to the championship with 60 points, three clear of Arsenal, the Keegan–Toshack combination weighing in with 26 goals.

As Anfield celebrated the title win following a goalless draw with Leicester in the final League game, Shankly's feeling for the fans was vividly illustrated. He went to the Kop to take their salute and as he walked away he noticed a policeman flicking a red and white scarf across the running track with his truncheon. 'What do you think you're doing?' barked Shankly at the officer. 'That scarf is somebody's life and you're grinding it into the dust!!'

His followers had even more to cheer because in Europe that season Liverpool marched all the way in the UEFA Cup, toppling ace German outfit Borussia Moenchengladbach on a 3–2 aggregate in the two-leg final.

The weather, fate and the keen eyes of Shankly, assisted by his backroom staff, played key roles in the first meetings at Anfield. On a rain-lashed evening on 9 May the game was abandoned after 27 minutes with the pitch waterlogged. Years later, one of the ground maintenance staff revealed to me that a blockage was found in one of the drain releases which contributed to the build-up of surface water.

Shanks had opted for Brian Hall in the first match with Toshack on the bench, but when the game was restaged the following night he reversed their roles after suspecting that the Germans would be susceptible to the big Welshman's aerial threat. This change of mind was a spectacular success. Toshack terrorised Moenchengladbach and, after two goals from his partner Keegan, and another from Larry Lloyd, plus a penalty save by Ray Clemence from Jupp Heynckes, Liverpool went to Germany for the second leg armed with a 3–0 lead. The penalty stop by Clemence proved to be critical and Shankly enthused about his England goalkeeper:

Ray is possibly the greatest factor of all in Liverpool's success because of the goals he prevents over the course of a season.

As well as penalty saves he keeps out shots that might sneak in and, very often, does it cold after a long period when he's had nothing to do. He's a brilliant man.

Thunder and lightning heralded the return match and the storm clouds were gathering for Liverpool as Borussia, inspired by the midfield craft of their skipper, Gunter Netzer, put Shankly's side on the rack...and by half time they had scored twice to slash the deficit to a single goal. But Liverpool held firm and the Germans visibly ran out of steam. A first European trophy was bound for the Anfield sideboard.

The fans turned out in their thousands to salute Shankly, captain Tommy Smith and the rest of the players as they toured the city with their coveted pieces of silverware, the first English club to achieve the double of Football League championship and UEFA Cup.

Cormack slotted superbly into the side that lifted the two trophies. Also, a future star from within the ranks emerged in the slender form of Phil Thompson.

Originally a midfielder, he settled into first team football as a centre back, going on to captain Liverpool and win 42 England caps. The defender came into prominence in 1973–74 after Liverpool had suffered the shock of going out of the European Cup following a rare home defeat by Red Star Belgrade.

Liverpool lost the first leg in Yugoslavia 2–1 with Chris Lawler's goal seemingly sufficient to give them a springboard to an aggregate victory in the Anfield return. However, the visitors, managed by Miljan Miljanic, proved too strong and skilful. Lawler scored again but two Red Star goals took them into the quarter finals on a 4–2 aggregate and left Shankly plenty of food for thought.

That European exit led to the biggest internal reappraisal

of Liverpool's style since Shankly first laid the foundations. And the main conclusion of a 'Boot Room' inquest held by Shankly, Paisley and the staff was that the game had to be played more 'from the back'. The era of the 'stopper' centre half was disappearing Defenders had to be creative as well as destructive, initiating moves in seamless links with midfield and attack. Football was witnessing a new fluency.

Significantly, Phil Thompson was installed as centre back partner to Emlyn Hughes, who had succeeded Smith as captain, while Larry Lloyd left that season to join Coventry.

'The Europeans showed that building from the back is the only way to play,' said Shankly.

It started in Europe and we adapted it into our game at Liverpool where our system has always been a collective one.

But when Phil Thompson came in to partner Hughes it became more fluid and perhaps not as easy to identify. This set the pattern which was followed by Thompson and Alan Hansen in later years.

We realised at Liverpool that you can't score a goal every time you get the ball. And we learned this from Europe, from the Latin people. When they play the ball from the back they play in little groups.

The pattern of the opposition changes as they change. This leaves room for players like Ray Kennedy and Terry McDermott, who both played for Liverpool after I left, to sneak in for the final pass.

So it's cat and mouse for a while, waiting for the opening to appear before the final ball is let loose. It's simple and it's effective. It's been built up over the years but it sometimes takes players time to get used to it.

It's also taken the spectators time to adjust to it. The British public are not totally used to slow build-ups from the back, of teams making 25 passes and only getting to the bloody halfway line!

But they're getting used to it gradually because I've
seen games where, not so long ago, all the people would
have walked out before half time!

The Red Star defeat was to prove Shankly's last European
engagement, although nobody knew it then.

Liverpool shrugged off that setback to finish second in the
League, five points behind great rivals Leeds, and to reach the
FA Cup final. Their Wembley opponents were Newcastle
United.

The build-up was dominated by the threat Malcolm
Macdonald posed to Liverpool's ambitions. The powerful
Newcastle and England striker was seen in Geordie eyes as
the explosive force to demolish Shankly's side and take the
Cup to Tyneside.

Shankly had other plans! Liverpool defused the threat and
overwhelmed Newcastle 3–0, Keegan bagging two goals and
Heighway the other, Lindsay had an apparently legitimate
goal disallowed for offside by referee Gordon Kew.
Macdonald hardly got a kick. Thompson, who had helped to
shackle the much-vaunted centre forward, offered the
unforgettable verdict: 'What about "Supermac" now? I'm
going to take him home and put him on the mantelpiece for
our kid to play with . . .'

It was the second time in a couple of years that Shankly
and his team had enjoyed the last laugh at the expense of
Macdonald and Newcastle. Shankly recalled their home
League duel with the Magpies in March 1972:

As the Newcastle team arrived and saw the sign 'This is
Anfield' above the players' tunnel Macdonald said to the
manager Joe Harvey: 'At least we've come to the right
ground, boss.' I said: 'Listen, son, you'll soon find out.'

That day we beat them 5–0. And, candidly, my own
opinion was that they were scared to death.

Shankly was a master purveyor of immortal lines, which he classically illustrated as he bathed in Cup-winning triumph that May day in 1974. As the travelling Kop sang his name a couple of them raced on to the Wembley turf and flung themselves at his feet. Shankly took stock of the situation then quipped: 'While you're down there give my shoes a quick polish!'

He was also in sparkling form at Liverpool's after match banquet at a London hotel where was interviewed by television pundit Jimmy Hill for the BBC. Surrounded by his victorious squad he told Hill how his second Cup win with Liverpool compared to the club's first in 1965:

SHANKLY: This game finished up very one-sided, Jimmy.

TOMMY SMITH: Hey! It's Benny Hill!! (*in the background amidst much laughter*)

SHANKLY: We were a little too cautious in the first final and Liverpool had never won it, you see. But today, in the end, it was very one-sided at the finish...a runaway victory, really.

JIMMY HILL: Could I have a word with you about Tommy Smith the man who's calling me Benny Hill, because I think his achievement is really remarkable and a good guide to a lot of footballers who take a bit of disappointment and give up? He took a bit of disappointment and fought back.

SHANKLY: Tommy and I had our differences during the season but we're not like the politicians, you know, we don't harbour it on till the end. Till the country drops down. If we'd been like the politicians Liverpool would've dropped down. The politicians carry on their grievances and the country falls down. But Tommy and I have patched it up and that was it...You saw Tommy today...

TOMMY SMITH: We're sleeping together now. (*laughter throughout the room*)

SHANKLY: Tommy's nearly as fast as me now!

Little more than two months after that afternoon of Wembley glory, Shankly shocked not just football, but the entire nation by announcing his retirement as Liverpool manager. It was a bombshell that carried no warning.

The Press were summoned to a noon conference at Anfield on Friday 12 July 1974 when the news was delivered. Even hard-bitten media men gasped in astonishment when the club chairman John Smith made the announcement of Shankly's departure shortly after he had been awarded the OBE for his enormous services to the national game.

The shrewd Anfield overlord, who had been elevated to the status of a demigod, was the most successful and charismatic manager in Liverpool's history at that time. He rejected a new contract offer, turned down the chance to take a break before resuming his duties, and had resited all attempts by the Anfield board to get him to stay. 'Coming to my decision was like walking to the electric chair,' said Shankly, graphically capturing the magnitude of his decision and giving us an insight into the pain of reaching it.

> But I've felt tired and the pressures are intense. My wife and I both felt that I needed a rest. I must say it's not been very fair to my wife. I don't go out to theatres or the pictures. I think we've only been out together twice in Liverpool since I arrived here.
>
> We went once to the theatre and once to a garden fête during the summer. Twice in 15 years... it must be a record! But Ness realises the situation. She's a sensible woman. She knows that Liverpool is a city that's football crazy.

The amazing twist in the plot caused by Shankly's departure from Liverpool was as dramatic and unexpected as in any of the America gangster movies he used to love. He revealed:

> I get guided by my conscience. My conscience is honest

so if I do something I'm doing the right thing. People might think that when I do something it's quick and erratic. No, no. I'm being guided by my own conscience. So that when I got the message I thought that was the right thing to do.

If you can't make decisions at this game, if you can't make decisions in life then you're a bloody menace. You'd be better becoming an MP!

I always had in mind that one day, maybe, I'd want to retire from Liverpool. I didn't know how old I would bloody be. But some morning when I woke up I was going to say: 'I'm going to lie in bed for another hour.'

But I didn't know whether I'd be 69 or 90 when I got the opportunity. Now I've got it and I'm going to see how it works.

Actually, I was tired at the end of the Cup final even though we'd won. I'd been in London on Wednesday, Thursday, Friday and Saturday that week and at the end of the game I sat down and ate a couple of meat pies. That built up my strength again.

I left Liverpool because I was manager. That's the satisfaction I got. Not that I was gloating about it. But I had won. So I left when I had conquered Everest. I left because I was satisfied. I had proved a point. I was manager of a big club. And if I'd wanted to buy a player or give a player something there were no arguments about it. All the arguments were won.

But Shankly insisted that while he was retiring from Liverpool the very word 'retirement' rankled with him.

It's the most stupid word I've ever heard in all my life. It should be stricken from the record. You retire when they put the coffin lid down with your name on top. Until then nobody can retire.

Look what happens in China. A leader dies when he's

78 and the man who takes his place is 71. They only start when they're 70. I've retired from Anfield, yes. But not from anything else.

But if ever a man lived and breathed football it was Shankly. At home he loved sitting and listening, with his dear wife Nessie, to singers such as Jim Reeves and Kenneth McKellar. And Pat Boone's album of hymns was a big favourite of Bill's. But most of his time away from Anfield was still filled with football.

He would walk down a street and see young boys playing football, and would get involved in their game. He had such a passion for it that he never really switched off. This was a point Ian St John made emphatically when he first heard of Shankly's shock resignation:

> The news came out, and I couldn't believe it, I thought I don't believe this is happening – that he just packed in at the end of that season, you know. They had just won the Cup and everybody thought, well it's ill-health and one thing and another but it was a case that he felt that he had done enough and was going to step aside. And I suppose that at that time retirement maybe looked very nice but, you know, he didn't have any other hobbies.
>
> He couldn't go playing golf like Joe Mercer and Matt Busby, men of his era. They'd go on the golf course and have a knock and had their little social life. The boss didn't have that. He only had the football and when he didn't have that he had this big problem of all this energy and restlessness and he couldn't get rid of it.
>
> Despite all the things he did...he would travel to games, he would talk at dinners, he would do books, he would do records, he did everything...he missed the involvement of the dressing room, being involved with the training and being in charge of a football team – which was what he was born to do really.

Denis Law, the star he helped develop at Huddersfield, said after Shankly walked away from Anfield and, effectively, from full time football:

> To think that many people in the game didn't realise at the time how much he did for football; there'll be some with a few pangs of conscience that he was allowed really to drift out of the game.
>
> Just think of what he could have done for Scotland, for example, or other teams. I know he did help some clubs but, really, not in the way he should have been asked to do.

Nessie shed light on Shankly's decision to quit when she said: 'Bill has resigned for my sake. He knew that the tension and strain of being married to Liverpool's manager was getting me down. I was highly strung and full of tension. The days the team was playing, whether Bill was home or away, were terrible. He gave so much of himself and you had to feel for him and with him. This was something I asked him. I wanted him to think about retirement – and he did.'

The news of Shankly quitting was so big that Liverpool's club record signing of Ray Kennedy from Arsenal for £180,000 that same day, was relegated to single columns in the newspapers. At 60 Shankly was walking out when so much more success seemed to be beckoning. He left behind a record of three League championships, two FA Cup triumphs, a UEFA Cup, as well as three Charity Shields (outright or shared), a Second Division title and various runners-up spots. He was also 'Manager of the Year' in 1973.

In 784 games in all competitions during Shankly's 15 years at the helm Liverpool won 408, drew 198 and lost 178. Of the club's 65 European matches (which are included in those overall figures) they lost only three times at home – to Ferencvaros, Leeds United and Red Star Belgrade. His wife, Nessie, said at the time that she felt her poor health had helped sway his decision. Others believed that Shanks just felt it was time to go after steering the club to such a pinnacle.

Shankly paid a public farewell as manager by leading out the team for the 1974 Charity Shield against Leeds at Wembley. The adoring fans, in turn, saluted him at his testimonial match at Anfield the following April between Liverpool and the side chosen by his old managerial foe, Don Revie.

After his exit he was always ready to offer advice and guidance from his vast well of knowledge to anyone who asked. His loyal assistant and club physiotherapist Bob Paisley, who had fruitlessly pleaded with Shankly to reconsider and even suggested he should take a cruise then return and resume command, reluctantly stepped onto the bridge himself. Paisley memorably declared: 'It's like being given the Queen Elizabeth to steer in a force 10 gale.' But he guided the ship to horizons undreamed of.

Shankly became a regular guest of many clubs, both in the boardroom and dressing room, and hosted his own chat show on local radio. He gave his producer, Wally Scott, nightmares. At various memory-jogging points in his interviews with football personalities, Shankly was prone to desert his microphone to kick an imaginary ball round the studio!

Although he never again managed a football club, he divided his time between his home life with Nessie, their two daughters and family, and regular visits to matches at all levels. Said Shankly: 'There's nobody closer to you than your own kith and kin, your own blood. I've got my wife, my daughters, four little grandchildren and my sons-in-law. They're the closest to me and I would die for them.'

Some time later he reflected on his decision to retire and insisted:

Nobody pushed me. Not even Ness. It was my own decision. It took a long time to make it. It was like waiting for the gallows, really.

I haven't regretted doing it. But my life's changed completely and I've been bored a lot of the time. Before, I had somewhere to go and didn't have time to be bored. Now I've got time on my hands.

I have done quite a few things. I've been to hospitals, made speeches and watched a lot of games. But not being connected with football in some capacity has bored me.

I'll always be a Liverpool man. I never resented the club after I left, as some stupid person wrote in the paper. I was so proud of what Bob Paisley achieved after I left because we worked together for so many years and I was a part of it.

It would have been a good thing if Liverpool had made me a director of the club or involved me in some capacity. I wouldn't have interfered with anybody at the club. I could adapt to do anything. I was in football for 43 years and all of a sudden I was out of it.

It was a revealing comment underlining that the man who always preferred a cup of tea to anything stronger craved for the drug of football even in retirement.

Shankly's assertion that he would have liked to have become a Liverpool director, or be given some other official role at Anfield, was echoed in many quarters. Pundits and punters alike pointed to Sir Matt Busby's situation at Manchester United where he filled various roles after stepping down as manager, including general manager, director and club president.

But Liverpool felt that the sheer force of Shankly's personality and his massive charisma would undermine the authority of his successor, Bob Paisley, who was as shocked as anyone about Shankly's decision to quit and, by his own admission, 'went down on bended knee to try to persuade him to reconsider.'

When Shankly turned up at Liverpol's Melwood training ground the players greeted him as 'boss'. Chairman John

Smith, later to be knighted for services to football, and his fellow directors had made unsuccessful pleas for Shankly to stay. Having failed in that mission they felt that if Shankly insisted on resigning as manager it would have to be a clean break, simply to be fair to his successor. Their view was that the former manager's regular presence at the club would compromise Paisley and tend to overshadow him in a managerial role he had reluctantly plunged into with no experience.

After a while Shankly ended his visits to Melwood and went instead to Everton's Bellefield training ground, adjacent to his house in West Derby in which he had lived for years. He also stopped sitting in the directors' box at Anfield, where he had been made welcome, preferring instead a seat in the stand. But he travelled with the club to the successful UEFA Cup Final in Bruges in 1976 and went to Rome a year later when Liverpool gloriously won the European Cup for the first time in their history.

In Bruges I was with him when he opened his wallet and handed money to Liverpool fans who told him they had spent all their currency and faced a problem travelling home. It was an act he had performed so often down the years, giving out match tickets and cash to supporters whose personal circumstances stirred the great humanity in Shankly, even extending to 'cheeky' Everton fans who wrote to him asking for derby game tickets!

In November 1974, just a few months after Shankly's resignation, the relationship between him and Bob Paisley was soured by an appalling misquote from a sportswriter covering Liverpool's 1–0 defeat at Ipswich. Paisley recalled:

A Sunday paper report the day after the Ipswich game quoted me as saying that even in Bill's days I used to run the show. It was totally untrue. I never said any such thing. And anyone who knows me and my feelings about Shanks knows I'd never say anything like that. But Bill read it and took offence. I apologised, even though I was in no way to blame. He was still free to come to our training ground, where the players still called him boss. But he took the decision not to come to Melwood any more. In the fullness of time we both agreed that his decision had been the right one even if it had been for the wrong reason. There is no way I'd have driven Bill away.

In his biography entitled *Shankly by Bill Shankly*, published by Mayflower in 1977 and which he wrote with the assistance of my journalist colleague John Roberts, he claimed that other clubs made him more welcome than Liverpool. 'Over the last few seasons I have been received more warmly by Everton than I have been by Liverpool,' said Shankly. 'It is scandalous and outrageous that I should have to write these things about the club I helped to build into what it is today.'

It was sad such a schism occurred between a man and a club that will forever be inextricably linked. The truth is that after his retirement he was a monarch without a domain, a master thespian seeking a role. But the imposing Shankly Gates at the Anfield Road end of the stadium and his magnificent statue at the other ensure for posterity the enduring esteem in which Liverpool Football Club hold him and their respect and gratitude for the pivotal part he played in the club's history.

Bill Shankly died at 1.20am on 29 September 1981 in Liverpool's Broadgreen Hospital, following a second heart attack. The nation grieved, tributes flooded in, and the Union flag few at half-mast above Liverpool Town Hall. His greatness was captured by Sir John Moores, the wealthy Everton benefactor, who had transformed Goodison fortunes two decades earlier.

'Bill Shankly MADE Liverpool FC,' said Sir John. 'Before he came as manager they were a very ordinary club. With Shankly in charge they became a great club, winning everything worth winning.'

Liverpool Football Club were doubly blessed. In Shankly

they found a man to create a kingdom. In Paisley, they had a successor who would take it on to unprecedented heights of achievement. Somewhere in the heavens right now the two of them are probably organising a celestial five-a-side match, just as they used to do at Liverpool's Melwood training ground, when Shankly would play until it was dark to ensure that his own side won. Asked how he would like to be remembered Shankly said:

> That I've been basically honest in a game in which it's sometimes difficult to be honest. Sometimes you've got to tell a little white lie to get over a little troublesome period of time.
>
> I'd like to think I've put more into the game than I've taken out. And that I haven't cheated anybody, that I've been working for people honestly all along the line, for the people of Liverpool who go to Anleld. I'd like to be recognised for trying to give them entertainment.
>
> I'd played at Anfield and I knew the crowd were fantastic. I knew there was a public just waiting. So I fought the battles inside and outside. I was interested in only one thing... success for the club. And that meant success for the people. I wanted results for the club, for the love of the game, to make the people happy.

That wonderfully achieved aspiration is proclaimed on the base of the bronze statue of Bill Shankly which stands outside Anfield's Kop stand. It says simply: 'Shankly – He Made The People Happy'. It is a legend that defines a legend. Shanks was more than a manager. He was a man of the people for the people.

2

One To One with Shanks

Some 17 months after Bill Shankly's bombshell decision to
retire as Liverpool manager I had the pleasure of sitting down
with him to record a relaxed, one-to-one interview on a variety
of topics. Some of the material has been drawn on for the
account of Shankly's life and career in the previous chapter. The
interview took place in December 1975 and I think it captures
perfectly the man, his pride and his passion... not just for
football but life in general. This is the text.

KEITH: There were three points that came through in your
later life. There was hardship, there was football and there
was also humour, and those three qualities, those three
things you had in abundance, didn't you?

SHANKLY: Well really I think... if you've 10 in your family
with your mother and father – I don't think you can say you
didn't have poverty. I remember very well having to go out
to get something to eat, which was a difficult thing, and I
don't think I was in a bath until I was 15 years old. I was in
a tub maybe washing myself. But I remember when we were
boys, there was an old lady who used to make potato
scones... and if you had a jam jar then it was worth a penny.
Now the jam jars are worth nothing. The quality must be
bad! So I used to get all the jam jars and collect them, and
for every jam jar you got a potato scone, you know...

KEITH: I see ...

SHANKLY: So we used to rush round to the old lady and she gathered jam jars, and she got the pennies, of course. If she had four dozen jam jars – she had four bob. So this is the thing... out of poverty, and out of a lot of people living in the same area, in the same house, you get humour.

KEITH: Yes. And there's a camaraderie, a feeling of being in it together – team spirit, if you like.

SHANKLY: Oh, yes. Well I think that's the kind of thing that breeds team spirit. And 'team spirit' is a form of socialism. I'm my own politics – I don't go in for politics. But that kind of forms a camaraderie, as you say, and it's a basis for socialism. And when you hear people running down fellers that are socialists I think they're wrong. They don't know what they're talking about. I'm not talking about militant people at all... who go and try to destroy everything...

KEITH: As a code of life...?

SHANKLY: I'm talking about life. I'm not talking about politics in the true sense of politics... I'm talking about humanity. People dealing with people, and people helping people.

KEITH: Sure. Being human beings to each other.

SHANKLY: When you're with your family and they're all there. Now there's nothing closer to you than your own kith and kin – your own blood. I've got my wife, my daughters, I've got four little grandchildren, I've got my sons-in-law... Now they're the closest to me, of all the people... and I would *die* for them. You see?

KEITH: Yes. But you also fostered a team, a family at Anfield, Bill, didn't you?

SHANKLY: Well, having been in that environment, and having been brought up that way, and having played football, I think that everything I have, or you have, John, is a natural thing. When I started playing, I played for my team. I played for myself as well, mind you, oh yes. But I played for my team, and everything that I did as a football player – it was all geared for to make the team win. And if the team won, then I had won! If I had anything else, over and above that, I gave it and got a little kudos for myself – like international caps.

KEITH: Sure, yes. Although you were denied a lot of those, weren't you, because of the war?

SHANKLY: Yes. I lost six years like everybody else – I'm not complaining about that. If you've one international cap, you're an international. If you've got a hundred, you're an international. So it doesn't make any difference.

KEITH: You were saying, Bill, about the days back in the village, and the team spirit and camaraderie – this gave you the psychology that you used right through, certainly in your days in management. Would you say today that footballers lack this hard upbringing? And perhaps, because of that, they don't put the 110 per cent into it, as some people claim they don't, would you say that?

SHANKLY: I think that's a possibility. This is 1975, and many things have changed. And I think this is a way of life, really. It's possibly crept into football as well, as it's crept into all walks of life. And I think there's more people working for themselves than working for each other. I think that it may have crept into some places and if it has then it's time that the gospel was preached. You can take the case in point of one man in particular, Ian Callaghan. He's a living example of a boy who plays for everybody else, by using all his own strength to play for that team – and Liverpool's got a number of them, of course. Emlyn Hughes has been a brilliant performer for Liverpool and all of them . . . Tommy Smith, every one of them. Kevin Keegan's been working and all of them. I mean the Tommy Smiths, who has been there a long time . . .

KEITH: Indeed, and Chris Lawler before him.

SHANKLY: Oh yes. Chris Lawler before him . . .

KEITH: Because this is the creed you and Bob Paisley have always preached, isn't it?

SHANKLY: Oh, yes! The preachings that have been preached, of course, fellers like Callaghan have picked them up. And there's one thing about this – he never has forgotten it. Now if you've got to keep drumming it into people, reminding them about it, it gets monotonous.

KEITH: Yes. But you still have to do it.

SHANKLY: Oh, yes. And they think you're repetitive, you see. And sometimes repetitive people can be boring. But sometimes it's a necessity.

KEITH: But it's effective, Bill.

SHANKLY: Well, I hope so... that it's been effective. All I was concerned about was the fact that we wanted a team in Liverpool. There's two teams in Liverpool, but the team I was with wanted to make half the population happy.

KEITH: But this psychology has been tremendous. Players have told me stories about your pre-match tactical talks where you've got the model players out on the model pitch and the team in white represent the opposition. And the first thing you do is take the opposition forwards off the board, put them in your pocket and say 'It doesn't matter about those because they can't play anyway!'

SHANKLY: (*Chuckling away*) Yeah – that's right!

KEITH: Now, this is tremendous, isn't it?

SHANKLY: Yeah, Bobby Charlton, Law and Best got put in my left-hand pocket. 'Don't worry about them,' I said, 'They can't play at all.' They were three of the best players in the game, of course.

KEITH: Indeed.

SHANKLY: I think, in fact, Anderlecht was the beginning of Liverpool, John.

KEITH: Well, I remember it, Bill. Apart from the fact that it was a magnificent performance, and apart from the fact that it was Tommy Smith's real baptism in the side in the number 10 shirt – which again was psychological by you. You didn't want to change them around, you left him in number 10, didn't you... and left Gordon Milne in number 4...?

SHANKLY: Well, I said that the numbers on the people's backs were only to identify the players – it wouldn't be anything to do with where they would be playing.

KEITH: But apart from all that, Bill, the atmosphere that night was absolutely incredible and I think one of the big points about that was the fact it was the first time you wore the all red, or all scarlet, strip which has become famous since.

SHANKLY: Oh . . . yes.

KEITH: And it seems to be a very emotive colour, Bill. It gives people passion, more than the old white shorts used to do.

SHANKLY: I think so, John, I think you're right. The introduction of Tommy Smith, the fact that we were playing Anderlecht, and I had seen them at Wembley playing against England. Joe Mercer sat with me. I said, 'We're due to play this mob, Joe. What do you think? How can we deal with them?' Joe said, 'Apart from shooting them I don't know!'

KEITH: Because they drew 2–2 with England, and they could have beaten them, couldn't they?

SHANKLY: Oh, they were winning. England were very lucky to get a draw.

KEITH: And you had seven of those players against you at Liverpool only a fortnight later . . .

SHANKLY: Including the great Van Himst who's still playing . . .

KEITH: Van Himst . . . Jef Jurion was playing?

SHANKLY: Yes he was.

KEITH: It was a good side, Bill, that.

SHANKLY: Oh, well . . . it was Belgium's international team really . . . and I think that the introduction of the all scarlet strip, I think, really and truly, that was a psychological effect. I went home that night and said to Ness, 'You know something? Tonight I came out onto Anfield and for the first time, there was a glow like a fire was burning. There was an atmosphere you could a' cut with a knife.' And Tommy Smith made his appearance, of course, centre back, sweeping up. The atmosphere was so unbelievable. Celtic was the next time it was like that.

KEITH: Incredible – you could bottle the atmosphere.

SHANKLY: Yea...I felt a glow and I thought...'Christ, there must be a fire out here!' And it was just the excitement. And we had scarlet jerseys on, and scarlet pants and scarlet stockings, and I said 'It made the players look bigger – it made them look more awesome'.

KEITH: Absolutely.

SHANKLY: And, of course, they were brilliant and they beat Anderlecht 3–0. Anderlecht was a great team, because in the return match, which Liverpool won as well, the great Herrera was there from Inter.

KEITH: Helenio Herrera?

SHANKLY: Yeah, and he said then he didn't want to meet Liverpool. He said that this was something 'extra special' in the way of British teams.

KEITH: Yes, it was, wasn't it? It was probably the most powerful side that's ever been seen, Bill, in sheer terms of they kept coming at you, didn't they? There was no way they relented, was there?

SHANKLY: Oh, no! They were all strong physically and strong mentally...but the psychology of all this...when Herrera came of course, Continental psychology is a little different. Now just the same as I would like to say to you, 'What about Continental newspapermen, John – their conception of reporting a match?' I have come out from the dressing rooms in Italy and Belgium and Holland and the Continental newspapermen have asked me a stupid question, you know? I know I've given them some terrible answers. One feller says, 'What is he saying?' and the other feller says, 'I don't know what he's saying – but I don't think it's very good!' (*laughter*)

KEITH: I think Press men, newspapermen, call them what

you will, are the same virtually the world over. I suppose Continental newspapermen probably have less direct contact with the clubs than we do here. By and large, they're pretty much the same, Bill. But your point about Herrera was interesting because their psychology is different, a Continental manager's psychology – they're more subtle, aren't they? They try and douse the fire.

SHANKLY: I think so, John . . . I don't think subtle's the word . . . (*laughing*)

KEITH: They're cunning aren't they?

SHANKLY: I think 'devious' is the word. I mean, you go across there and you meet somebody and they say 'Oh . . . Liverpool . . . ! Too strong . . . too good . . .'. This is to soften you up, you know, and simmer you down – and then maybe beat you. And sometimes they did, of course they did beat us. We met Ajax once and we'd never heard much about them. I remember we were in Rumania when we heard the draw. We were coming back from Bucharest and we knew that there was a lot of very good teams that we knew about – but Ajax of Holland? I said, 'Now, if I get the pick I'm gonna pick them . . .' (*laugher*). And sure enough we met them and we went over there and they belted the life out of us!

KEITH: In the fog.

SHANKLY: That's right.

KEITH: A very foggy night.

SHANKLY: Now that was another thing about newspapermen. We sat at the front and we could only see just inside the touchline and the newspapermen reported the match. Now I couldn't see the game. As a matter of fact, I'll tell you a story. I was *on the pitch*.

KEITH: (*In an amazed tone of voice*) Were you?

SHANKLY: Oh, yeah. We were down two-nothing. So I ran on to the pitch in Holland and I'm saying to Willie Stevenson and Geoff Strong, they're defending and they're up the pitch trying to score goals, we're only down two-nothing . . . I said, 'Listen, boys there's another game to play at Liverpool – it's not even half time yet!' Of course, we got beat 5–1 and it was only through haphazard stuff. But the parts of the game we saw of course, they were better than us.

KEITH: But you actually ran on the pitch?

SHANKLY: I was on the pitch, yeah!

KEITH: Without the referee knowing?

SHANKLY: Oh, the referee didn't know anything about it. Oh, no. (*Laughter*) It was so foggy that even the Press men didn't know I was on the pitch . . . this is an amazing thing.

KEITH: There's some very funny tales on these foreign trips, but there was one I believe (I wasn't there) in Hungary when you played Ferencvaros. In the foyer of a hotel you were having, shall we say, an argument with one member of the English Press? And a Continental press man, who couldn't speak any English, was watching, and realized you weren't very happy and he tried to find out what you were saying and you said, 'Go away! I'm talking to one of my friends!' (*Much laughter*) Is that right?

SHANKLY: That's right, yeah . . .

KEITH: . . . and he couldn't believe it!

SHANKLY: Yeah, I was giving him a terrible doing and he said 'Can I help you?' I said 'Listen – you GO AWAY! I'm talking to a friend of mine!' That's true, John, yeah.

KEITH: Tremendous, yeah . . .

SHANKLY: I'll tell you a story about when we were playing Cologne at Rotterdam.

KEITH: In the play-offs . . .

SHANKLY: Yeah, the play-off It was another big night an' all. Er . . . number six got injured. He was a well-known player. He scored a goal in the World Cup Final at Wembley. He scored the equalising goal and made it 1–1. He was injured badly in this game at Cologne and we were winning 2–0, you see. Just before half-time they scored and made it 2–1 and this guy was limping off . . . er . . . er . . . it's a well-known name in Germany . . . ?

KEITH: Was it Weber? There was a Weber...

SHANKLY: Weber – Right! That's him – Weber! That's the name. So it's a very muddy night in Rotterdam and he's covered in mud, you see. So I thought, well, I'll er... knowing everything's strange across there and you can expect anything to happen at all. So, I got a little guy, he was a Belgian. I said 'Mister so-and-so, would you stay with me?' He said, 'Yeah... why?' I said 'Well, there's one of these players, Weber, he's injured. I just want to see if he comes out at half time... (*laughter*) – or somebody else comes out in his place.' I thought maybe they'd put the dirty strip on him, you know, and send him out...

KEITH: Exactly, yeah...

SHANKLY: So I said to this guy 'Do you know him?' He said, 'Yes, I know him personally.' So he stood alongside me. He didn't come out in the second half, and, of course, we only got a draw. We won on the toss of a disc.

KEITH: And then you went on to beat Chelsea in the semi final at Villa Park only three days later.

SHANKLY: Yeah, we played extra time then we came back and played Chelsea. Tommy Doc was with Chelsea then. But I remember that one – that Weber boy – and not knowing what was going to happen. And anything can happen on the Continent. I thought, 'Well, I'm going to be doubly sure.' And not knowing the players as well, if it was an English player or a British player you'd know him. But a lot of these Continental boys look alike, and I couldn't really tell the difference between them.

KEITH: We have that problem, Bill, when we don't know the teams, and we don't know what the players look like.

SHANKLY: Well South Korea, was it Korea played here in the World Cup?

KEITH: North Korea, yes.

SHANKLY: North Korea, well I think if they'd sent out another 11 in the second half nobody'd have known, would they?

KEITH: No...they were all the same size and looked alike (*laughter*)

SHANKLY: You couldn't tell them apart. They could've sent another team out – they were winning as well – against Portugal...

KEITH: Yes, exactly – against Portugal, until Eusebio stepped in.

SHANKLY: And if they'd sent 11 new players out, grinning, nobody'd known who they were.

KEITH: Nobody would've known.

SHANKLY: So this was the same thing. You don't know the Continental players. I wasn't thinking that they were trying to cheat us, but I thought, 'Well, I'll just be watching. Anything can happen.' You can't be too careful.

KEITH: No. Continental football, however long you're in it, it's always a trip into the unknown to some degree, Bill, isn't it?

SHANKLY: Right. That's a good point, John. You could play for 20 years in it but still when you play again next season, or the next game, there's always the unknown, the uncertainty. You don't know who's gonna turn up, or what's gonna turn up.

KEITH: Getting back to the point of your great psychology, Bill. Now it has been said, by certain people, that you, er...I mean you built two sides. But the team of the sixties was heralded by a lot of people. It's been said that perhaps you made them greater than they really were.

SHANKLY: Well, I think they were better than I thought they were. I thought they were er...you know, indestructible. And I think if I could add about three players from the present set-up at Anfield, that would make 15, I think they could have been the greatest team in the world.

KEITH: Now that's a fascinating thing because now you're comparing two teams of different eras which always fascinates people. You mentioned that with three players from the present team, the old team would have been

Bill Shankly returns the salute of the fans.

Shanks and John Keith in conversation in 1969.

A moment to cherish . . . Bill Shankly sits in the Goodison Park dug-out prior to the 1966 Charity Shield match between Liverpool and Everton. The trophy nearest him is the League championship won by Liverpool and next to it the World Cup lifted earlier that summer by England. Also on parade that day was the FA Cup won by Everton.

Solitary Shanks . . . the legendary manager emerges from the players' tunnel ready to see his team embark on another 90 minutes.

*Shankly proffering his after-match views to the Press after a 2-0
Mersey derby win over Everton at Goodison in March 1973.*

*Communion at the Kop . . . Shankly and the Anfield faithful
celebrate Liverpool's 1973 championship triumph.*

A Wembley farewell from Bill Shankly after the 1974 Charity Shield between Liverpool and Leeds.

*Shankly and his 1974 FA Cup winners. Back row (left to right)
Kevin Keegan, Brian Hall, Alec Lindsay, Ray Clemence,
Phil Thompson, John Toshack, Chris Lawler. Front row:
Tommy Smith, Ian Callaghan, Shankly, Emlyn Hughes,
Steve Heighway, Peter Cormack.*

probably the best ever. We're just interested – which three players, Bill?

SHANKLY: Well, there were 11 players who played regular, and there was Geoff Strong. Er...that was 12 and you could add Alf Arrowsmith until injuries crippled him. That would have been 13, 'cause he could score goals. And if you'd like to add Ray Clemence, Emlyn Hughes and Kevin Keegan to these 12...these 13. That would make it 16. Well, if I had these 16 now, then I would have asked for nothing else.

KEITH: Yes. Tremendous squad.

SHANKLY: I would'a taken them and I would've said to them – Herrera and them all – 'You can all come now. I'm not concerned about you.' Because they would've had the guts, they'd have had the guile – they'd the strength they'd had the pace – they had everything. And, really and truly, it would have been an awful awesome sight to see...

KEITH: Tremendous, yeah, 'cause if one went off you'd a great player to come on in his place.

SHANKLY: Oh, dear me! That would'a been ma greatest wish...to have these 12, 13 boys, because Arrowsmith played in the '64 championship.

KEITH: Yes, I remember, yes, he did. In fact it was in the Charity Shield his cartilage went, on the touchline.

SHANKLY: Yes, he did – against West Ham. He turned round then he went down, and he played no more.

KEITH: Tragic, really.

SHANKLY: He played a little bit, but not very much.

KEITH: He was never his old self...

SHANKLY: And then, of course, there was a man who never got...he got credit, but not a lot...and he'd to pack up early – Gerry Byrne.

KEITH: Oh yes.

SHANKLY: He did himself the first match of the season, after the 1966 Charity Shield at Goodison in our opening League match against Leicester. He went down, and he never got over the injury. Prematurely finished – and he was a *brilliant* player. Nobody knows how brilliant he was.

KEITH: Yes. In fact, I once asked you if you could pick out the one Merseyside player and you picked Gerry Byrne.

SHANKLY: Aw, Gerry... Who could've played at Wembley Stadium for two hours with a broken collar bone?

KEITH: Unbelievable, wasn't it?

SHANKLY: But the greatest thing of all was the fact that we never disclosed it.

KEITH: I know. And he didn't disclose it.

SHANKLY: No. This was the greatest thing – that nobody knew till after the game, barring Bob Paisley and myself... and the doctor... and the players, of course, at half time because the bones were gritting together. We kept it and we didn't disclose it to Leeds. So they were unaware that this had happened.

KEITH: Which is incredible – that a player can hide that...

SHANKLY: Well, if we'd switched Gerry Byrne to outside left, say, or outside right, then we'd have disclosed it. We'd have given our hand away.

KEITH: Yeah, if you were playing poker you'd have given the game away.

SHANKLY: We'd have given our hand away and Leeds would have known we were a man short. So we said, 'Soldier on, Gerry', knowing who Gerry Byrne was of course. Some players you couldn't have done that with Gerry Byrne, yes. Because he dislocated his elbow at – Celtic Park and played on. You should've seen his arm. It was black an' blue – that was a Thursday night match an all... and he came back here on the Saturday and played.

KEITH: He was one of the hardest men ever, wasn't he?

SHANKLY: Gerry Byrne was not only a hard man, Gerry Byrne was a great player...

SHANKLY: Being a newspaperman you've done a lot of

'ghosting' as well, of course, for Kevin Keegan for instance . . . with the articles.

KEITH: Yes, that's right, in the *Express*.

SHANKLY: And you also have done a bit for the Ian Callaghan book, which pleased me very much, because ma name was mentioned a few times in it . . .

KEITH: It was, wasn't it?

SHANKLY: I'm not looking for publicity – but I thanked Ian Callaghan for it anyway.

KEITH: Well, of course, Ian had a tremendous amount of respect for you and therefore your name kept cropping up, because his debut in the team came a matter of only months after you took over at Liverpool. You took over in December '59 and Ian Callaghan made his debut in April 1960, so it was only four months later. So, obviously, his time at Liverpool just completely overlapped your time at Liverpool. But it was very interesting to do those things with Kevin and Ian, because I think you get to appreciate about the game, and about a player's life that you wouldn't necessarily appreciate otherwise.

SHANKLY: Both genuine boys, John.

KEITH: Oh, tremendous!

SHANKLY: You must have found them wonderful to work with.

KEITH: Oh, absolutely! Well, Kevin used to come along . . . people have an idea that 'ghost-written' articles, of which there are not a lot now, are not at all representative of the subject – in other words that you just write them. Well, that wasn't the case at all. Kevin used to come along with his own ideas written down. I had an easy job with Kevin – and with Ian. He's got such a wealth of experience that we just got a tape recorder and talked into it – and I think that's the way to do it. And while I'm on the subject, I believe that a colleague of mine, John Roberts of the *Express*, is now working with you on a book of your great career and life.

SHANKLY: Yes. There was a promise given by word. I gave a promise a long time ago that that would happen – if I was going to do it. That company, a certain man got a promise from me, and of course I kept my promise. It wasn't in writing. I give nothing to anyone in writing. It was word of mouth, and it's going to be from the cradle.

KEITH: Gonna be a fascinating tale that.

SHANKLY: And the days when I was a boy, and how I lived, and how I used to do a paper round, and work at the pit. Cycle 15 miles to play a match and cycle 15 miles back home again. All the things of the era and all the snags. At the same time, some people think these are sad things, but not for us, no. I think that I'd rather've had that way of being brought up. I had good people. Good parents. Good brothers and sisters.

KEITH: Which is a lot more than some people have, Bill.

SHANKLY: I think so. If I had the chance of changing my life I would have changed some . . . one or two things . . . but not the major things. And the major things were being brought up the right way, being brought up to respect people, and to fear your parents – and even to fear your schoolteacher. But the man I feared most was my father.

KEITH: You actually feared him?

SHANKLY: Oh, yeah! Oh, yeah! Yeah, he took his hand and gave you a belt on the jaw – when you needed it. And he was right.

KEITH: That's a very interesting point, Bill, about the fact that you feared your father, you say, and that he wasn't loath to give you a belt, or a sock on the jaw now and again. Do you think that perhaps today our society's become too soft? That juvenile crime is rising, hooliganism, crime in general is rising? Do you think that we need to be more strict?

SHANKLY: Well, I think the community part of it makes a difference. I mean, we're in a big city . . . and Manchester and all the big cities, and Glasgow. Ours was a smaller community, and consequently there weren't as many places to damage, actually, for hooligans. There's always been boys who would cause trouble, no matter where you go. But I think there could be something done about a lot of the trouble.

It's possibly because they're unemployed, there's some of the boys bored, they don't have enough to take up their attention. And when I see it, it galls me to think that there is that kind of thing. But at the same time, it's a very difficult thing to stop. And whoever's going to come up with the answers is going to be very lucky.

Getting them work – getting them interested in something. Having clubs, having places to go. I think if you've something to do – this is the thing. Then there would be less trouble. Boredom's a bad thing.

KEITH: Oh, sure. It breeds all sorts...

SHANKLY: Idleness. Idleness can cause your mind to be warped.

KEITH: Mm...the Devil finds an empty mind something to do?

SHANKLY: But I think where there's more people then you've got more trouble. But I was lucky. I was in a small community. There was still trouble but not as much as there is today.

KEITH: What do you think about the current trend in management, Bill? I'm not referring to any local players, thank goodness, but there are occasions when players go off the rails today. Seemingly more than did perhaps even 15, 20 years ago. Do you feel that the temptations are now much greater for players, Bill?

SHANKLY: Well, I think you're talking about the 'awkward squad' now, John. The boys who have been running away from the clubs and saying that they're not going to play again...and have left England international teams. And when I see these things it makes me sick, you know? To think that somebody could run away from an international party...I really and truly don't understand it. It makes you wonder how it's possible for that to happen.

I mean, it's pride, whether you're English, Scottish, Irish, Welsh – anything at all. To be picked to play in a team! They don't do it with their own clubs, funnily enough, most of them. It seems to be when they're away with the international team. But to be picked to play with your country, or to be in the party even – that's an honour. And then you pick up the paper and see 'so-and-so's absconded from the international team', whether it be England, Scotland, Ireland or Wales. It's a terrible thing. I don't know what you could do about it. Really and truly, the question should be asked of them, 'If you don't want to play, all you need to do is say so.'

KEITH: Somehow you kept the wheels rolling at Anfield and Bob Paisley's doing the same.

SHANKLY: Oh, well, we had one or two problems at Anfield, but we got over them. Sometimes a player does things and he's sorry for them after. And if they're sorry for them after that, that could make me feel sorry for them, you see. So that I dealt with it in my way. So that anything that I've done, if people thought I'd done it the wrong way, then that's their opinion.

KEITH: You did it your way.

SHANKLY: I did it my way. And if I did it my way, then I was quite satisfied in my mind that I'd done right. I did what I thought, and I did what was honest.

KEITH: Bill, in this city you can never come away from the point that across Anfield there is Goodison Park. Now your comments over the years about Everton have been, er...can I say outrageous at times? I wonder deep down, I know you had a very good relationship with Harry Catterick beneath it all, but I wondered what you said about Everton – was that purely for motivation? For the players...and for the jokes among the fans...you came out with some pearls didn't you?

SHANKLY: Well I did...if you're in a city where's there's two teams, like Celtic and Rangers, United and City in Manchester, and Liverpool and Everton, I mean, if you're in a city like that, then that's the ultimate. Jock Stein says when they play the Rangers 'That's the ultimate'. The whole week everybody's keyed up. When we're gonna play Everton in a match, I mean that's the ultimate, and it's the same before the season starts. Everton and Liverpool people have a bet on, a lot of them, that 'We'll finish above you', you know. So that it's great to have a good team and win something for your fans – but to beat the local team is really something.

KEITH: It's like an extra point if you win, isn't it?

SHANKLY: It is. It's a bonus. An' I have said things which people have exaggerated, because when we make them...(*laughter*) I mean, I got to the point where I was frightened to say anything because somebody was going to exaggerate it! I said something and, of course, since I've packed in managing Liverpool things have changed a little bit. And I get well treated at both places.

KEITH: Oh, yes. I know you do.

SHANKLY: Yes, I get well treated at Everton an' all. But I think that I've said some things that didn't...that people didn't like...and which I meant, of course. But I've said some things, that have been exaggerated. Harry and I had...Harry was withdrawn...quiet. He was a different personality from me. Harry looked on it in a different light. I think I could make more excuses than Harry. I think my excuses were better than Harry's! (*Laughter*)

KEITH: Yeah, tremendous...What always interested me, Bill, was how you, who absolutely ate, slept, drank football, Liverpool, how you switched off. You went home, what did you do? I know Nessie, your wife, often said that if you lost, which wasn't very often, you used to clean the cooker, didn't you?

SHANKLY: Yeah (*chuckling*).

KEITH: And mow the lawn about five times in the same afternoon.

SHANKLY: Yeah, I wanted something to do, if we got beat. If Everton beat us, you know. Once Everton beat us an' I went home an' washed all the back kitchen that night. It was a Saturday night. (*Laughing*) I just wanted something to do... an' it took my mind off it an' I got over it. An' the next day after it, when you get out of your bed in the morning, an' you've lost a match that was important. It's a terrible feeling. Oh, terrible. Then maybe the day after, Monday, it's a bit easier. Then Tuesday... It's like cutting your finger. It's very sore to start with.

KEITH: It just heals?

SHANKLY: After a few days it heals up. And then after a week you've forgotten, until the next match. But when you play a local derby, an' you lose it – it's a terrible feeling.

KEITH: It must be sickening...

SHANKLY: Aw... unbelievable. We used to have an expression at Preston, if we were playing an important match, you see, an' we got beat. We didn't play very well, you know, and some guy would be laughing in the dressing room, or in the bath. And I remember me saying to, I think it was Jim Milne, Gordon Milne's father, after we'd got beaten. This feller was laughing in the bath. I says: 'Laughing? You've just got bloody beaten out there and you're laughing! I'll tell you something. You should be barred from laughing till next Saturday!' So, at Preston we used to say: 'If you've got beat you can't laugh till next Saturday. It's a week before you can laugh again.' The whole thing's so serious. And by taking it so serious, I mean, you eventually get results. You're eventually successful.

KEITH: Sure. In other words, if you do anything do it properly, take it to the ultimate.

SHANKLY: Yeah. Oh, yeah. That's the only way, right to the peak.

KEITH: But how do you switch off at home, Bill?

SHANKLY: I like to listen to records. I've got a few records of all people. McKellar, who's a very good singer, I think he's at his peak now...of Jim Reeves, gone of course, unfortunately. Pat Boone. A lot of folk singers as well. And there's a Scottish singer called Daley, he's a good singer. Glenn, I think it's Glenn Daley. But we've got a lot of Pat Boone's records, and we've got Harry Secombe. I like Harry. I think Harry's a very funny man – his records are very good too but I like to see him in person because Harry can make people laugh.

KEITH: Yeah. He's got two gifts. He can make people laugh and sing well as well.

SHANKLY: Pat Boone sings hymns, and I've got a lot of his hymns.

KEITH: Do you like hymns?

SHANKLY: Aw...I love them!

KEITH: Do you?

SHANKLY: Oh, yeah! The hymns that I used to remember as a boy. I can tell you all the words now. When one comes on I know all the words that are in it, an' that's only from being a boy. You heard them out in the street – the Salvation Army, singing their hymns. Pat Boone 'n' them sings hymns like that, an' Boone, of all of them, I think his records are the best.

KEITH: Talking about relaxation, Bill, you were never one to take off to Spain, or Italy, or the beaches of Majorca. It was Blackpool, wasn't it, all the time?

SHANKLY: Well I travelled all winter, John, and the last 12 years I've been abroad an' we've been to Las Palmas an' a few places an' Ness doesn't fly. So, she doesn't like travelling and I don't want to go too far away. I mean, even going home's a chore for me. So I used to go to Blackpool because I was at Preston at one time – for 10 years actually in the war and 16 years all told. So, I felt Blackpool was a very bracing place, through going 'special training' with

North End. And, the travel's very short. You see, you can go in the car and if I got a puncture I could always walk home (*laughter*) . . . It's not very far to get home!

KEITH: Yes. And also I know you played football with porters at Euston Station once and you used to castigate them if the ball went on the lines. Did you used to do the same with waiters at Blackpool?

SHANKLY: Oh, I had a game with the waiters, yes. There was a bunch of little Greek boys over there once an' we had a game – oh, umpteen games. In fact, I came back from Blackpool one day an' I was jiggered. I had a bad back and everything from playing in the sand, you know.

KEITH: But you used to take them very seriously, Bill. You used to tell the waiters they had to play.

SHANKLY: Oh, yes! There was no messing about – these little Greek boys could play. Oh, yes – but I always made sure I was on the team that won, you know! (*Laughter*). If we were getting beat we played on for about an hour and a half . . .

KEITH: That's what you used to do at Melwood – in the five-a-sides . . . And if your team was losing you'd play till it was dark, didn't you?

SHANKLY: Yes. I refereed the matches at Blackpool, but we always won. We always finished up winning and this makes you feel good, when you win. But I like Blackpool and the fact was that it wasn't very far away, and it was bracing. I think that if you're enjoying a holiday it's the main thing. The sunshine is good for people. A fortnight in the sun's a good thing, but I think that if you enjoy something then I think it must be good for you.

KEITH: Yes, a little bit of what you like does you good . . .

SHANKLY: Yes, even better than the sunshine.

KEITH: Sure, really – because that's a part of a footballer's game. He's got to relax as well as play.

SHANKLY: If he's enjoying playing then he's playing well.

KEITH: Bill, I've thoroughly enjoyed this but I'd like to ask, if I may, one question I think everyone on Merseyside and throughout England, Britain, whatever you like, wants to ask you – are you going to come back into football, Bill?

SHANKLY: Er... well, I do a little bit here and there, you know. People are on to me every day really about asking questions about players and things. I think, in some kind of capacity, I would like to take part in it. With one particular club. I go from place to place now an' give information to people, an' advice, of course. I don't know how many people has been on to me an' I've been to a lot of grounds, incidentally. An' I've travelled quite a long distance to one of them. I think that I've given a lot of advice an' I may take a job, not fully occupied, no. Not fully involved, oh no. No way, no.

KEITH: But using your great knowledge, your vast store of knowledge about the game, surely, you've got a lot to give to the game even now?

SHANKLY: I've had an interesting time up to present this season. I've seen a few players who have been unknown till recently, an' they look like being players. An' I've got a number of players on my list an' all who I think can play. If I can help anybody, I'll help them in the game. And in that way, that would be interesting.

KEITH: I'm sure...

SHANKLY: Just helping somebody else. There might be a problem they've got that I've had before an' I've dealt with it the right way. An' so I can advise people.

KEITH: Yes, it's only learned by experience.

SHANKLY: Yes. They might phone me, and they do, an' they say, 'I've got a problem' an' I say, 'Oh, well, I had the same problem' and 'How do you deal with it?' So, maybe my dealing with it was the right way and of course, I give advice to people. And this happens regularly.

KEITH: It has been mooted that it might be as an assistant to an international team, Bill. Possibly that is one way you might come back again into the game.

SHANKLY: Well, that's a kind of part-time job as well. That's a job that would interest me, yeah. I mean, I think an international job's really a part-time job in any case.

KEITH: Do you really?

SHANKLY: Well I think I could do that and paint the house ... (*laughter*) ... at the same time.

3

Funny Gags and Short Jabs

When Shanks saw Harry

I am often asked what was Shankly's attitude towards his Merseyside counterpart Harry Catterick, the Everton manager, and the Goodison club in ceneral.

Despite Shankly's outrageous public observations about Liverpool's arch rivals, just three-quarters of a mile away across Stanley Park, he needed them to bounce off. He would not have liked to operate in a one-club city and during the 1960s Everton had their own share of success, which provided the perfect springboard and catalyst for banter between the rival sets of supporters . . . and Shankly.

Catterick was a very different character. A taciturn figure, he was the antithesis of Shankly who embraced the public and the media with gusto. The two men were poles apart.

A story Harry recounted concerned his return to work following a heart attack in the early 1970s, when he was swamped with telephone calls and telegrams from other managers welcoming him back. But from Shankly . . . nothing!

Then, late in the afternoon, Catterick heard footsteps up the spiral staircase leading to his office at Everton's Bellefield training ground. And, there, standing in the doorway was Shankly with two cups of soup.

'Here you are Harry, hope you're better,' said Shankly.

'Now, how much do you want for Joe Royle and David Johnson?'

High Steaks

One enduring tale concerns a young player of whom Liverpool had high hopes to replace the great Ian Callaghan. They thought that the only problem with the young man was that he wasn't strong enough. So they had a 'council of war.' There was Shankly, Bob Paisley and Joe Fagan and they came to the conclusion they would employ the traditional Anfield solution – give him steak! So Shankly said: 'D'yer know the family, Bob?'

'Well, I know the butcher around the corner like . . .'

Shankly said: 'Get the steaks every day!' So Bob Paisley made arrangements for steak to be delivered to the family daily. This was towards the end of the season and continued right through the summer. On the first day of pre-season training the player came in and knocked on Shankly's door.

'Jesus Christ, son . . . you look like physical poetry – you're muscular. Oh! It's great – you're a prize specimen – the steaks have done the trick,' said Shankly.

The player replied: 'Actually boss, I wanted a word.'

'Oh no,' said Shankly. 'Christ you look well.'

The player insisted: 'No, boss, I wanted to tell you – I'd like a week off.'

'Why, what's the matter, son?'

'Well, I've got a girl in the family way.'

Shankly raced to the door of his office and shouted down the corridor: 'Joe, Bob, come quickly . . . we've reared a bleeding monster!'

Shankly to Tommy Docherty 1

Shankly as a Preston North End player to Docherty, as he prepared to make his debut for the Lancashire club in 1949, as Shankly's successor at right half:

'Don't worry about anything, Tom...that No. 4 jersey knows its own way round.'

Shankly to Tommy Docherty 2

Shankly talking to fellow manager Docherty, who sold him Tony Hateley from Chelsea for £96,000 in 1967, a player Shankly sold on to Coventry after 28 goals in 56 Liverpool appearances...

DOCHERTY: 'You've got to say that Tony's good in the air, Bill.'

SHANKLY: 'Aye, so was Douglas Bader...and he had a wooden leg.'

Shankly to Tommy Docherty 3

When they met as respective managers of Liverpool and Chelsea in the 1965 FA Cup semi final at Villa Park, Shankly led his side into the home dressing room and when Docherty arrived with his side said to him: 'Tom, I think your team's good enough to win the Cup next year!'

Tea for Two

Shankly and Liverpool coach Reube Bennett were sitting in a hotel in Rumania on a European trip and ordered a pot of tea. The waiter duly brought it. But when Reuben poured some and tasted it he almost spat it out, exclaiming: 'It's like maiden's water it's so weak!'

Shankly barked: 'Reuben, give him that tea you've got in the bag in your room and tell him to make a proper pot.'

Some 20 minutes later the waiter, having been given the tea by Reuben, returned with a fresh pot. Shankly poured some out then exploded:

'Jesus Christ...it's INK...he's put the whole bloody packet in!'

Bob-a-Job

Liverpool arrived at London's Euston Station and Shankly headed for the toilets, which had recently been modernised. When he discovered it cost five pence to go through the barrier and into the toilets he shouted at the attendant:

'The Scots boys will be down here for next week's international and when they find you've put a shilling on the piss they'll slit your throat from ear to ear.'

Brief Encounter

Shankly met former Newcastle and Liverpool centre forward Albert Stubbins, by chance, on the platform of Crewe railway station... the first time they'd met in 20 years. Dispensing with the usual pleasantries, Shankly said:

'Hello Albert... if the opposition centre half moves up into the attack, d'yer think your centre forward should go with him?'

Channel Hopper

Liverpool were staying at a hotel in Porthcawl, prior to a game, and the television lounge was populated by two old ladies wanting to watch *Coronation Street*. Then Shankly and all the players walked in. When they all sat down Shankly discovered there was boxing on another channel so he said: 'Hello ladies! What are you watching?'

'We're watching *Coronation Street* – it's our favourite programme.'

'Do yer like it?'

'Oh! we never miss it.'

'Well... er, there's boxing on the other channel – we want to watch that.'

'Well, we would like to watch *Coronation Street*.'

'Tell you what I'll do – I'm a democrat. HANDS UP IN

THIS ROOM WHO WANTS TO WATCH BOXING!'

A Bouncer for Ball

When Everton signed Alan Ball for £110,000 in 1966, just two days after losing 1–0 in the Charity Shield to Liverpool, Shankly rang him.

'Congratulations on your move, son,' he said. 'You'll be playing *near* a great side!'

Shankly meets the Martians

Shankly and Bob Paisley drove into a garage. Shankly was driving and he parked alongside the petrol pump. Nothing happened. Shankly said: 'Jesus Christ, where are they? The service is slow tonight.'

Bob chipped in: 'It's one of these new-fangled things like ...'

'Jesus Christ, Bob, what's going on?'

Then suddenly a disembodied metallic voice shouted: 'Choose your grade. Choose your grade.' So, Bob said: 'I'll go out and have a look...

Bob got out, came back and said: 'It's one of them self-service...' So Shankly jumped out of the car, ran to the window and said:

'I don't know who you are, but if any of my players were as lazy as you I'd sack the bloody lot of them!'

Then he drove of

Starring Role

Bill Shankly to defender Peter Wall:

'I have my spies out and I'm told you were in a nightclub until three o'clock in the morning. Who do you think you are... Errol Flynn?'

Red Neck on a Bus

Shankly's native cunning was a quality to behold . . . as long as you weren't the target of it when his team had lost. One referee who handled a Liverpool game at Southampton will never forget the day he fell foul of Shankly's wrath.

Southampton won with a highly disputed goal, one that Liverpool insisted should have been disallowed for offside. Shankly, Bob Paisley and the rest of the Liverpool camp were furious at the referee for letting it stand. After the game, the Liverpool bus was about to leave the Dell when the referee a married man to whom we will give the protective pseudonym of Jack – came running out with a young lady on his arm.

'Any chance of a lift to Euston on your coach, Bill?' asked the referee.

'Of course,' said Shankly, 'get on.'

Shankly put 'Jack' and his female companion at the front of the bus, then darted into the seat right behind them, alongside journalist Chris James. 'Hello, Chris,' said Shankly. 'See that referee today? He's a cheat. He's not straight. He should be banned from ever setting foot on a football pitch again. He should be strung up . . .'

The Shankly tirade lasted all the way from Southampton to Euston with the referee's neck turning purple with embarrassment. He was trapped! He couldn't report Bill to the FA because he was a guest on the Liverpool bus. And he was also in the compromising position of being a married man accompanied by a young lady.

Euston could not come quickly enough for 'Jack.' When the coach pulled into the station he and the girl raced down the steps, heading for the door to escape their tormentor. But Shankly was just as quick. He called the referee's name and as 'Jack' turned round and muttered a hurried 'Thanks, Bill,' the Liverpool manager delivered the verbal kill by declaring:

'You're welcome . . . any time you want a lift, you've only got to ask!'

Upstaged

Bill Shankly was equally at home on the showbiz stage as he was on the football pitch. He was once asked to go on the *This Is Your Life* TV show when Jimmy Tarbuck was the subject. Shankly was introduced. He walked on and as he passed Eamonn Andrews he said:

'You know Eamonn, I've been on this show more than you!'

The Life and Sole

The Liverpool squad, in London for a match, went to see Tommy Cooper perform at the Palladium. Shankly went backstage to meet the great comedian and was stunned by the size of Cooper's feet.

'Bloody hell, Tommy...what size shoes do you take?' Shankly inquired. 'I've sailed to Ireland in boats smaller than those!'

The Flip Side

Shankly's first managerial job was at Carlisle United, where he was in charge from 1949 until 1951. In one game they were 2–0 down at half time. When the players returned to the dressing room Shankly rounded on skipper Geoff Twentyman.

'What did you call at the pre-match toss-up?' demanded Shankly.

'I called heads, boss,' replied Twentyman.

'Jesus Christ... *never* call heads,' roared Shankly.

Nessie's treat

There is a time-honoured, apocryphal story of Shankly taking his wife, Nessie, to watch an Accrington Stanley game on their wedding anniversary. He was quick to put the record straight.

'D'yer think I'd have got married in the football season?' Shankly blasted. 'I'll tell you the true story... it was her birthday and we went to watch Tranmere Rovers.'

Secure Positions

As Shankly left the Liverpool dressing room and walked down the corridor following a Saturday match at Anfield, a journalist shouted to him: 'Hey, Bill, Manchester United and Manchester City both lost. They're bottom and next to bottom of the table.'

'Aye...' boomed Shankly, 'and they'll take some bloody shifting...'

Spicing the Currie

Sportswriter to Shankly after seeing Tony Currie star in a match during the 1970s:

'I think Tony's display was reminiscent of Tom Finney, Bill.'

Shankly: 'You could be right. Mind you, Tom's 57.'

Virtual Reality

Shankly had been a team-mate of Tom Finney at Preston North End and he rated the England forward as the greatest player he had seen. In 1973 the *Daily Express* ran a computer international match between the England team of that time and an 'old' England side. I picked the two teams, and fed the full details of every player into the computer at Liverpool Polytechnic. Eventually, it chattered out a match report which was printed in the *Express* next morning. Part of it read: 'Tom Finney was stretchered off after a 75th-minute tackle by Emlyn Hughes.'

When the Liverpool players reported for training that day, Emlyn was getting changed when Shankly burst in, threw down a copy of the paper and yelled at the nonplussed England star:

'Listen, son! If you touch Tom Finney again I'll kick you up the arse!'

Hot Airwaves

Many Merseyside people will affectionately remember Bob Azurdia, the late broadcaster, who was a friend of mine. Shankly had a 'love-hate' relationship with Bob. They liked each other really. But professionally it was always 'war' and Bob was more 'banned' by Shankly than 'unbanned' for his highly individual observations, and colourful opinions on football and multifarious other topics.

Once on a trip to the Bulgarian capital, Sofia, which coincided with a state visit by Nikita Khrushchev, Bob's bearded countenance led to the Soviet supremo embracing him and declaring '*Cubanski! Cubanski!*' confusing him with the Cuban dictator Fidel Castro.

But there was no confusion by Shankly, who refused so many interviews with him that Bob would smile and say: 'I'm not banned this week,' as if it was news in itself!

During BBC Radio Merseyside's early months on the air in 1967, when, for a brief period, I read the sports results, Bob went to Shankly to do one of his first interviews with him. 'Right . . . testing one, two, three,' said Bob. Then off he went 'Mr Shankly, why is it that your team's unbeaten run has suddenly ended, and you find yourselves struggling to recapture your best form?'

'Why don't you go and jump in the lake?' Shankly responded, summarily ending the interview.

This cosy relationship continued until one day Shankly, with typically outrageous hyperbole, announced:

'D'yer know something, Azurdia? I've been asked a *million* stupid questions in my time . . . and you've asked *all* of them!'

But Bob took it all in his usual philosophical manner and

held Bill in high esteem, as he wrote in Shankly's testimonial match programme in April 1975:

> From Liverpool to Leningrad, wherever football is played and talked about, the name of Bill Shankly is invariably mentioned. His is the ONE name about whom there's always a story.
>
> This is one of the unique features of the man who put Liverpool Football Club on the map . . . who made them great.
>
> Bill Shankly holds this supreme position because of his single-minded dedication to his cause. Transparently honest, his integrity comes through to the fans – the people. The peak of his incredible relationship with 'the people' was surely his historic 'Chairman Mao' speech when 100,000 people turned out to see Liverpool – and Bill Shankly – after the team LOST!
>
> A man sincere in his simplicity – 'Every day's a bonus for me, it's a holiday just to get out of my bed' – Bill Shankly is a broadcaster's dream. Articulate, outspoken – though NEVER malicious – his biting wit has made many a programme when the prospects had seemed dim.
>
> I recall arriving with Bill and the Liverpool party at a Frankfurt hotel before a UEFA Cup-tie. There were pre-World Cup estensions being added to the building and a degree of noise was made by the workers. Bill was across like a shot.
>
> 'They'll no' be starting work before 10 tomorrow morning,' he declared, with satisfaction.
>
> 'I put a stop to THAT while players are trying to sleep.
>
> 'But the PAINTERS – they can start.'
>
> For me, Bill Shankly is my 'most unforgettable character' – anywhere. And for thousands of Merseysiders as well as millions elsewhere the same must be true.

A Belting Story

Bill Shankly, Bob Paisley and other members of Anfield's famous 'Boot Room', football's equivalent of the Brains Trust, were going to watch Scunthorpe goalkeeper Ray Clemence with a view to signing him. (They actually watched Ray Clemence on eight occasions before the transfer was completed in June 1967 for a bargain £18,000. The reason for the deal being protracted was the fact that Clemence was left-footed and right-handed, a 'diagonal' that Shankly took time to fathom.) As the Anfield posse set off on one of their spying missions on the future England goalkeeping great – with Paisley driving – Shankly said:

'Bob, can we go via Manchester, because I need a new coat and Kendal Milne always have a good selection?'

Now, when Shankly wanted a new coat, it was a production of which Barnum and Bailey would have been proud. He was an avid fan of 'B' movies and gangster films of the James Cagney genre. He liked coats that gave him the look of Elliott Ness in *The Untouchables*, the television series he compulsively followed. The Liverpool party, also including Joe Fagan and Tom Saunders, duly arrived at the Manchester department store and headed for the gents' coats section. Shankly put on one of the coats and began to pose in the mirror, adopting various stances and postures.

'What d'yer think Bob...?' Shankly demanded of Paisley.

'Aye, you look good in that, Bill,' said Bob, eager to do the business and get back on the road.

'No, not quite right... give me another coat, son,' he said to the young assistant, still in his teens and in his first job.

'This one's alright, son... but, er, I don't like the belt... cut the belt off!'

The young assistant did as instructed and cut off the belt. Shankly put the coat back on and then said:

'Nar... I don't like it.'

He handed the beltless coat back to the lad and swept out of the shop, leaving a horrified young salesman rooted to the spot. Bob Paisley walked over to the trembling lad, asked him the price of the coat, opened his wallet and handed him £35 . . . one of the few transactions he had nothing to show for!

Confidence Trick

Shankly was known as a great motivator. One of the early examples of his motivational psychology was when Liverpool played in their first season in the European Cup. It was 1964, and they were drawn to play Anderlecht, a crack team at the time. Seven of their players had played for Belgium when they had drawn with England at Wembley a fortnight earlier. In the Anfield dressing room pre-match talk Shankly said:

'You're OK boys, you're playing a load of rubbish tonight.' Liverpool went out and won 3–0. When they came back in again Bill said:

'Congratulations lads, you've just beaten one of the best teams in Europe.'

It's All Foreign to Bill

Bill Shankly was very suspicious of foreigners. He once said: 'You know, what they're like abroad . . . a load of thieves, rogues and vagabonds, living on their wits in the gutter.'

He used to talk about how foreign managers were devious and cunning. So, clearly, when Liverpool played in Europe he was always on his guard – but it wasn't just in Europe.

Liverpool had an amazing trip to America in 1964. New York is five hours behind Britain and one of Bill's ambitions was to go to Jack Dempsey's bar, which he did. He had been in there only 20 minutes when he said to Bob Paisley: 'Well Bob, I'm off to bed.'

Bob said: 'But it's only bloody nine o'clock!'

Shanks said: 'It's two o'clock on my watch and no bloody Yank's telling me the time.'

If that wasn't bad enough, Shankly put up the team sheet on the wall in the hotel at six o'clock in the morning.

On that same tour of the US and North America, Shankly took the Liverpool team to Soldiers Field, Chicago, venue for the famous 'long count' world heavyweight title fight between Jack Dempsey and Gene Tunney in September 1927, when Tunney retained the championship with a points verdict. Dempsey had felled Tunney but failed to go to a neutral corner, when ordered by the referee, and after being down for an estimated 14 seconds Tunney regained his senses and went on to score his second successive points win. When Liverpool arrived at Soldiers Field, Shanks sought out the groundsman and asked:

'Now then, where did this fight take place?'

The guy said: 'Well around about here you know...just here...'

'Right,' said Shankly to his players, 'get stripped. I want you to play a five-a-side game on the very spot.'

And he made them play on the very site of the Dempsey/Tunney fight.

On the same 1964 tour journalists Colin Wood of the *Daily Mail* and Derek Potter of the *Daily Expess* had to make an early-morning trip across Detroit from their hotel to the Liverpool hotel to link up with the team for an airport departure. Wood recalls:

We got there about six o'clock and we encountered Shanks prowling around the hotel lobby to the sound of vacuum cleaners and floor polishers. We were looking for breakfast but Shanks said: 'There's no breakfast here yet. We'll go out and find some.'

We suggested it would soon be served in the hotel because the team were leaving early for the airport. But he wouldn't have it. He insisted on taking us on a march across the city. We must have walked three miles.

Eventually he stops at this dreadful place, full of

dropouts and drug addicts. Shanks walks straight in and says to this six feet five inch, 18-stone guy chewing gum and wiping the counter: 'Right...bacon, eggs, sausage, tomotoes, fried bread and tea for three.'

This huge guy just pointed to the menu board and drawled: 'We only do hot dogs and hamburgers in here.'

Shanks was so angry that he leaned across the counter, picked up this enormous feller and roared: 'Jesus Christ... nobody eats a hamburger or a hot dog for breakfast!'

So we walked out and found out we were double losers because when we got back to the hotel all the players had enjoyed a lovely breakfast and we'd missed it!

Wood also remembers an amazing scene before the game in Chicago beween Liverpool and German club Meiderich, later to become Werder Bremen:

The kick-off was approaching and we looked out and saw a figure go to the centre spot, pick up the ball and kick it in the air before it disappeared into his raincoat. He did this a few times with other balls. It turned out to be the Meiderich coach and the next thing is that Shanks goes over to him, kicks this fellow up in the air and the ball pops out of the top of his coat like a pea from a pod.

Apparently the German was trying to deflate all the footballs to a pressure that would suit his team best. But Shanks had seen him. So Shanks made Bob Paisley go to the referee and get all the balls reflated. Nobody but Shanks would have the gall and the nerve to do what he did. Many have felt the rough edge of the Shankly tongue – and got the message without the aid of an interpreter. But it was all for the Liverpool cause. Many tasted the indominatable spirit that made Shankly and his team so successful.

At Lake Como before the infamous Inter Milan

European Cup semi final second leg he tried to silence the church bells. In Amsterdam, the morning after a crushing 5–1 defeat by the then little known Ajax, he announced loud enough for everyone in a crowded airport lounge to hear that Liverpool would not only win the second leg, but win the tie.

And there were countless moments when he showed his soft centre. I recall particularly Malmo, Sweden, in 1967. One of the reporters with the party was taken ill after we had exerted ourselves in a kick-about with the players.

Shankly took charge. The hotel staff said there was no fresh orange juice. Shankly made sure there was fresh orange juice. Then he ordered the rest of the Press party to go out and enjoy themselves and sat up with our sick colleague.

But the greatest pleasure of all in travelling with this man was to see his reactions to people who showed enthusiasm for the game.

When we arrived in Dresden there was just about the noisiest reception I can ever remember the team getting abroad. Thousands of youngsters stood outside the hotel chanting 'Dresden, Dresden'.

The natives did not look too friendly to me, and other members of the party felt they were waging psychological warfare against the Liverpool team. But within minutes Shankly was out amongst them distributing badges, shaking hands, chatting, laughing.

'They're good people,' he said – after performing the kind of act that made him a wonderful ambassador for our game. Iron Curtains and language barriers meant nothing to such a man at times like these.

Something in Reserve

Scotland forward Lou Macari arrived at Anfield from

Celtic in January 1973 for transfer talks with Shankly. A deal seemed to be imminent. But at the last minute, Macari pulled out and travelled down the East Lancashire Road to sign, instead, for Manchester United. It caused consternation in many quarters at Liverpool, but Shankly responded with characteristic bravado.

'It doesn't matter,' he said. 'I'll have to find someone else for our reserves.'

Selection Box

England defender Phil Thompson, later to be Liverpool captain, was upset at being left out of the team by Shankly. Liverpool lost the game and on Monday Thompson went to see Bill to tell him how disappointed he was at not being picked.

'Disappointed, son!' exclaimed Shankly. 'You should be grateful to me not to be part of a team that played so badly. You should be *thanking* me!'

Thompson left Shankly's office highly encouraged, looking forward to a recall in Liverpool's midweek game. But he had simply been mollified by Shankly. He was left out again!

Pick-pocket

Shankly on pre-match tactical talks:

> At one pre-match tactical talk before we played Manchester United I took the models of Bobby Charlton, Denis Law and George Best off the model pitch and put them in my left-hand pocket. Then I told our players: 'Don't worry about them . . . they can't play at all!'
>
> It was psychology, of course. Charlton, Best and Law were three of the best players in the world.

Bill's Politics

Asked about his political views, Shankly said:

> I'm a socialist naturally, because I worked at the coal mine. But I think a man's politics really is himself. I try to help everybody I can. I don't try to hinder anybody. That's my way of socialism.
>
> If you're a good man and you can earn money, even if it's more than somebody else, I don't think anyone should come along and steal that money off you.

One-liners

Shankly to aspiring young player: 'The trouble with you, son, is that your brains are all in your head.'

Shankly on referees: 'They know the rules – but they don't know the game.'

Iceland Here We Come

Liverpool's first ever game in European competition was against Reykjavik in Iceland in the Champions Cup on 17 August 1964. They were to fly there from Renfrew and the club party arrived in Scotland with hours to spare before their flight. Shankly said: 'I know what we'll do to kill the time. We'll go to Butlin's at Ayr.'

The coach driver was given the instruction and off they went. When the team coach pulled up at the holiday camp gates Shankly, expecting to be recognised, was off in a flash and shouted at the commissionaire:

'Hello . . . Liverpool Football Club . . . we're on the way to Iceland.'

Back came the reply in thick Scottish brogue:

'Aye, I'm thinking you've taken the wrang road!'

No Bones About It

Shankly hated players being injured – or even talking about it. He used to say: 'They should all be like Ian Callaghan. He's a rubber ball. When he gets hurt he just bounces up again.'

But this attitude extended even beyond his team. Journalist Mike Ellis was involved in a road accident and was on crutches when he returned to Anfield on newspaper duty. Shankly walked straight past him, an incident often repeated as the weeks went by. But the day after Mike threw away his crutches Shankly saw him in the corridor and exclaimed:

'Mike . . . nice to see you . . . you haven't been here for ages.'

Fit for Duty

Chris Lawler was in the Anfield treatment room after making 241 consecutive League appearances for Liverpool over a span of six seasons from October 1965 to April 1971. Bob Paisley, a master physiotherapist, said to Shankly: 'There's no way Chris can play in our next game at Manchester City . . . his ankle's swollen up like a balloon.'

'He's a bloody malingerer!' barked Shankly.

Just Friends

A former journalist colleague of mine, Horace Yates of the *Liverpool Daily Post*, was standing in the foyer of a Budapest hotel prior to a Liverpool European fixture against Ferencvaros. Horace, clearly, had written something Shankly blatantly disapproved of. He walked up to him and bellowed: 'I'm not talking to you or your paper again . . . the stuff you write is crap, crap . . . it's bloody rubbish . . . I wouldn't wipe my backside with it . . . so don't ever come to me again . . . d'yer hear?'

At that moment, a Hungarian tapped Bill on the shoulder. Shankly wheeled round and boomed:

'Will you bugger off . . . ? I'm talking to a friend of mine.'

Signal Box to Penalty Box

When broadcaster Alan Jackson began as Anfield's public address announcer, he was approached by Shankly who said:

'Alan, I believe you're on the Tannoy?'

'That's right, Bill,' said Alan.

'Well, will you make sure that we're not near the opposition box when you make an announcement?'

Jackson recalls: 'Obviously, I'd gone on the speakers at some stage when Liverpool were on the attack and Shankly felt that it distracted the players and fans. But I had a big problem... because when I was announcing I was facing a wall and could not see the game. So I had to get a guy positioned who could see the match – then he'd give me the signal of when to speak!'

Not-so-Silent Night

Shankly hated defeat... even in the five-a-side games at Liverpool's Melwood training ground, in which he passionately participated. His team always had to win.

One day, late in the afternoon, his side were losing and it was getting dark. Then one of his team shot and Shankly shouted: 'Goal! That's it, 2–2. Let's pack it in.'

But the other team, also a mixture of players and coaching staff, including England defender Chris Lawler, were insistent that the ball had not crossed the line. A row ensued and Shankly announced: 'I know how to settle this.'

Lawler, a scoring prince among full backs who amassed the remarkable total of 61 goals without taking penalties, was nicknamed *Silent Night* by his team-mates, because he was so quiet and undemonstrative. Said Shankly: 'Chris, you're an honest man – was that a goal or not?'

'Sorry, boss,' Lawler replied. 'The ball didn't cross the line.'

'Jesus Christ,' retorted Shankly. 'You don't open your mouth for five years and when you do it's a bloody lie!'

The Blood Runs Red

Tommy Smith, the 'Anfield Iron' himself, had the rare experience of going off injured during a match. Shankly dashed from the dug-out to see how he was:

'Are yer alright, son?' Shankly inquired in concerned tones.

'It's my so-and-so leg, boss – it's killing me.'

'Correction, son,' said Shankly. 'It's not your leg ... it's *Liverpool's* leg.'

A Heart-felt Response

Manchester City were being trounced at Anfield. During the half time interval one of City's backroom staff, responsible for an injured player, knocked on the Liverpool dressing room door and asked if a doctor could assist. Shankly unimpressed by City's lukewarm display, replied:

'I think you need Christiaan Barnard.'

No Thanks, Pelé

Liverpool's England goalkeeper Ray Clemence loved to play outfield in training and jokingly called himself 'The White Pelé'. But his enthusiasm got the better of him, especially when it came to tackling. One day at Liverpool's Melwood training ground Shankly took action. He called Clemence over and said:

'I'm banning you from playing anywhere but in goal ... you've very nearly broken Alec Lindsay's leg.'

Maradona ... by Shankly

Shankly offered an intriguing verdict on a rising star called Diego Maradona after watching his Wembley performance for Argentina, then the reigning world champions, in their 3–1 defeat by England in May 1980:

Diego Maradona is possibly the best player in the game at the moment even at the age of 19. I saw him when England beat Argentina at Wembley. He's got all the natural skills of a Tom Finney or a Cruyff. He's a different build but he's sturdy and very clever at beating his man.

He does things in a bigger hurry than Finney who was more deliberate and composed. Maradona goes at a breakneck speed. Maybe he'll learn that he can slow down a little and have a bit more composure.

He's full of enthusiasm and ability but if he'd gone just a bit slower he might have got past the fellow and scored at Wembley instead of getting the penalty. A goal is better than a penalty.

I thought that instead of dashing all over the field if that boy had stayed up in the area where Roger Hunt used to play for Liverpool and kept his strength then he'd be a terrible handful for anyone to cope with. He worked really hard at Wembley but he must have been tired after covering so much ground.

I know he's young. But you can't burn yourself up all the time. You need to conserve your energy. He showed he can be lethal inside the box. Now the pitch is not very big inside the box but he was still beating England defenders. So I would keep him around the box and let someone else do the fetching and carrying. If Maradona did that it would give him much greater finishing strength.

Express Reception

Liverpool were travelling by train to London over an Easter holiday and there was an afternoon football match commentary on radio. Club coach Reuben Bennett had brought a battered old wireless with him and tried, with little success, to tune into the football broadcast.

'Give it to me, Reuben,' ordered Shankly, who shook the set several times without finding the radio station. Becoming increasingly exasperated, he opened the window and stuck out the aerial to its fullest extent.

After a minute or two of crackled commentary there was an almighty crack as another train roared past in the opposite direction. Shankly retrieved the aerial which was now bent at right angles and almost in two pieces. Then he said, in somewhat shocked tones:

'By Christ, Reuben! That was travelling!'

Mistaken Identity

Shankly to newly signed wing half or inside forward Alec Lindsay from Bury, who cost £67,000 in March 1969 and was converted at Liverpool to an England international left back: 'Listen, son, I want you to do for us what you did at Gigg Lane ... take men on, go past them and lash in those shots that brought you a few goals.'

But that wasn't me, boss!' insisted Lindsay. 'That was Jim Kerr.'

'Jesus Christ, Bob,' Shankly said to Paisley. 'We've signed the wrong player!'

Live-in Job

On a European trip, behind the Iron Curtain, the Liverpool party were signing the hotel register. The desk clerk said to Shankly, in broken English: 'Excuse me, Mr Shankly, but, where it says "home address" you've written "Anfield".'

'That's right,' said Shankly. 'That's where I live.'

The Master's Voice 1

Brian Hall, a university graduate, who played for Shankly's Liverpool and later became the club's public relations executive, provides a classic illustration of Shankly's own grasp of public relations.

Hall and the rest of the victorious 1974 FA Cup team, who trounced Newcastle 3–0 at Wembley, were parading the trophy next day through the streets of Liverpool. Hall recounts:

> We were approaching Lime Street on the open-top bus when Shanks tapped me on the shoulder and said: 'Son, you know about these things. What's the name of that Chinaman...? Y'know...? Red Book... all those sayings...?'
>
> I thought... 'Hello!! The boss has gone – he's flipped.' But I replied: 'Do you mean Chairman Mao, boss?'
>
> 'That's the feller,' said Shankly.
>
> When we came to St George's Hall and we filed onto the balcony there were probably 300,000 gathered in the streets below. It was incredible. But when Shanks held up his hands there was complete silence. Then he said:
>
> 'Even Chairman Mao has never seen a greater show of *red strength* than this!'
>
> The place erupted... they went completely mad... and I remember thinking to myself: 'You're not just a clever so-and-so. You're a genius, you are.'

The Master's Voice 2

Following Liverpool's 2–1 defeat by Arsenal after extra time at Wembley in the 1971 FA Cup final, the team, Shankly and club officials toured the city next day, when thousands turned out for a Sunday salute to the gallant losers. Shankly addressed them in the city centre and proclaimed in outrageously militaristic terms: 'We've lost the battle – but we will go on to win the war.'

Observing the mood of the crowd, club secretary Peter Robinson was moved to make the aside:

'Bill's got such power of oratory that if he told them to

march through the Mersey Tunnel and pillage Birkenhead
they'd do it.'

On The Record

In those rare moments when football was not consuming his
attention Shankly liked to listen to records:

> I've got a radiogram at home and I love the songs of
> Kenneth McKellar, Jim Reeves, Pat Boone, Moira
> Anderson and Harry Secombe. The funny thing is most
> of them are hymns and a lot of them are Scottish.
>   Basically I'm religious. I think most people are. I don't
> go to the church but that's not to say I don't believe. I've
> got more hymns amongst my records than possibly
> anyone in England.'

A Laughing Matter

For a man who raised many a laugh himself Shankly had a
great appreciation of comedy, insisting:

> If there was no sense of humour, if there were no funny
> men and no music the world would be a terrible, dull
> place. And if I've been born with a sense of humour I
> think I should use it.
>   Sometimes my humour aggravates people because I
> catch them so quickly. When they open their mouths I
> can shut them up right away with something funny. But
> I should use my humour and so should everyone who
> has it because it brightens up the world.
>   I think Bob Hope is a very funny man and I love Phil
> Silvers as Sergeant Bilko. The mischievous, unbelievable
> stuff he gets away with is like a tonic to me. And the
> quick, short jokes when *The Comedians* series first
> started on ITV were tremendous.

Troublesome Foe

Shankly saluting the great Northern Irish inside forward Peter Doherty, who played for Blackpool, Manchester City, Derby County, Huddersfield and Doncaster:

'He gave me great trouble whenever I played against him. He was perpetual motion. You could dog him, challenge him and even hurt him. But you couldn't dismay him. He kept coming.'

Problematical

On encountering Everton defender Terry Darracott by chance one day, Shankly asked: 'How are you, son?'

'Fine, Bill, no problem.'

'No problem? Don't say that, son,' rapped Shankly. 'I've got problems, you've got problems. When you haven't got a problem that's the problem.'

Exit Darracott, scratching his head and deep in thought.

Be Prepared

Stamina was a central prop of Bill Shankly's football creed. He observed:

'It's a 90-minute game – but I used to train for a 190-minute match so that when the whistle blew at the end I could have played the game all over again.'

A Stitch Before Time

Prior to Liverpool's 1971 FA Cup semi final against Everton, at Old Trafford, Shankly went for a suit fitting to his tailor, Denis Newton:

'I'll take this one for Wembley, Denis,' he declared.

His confidence was not misplaced. Liverpool beat their arch rivals 2–1 to reach the final.

Off-Peak

When a sportswriter suggested that Liverpool's form had dipped, he replied:
'Aye…you're right. We're struggling at the top of the League.'

Home Promise

Liverpool lost their first three home games of the 1963–64 campaign to Nottingham Forest (1–2), Blackpool (1–2) and West Ham (1–2). After the defeat by Blackpool Shankly quipped:
'The Football League are not going to believe this result!'

And, after losing to West Ham, he told the Liverpool directors:
'I assure you, gentlemen, we WILL win a home game this season.'

He was as good as his pledge. In Liverpool's next Anfield outing they walloped Wolves 6-0 and finished the season as champions.

Dressed for Action

Shankly, in one of his many salutes to his hero Tom Finney, enthused:
'He was a "ghost" of a player – but grisly strong. He could have played all day in his overcoat.'

Summertime Blues

Shankly was once asked what aspect of the game he most disliked.
'The end of the season,' was the instant reply.

A Cut Above

One day in 1963 Shankly went for a haircut. He sat in the chair and the barber asked: 'Anything off the top, Bill?'

'Aye,' replied Shankly, 'Everton!'

His wish did not come true. Liverpool's neighbours from across Stanley Park swept to the championship under manager Harry Catterick, in only his second season in charge at Goodison.

No Scotch for this Scot

After being presented with two gallon-sized bottles of Bell's whisky, as Manager of the Month for September and October 1972, Shankly announced:

'I never touch the stuff. I'll donate one for the police raffle . . . and keep the other one for embrocation.'

Losing your Bottle

Liverpool and Celtic collided in a tumultuous battle in the second leg of the European Cup Winners Cup semi final at Anfield on 19 April 1966. Liverpool won on the night to go through to the final on a 2–1 aggregate. But in the cold light of the ncxt day the stadium was littered with bottles discarded by the travelling army of Glasgow fans. Shankly said to his great friend, and rival manager, Jock Stein:

'Do you want your share of the gate money, Jock, or shall we just return the empties!'

Explosive Talent

One defender who played against Shankly's Liverpool in the early 1970s must have felt his ears burning when his name came up in the Anfield boss's after-match press conference.

'If he had gunpowder for brains he couldn't blow his cap off!' was Shankly's withering appraisal of the player.

Family Trait

During Shankly's playing days, he was asked if it was true

that he would have tackled his own grandmother.

'That's a stupid question,' he retorted. 'She'd have had more sense than to get in the way.'

Dry up, Cloughie

Shankly was asked his opinion of Brian Clough in the aftermath of yet another media tirade by the Nottingham Forest manager.

'He's worse than the rain in Manchester,' said Shanks. 'At least God stops that occasionally!'

Relatively Speaking

Leeds United boss, Don Revie, one of Shankly's great managerial rivals, recalled: 'Whenever 1 mentioned one of our players to Bill he'd say, "Yeah, he's nae bad...a fair player...nae bad." I don't know how we ever won a match! But when it came to his own team every one in that red shirt had everything – left foot, right foot, tackling, heading, stamina. They didn't have a weakness. They were the best in the world in each position. There was no stopping his torrent of adulation.'

Blues in the Afternoon

Jenny Davies, a cleaner at Anfield and dyed-in-the-wool Liverpool fan, related a tale of Shankly and Everton during the three-day week power crisis in 1974:

He was a marvellous man and he even coaxed me to go to Goodison Park, a ground I'd never stepped foot inside in my life.

During that emergency period in the 1970s all the matches had to be played in the daytime because, to save power, floodlighting wasn't allowed. Bill was going through the door one afternoon and said he was going across the park to watch Everton.

'Why don't you come with me?' he asked. I said: 'I couldn't do that. I couldn't go to watch that shower!'

'Oh, come on over and have a look,' he insisted. So I did. Bill actually got me inside Everton's ground. But I didn't enjoy it...in fact I came out just after half time! When he saw I was ready to leave he said: 'I'm ready to go, too.'

He was a great man and the greatest personality I've ever met.

In Old Bucharest 1

The needs of his players were paramount to Bill Shankly. In the Rumanian capital of Bucharest, he learned that the hotel had no Coca-Cola for his team to drink. His fury visibly rising, he stormed:

'It's a conspiracy...a war of nerves!'

In Old Bucharest 2

The lack of Coca-Cola did not prevent Shankly's Liverpool from making their Bucharest visit a winning one in their Fairs Cup second round second leg duel with Dinamo on 4 November 1970. And it holds a unique place in the long history of the Anfield club...the one and only time an airline employee has ever sent on a Liverpool substitute!

The man in question was Jim Kennefick, then a representative of Irish national airline Aer Lingus, regularly used by Liverpool for their European missions. He was sitting on the Liverpool bench alongside one of the substitutes, Phil Boersma. As the game was in progress Jim turned to the player and offered the pleasantry in his rich, resonant Irish tones: 'PHIL BOERSMA...Alright!!'

Boersma's name was heard by Shankly's assistant, Bob Paisley, who told him to take off his tracksuit top then sent him on to replace Alun Evans. The move paid a handsome dividend. Boersma scored in a 1–1 draw to secure Liverpool's passage on a 4–1 aggregate.

'Sending on Boersma was a great decision, Bob,' Shanks beamed afterwards.

'Nowt to do with me, Bill,' said Paisley. 'I thought I heard *you* shout his name!'

It was only on the coach heading for the airport that the 'mystery man' responsible for the inspired switch was identified as Jim Kennefick. Jim later joined Liverpool ... but in an executive role – not on the coaching staff!

Red Spy

Bill Shankly's suspicions of dirty tricks in foreign lands were always at their height when Liverpool travelled behind the former Iron Curtain. On one trip into Eastern Europe, a member of the club party called at Bill's hotel room and found him standing on a chair talking at the ceiling light.

'I know you're there ... you're spying on us,' he shouted, borrowing nothing from James Bond. Then, still glaring upwards, he demanded:

'Why don't you come out, you cowards?'

Not Like it Seems

A classic example of Shankly's passionate refusal to accept defeat, and see only positive factors for Liverpool, was provided by Bill Nicholson, during his days as manager of Tottenham. Recalled Nicholson:

Bill phoned me one Sunday morning and, after the usual 'hellos', I said to him 'So you got beat 2–0 yesterday, Bill?' But, quick as a flash, he replied, 'No, no, Billy. We murdered them! We were all over them. They never got a shot at our goal. Their first goal wasn't a goal at all, and the second . . . well, you've never seen anything like it!

That was Bill Shankly . . . he never lost, even in defeat.'

Wine, Women and Medals

England winger Peter Thompson, Shankly's inspired £35,000 signing from Preston in 1963, tells of the day Bill 'read the riot act' to his squad when results started to dip.

He arranged personal interviews with all the players. He started with our goalkeeper, Tommy Lawrence, who went into Bill's office at one o'clock and emerged at 2.15. Because I wore the No. 11 shirt, by the time he'd seen the rest of the team, position by position, it was five o'clock when my turn came. To be honest, I was playing well, so I wasn't too worried. But, to my amazement, he said, 'Son, you're smoking yourself to death!'

I said: 'I don't smoke, boss.'

He just carried on and added: 'You've been on the town with women in nightclubs . . . every night a different woman.'

I tried to explain that I didn't do that sort of thing. But he kept going on and then said: 'I know exactly what you do . . . you're drinking yourself to death. I've heard from sources in town that you're practically an alcoholic!'

I insisted: 'Boss, I don't do anything like that!' Shanks replied:

'Well, son, the way you're playing at the moment you're doing ALL of those things . . . AND plenty of other things I can't find out about!'

(Consistency note: Thompson missed only nine League games in his first seven seasons at Liverpool – in three he was ever-present – and he won two championship medals and one FA Cup winners medal.)

Song of Praise

BBC broadcaster and journalist Bryon Butler provided one of the most colourful appraisals of Shankly whom he described as:

> Lord of the fanatics, all Scot and all Scouse, a legend in a tracksuit, the embodiment of Liverpool, the master of Anfield . . . a man who turned a game of sweat and blood into a faith.
>
> Shankly had a way with him. He was a master of what he called the true joke, a wicked mixture of exaggeration, whimsy and ego.

Dressed for the Queen

Shankly on going for his OBE:

> I'm looking forward to going to Buckingham Palace to receive my award from the Queen. But it's not necessary to wear top hat and tails, you know. When Frankie Vaughan went he wore a dark suit and waistcoat. That's good enough for me. As long as it's within the rules I'll have the minimum of pomp.

Scot On!

Shankly's managerial friend Jock Stein, of Celtic and Scotland fame, gave him a massive salute by saying:

> No Scot ever made a bigger impact on a club than Bill Shankly.
>
> Others may claim an equal share of trophies – and

Matt Busby comes to mind with his wonderful record crowned by the European Cup – but not even Matt would claim the kinship with the fans that Bill enjoyed. He was what football was all about. I can't praise him higher than that.

Comic Entrance

Top comedian and lifelong Liverpool fan Jimmy Tarbuck was given a special privilege by Shankly. Recalled Tarbuck:

Shanks invited me into the dressing room with the team and I was the only one outside the club who got that honour. It was something I guarded ever so jealously. I was thrilled to be in there. It was the next best thing to playing for Liverpool.

I used to travel with the team, too, and have dinner with them the night before games. Shanks used to tell them: 'Look after your body boys... you as well, Tarbuck!' I'd just say: 'Yes, Bill.'.

I'd train with them which was another great thrill. Shanks played so passionately in the five-a-sides. On the testimonal match night for Gerry Byrne, which drew a huge crowd to Anfield despite bad weather, I was due to play in a five-a-side game on the Anfield pitch before kick-off and I wanted to lead out a team wearing the Liverpool red.

I told Bob Paisley to ask Bill if that would be OK. But when Bob told Bill it was my ambition to lead out a team at Anfield in red jerseys Shanks replied: 'His ambition? Tell him it's my ambition, too!'

Bill's team played in red... we had to wear all yellow.

Tea For Two

His former captain Emlyn Hughes kept in regular contact with Shankly.

I used to ring him at least two or three times a week and whenever I was in Liverpool I used to go to see him.

He ordered me to have a cup of tea with him. That was Shanks. You always did what Shanks said. He used to come across as a very funny guy with people laughing at what he said. But what he used to say was sense. He was a magnificent man.

A Fare Point

Ray Clemence on Shankly:

I saw him many, many times pay for young fans on the train. They'd got on and not had the money to pay their fare. Rather than see them turfed off the train by the guard he'd pay for them. That was the gentle side of the man.

The humorous side of him was shown on the day he signed me from Scunthorpe in the summer of 1967. I took very little persuasion, anyway, to sign for Liverpool but Shanks told me: 'Carry on improving the way you are doing and you'll be in our first team within the next year. Tommy Lawrence is 30 coming up 31 and he's past his best. There's no problem for you.'

So I went home and told my mother and father what Shanks had said. When I reported for pre-season training a few weeks later I soon found out that Tommy was only 27 and at his peak. I had to wait two and a half years to get into the team! But Shanks could get away with that sort of thing.

Nessie's Eye Test!

Journalist John Roberts recalls the moment when he first saw Shankly use a pair of spectacles:

I remember during the time I was compiling Bill's autobiography he picked up a newspaper one day and wanted to criticise something that had been printed.

Almost absent-mindedly lie picked up a pair of spectacles which I'd never seen him use before. He looked at me very defensively and said: 'These are just for very close work. I came home from a match at Anfield last week and I said to Nessie: 'Liverpool had a penalty awarded against them today and, do you know something, I agreed with the decision.'

Nessie said: 'Bill, if you're starting to agree with referees' decisions you'd better get yourself a pair of glasses.'

Scots Guard

Scotland's shambolic performance in the 1978 World Cup in Argentina, when they were the only British nation to qualify for the finals, brought a passionate tartan blast from Bill Shankly who rapped:

Scotland had a fanfare of trumpets before their last match at Hampden prior to leaving for Argentina. They did all their shouting before they'd kicked a ball. Scottish people have a habit of doing that. And I'm Scottish to the core. When we have a fighter we say he's the greatest fighter in the world. But the world's a big place and the football world's a big world.

I remember Scotland playing England on a bone hard end-of-season pitch at Hampden Park in April 1962. England were favourites to win but Jim Baxter and Pat Crerand conducted the orchestra brilliantly. They played on that hard pitch as if it was soft.

They pulled the ball down and utilised it so well. Denis Law was also in the team and he was brilliant, too. They beat England 2–0. What a display! It was the first time I'd seen a Scotland team do a lap of honour.

It riles me, frustrates me and annoys me to think of all

the great players Scotland have had over the years and yet they haven't done anything. It's criminal after all the talent we've had that there's not been a really successful Scotland team.

Nature Not Nurture

When asked once if players are born or made Shankly replied:

Anything that a man is is inborn. If he's a football man he's been born with that in him. I had four brothers and they were all professional players. And my mother's brothers were professionals, too. So it's been hereditary. Football's an inborn thing. Nobody makes players except mothers and fathers. Not coaches. Time matures players but it doesn't make them.

Chopping the Forest

Shankly speaking at a *Daily Express* football forum in November 1980 when Nottingham Forest were European Cup holders under Brian Clough:

They've won the European Cup for the past two seasons as well as having success in the championship and the League Cup yet they can't fill their bloody ground! What more can Forest do? I don't think the people of Nottingham deserve football. I think it should be taken off them.

Cloughie's been lucky to have players like Archie Gemmill and Roy McFarland. Gemmill has been one of the best players in this country since the war. And Cloughie 'stole' McFarland from me when the boy was playing for Tranmere.

A Man and his Magic

Journalist Frank McGhee said of Shankly:

For sheer tactical and technical knowledge I would imagine that some of the South Americans and Germans could probably beat him. But for honesty, determination, dedication and motivation I don't think there's a manager anywhere in the world to compare with him. He took over Liverpool when they were nobodies and turned them into a very considerable European force.

I've resented how sometimes he's been turned into something of a clown. He was never a clown. He was a very funny man. But he wasn't always funny. He could be ruthless and cruel and harsh.

It was a crime under him at Liverpool for anyone to be injured. He thought that unless you'd got a broken leg you were fit enough to play. He didn't believe in bruises and strains.

There he'd stand with his hands jammed in his pockets and his face would light up if you were a friend of his. You'd get that handshake and those eyes that always looked straight at you and you'd hear that lovely Ayrshire voice. Then you knew you were in for 10 minutes of magic.

Shanks's Welcome

On match days Shankly would wait in the corridor for the visiting team to arrive. And he was never short of a greeting.

I used to call them all by their first names, 'Harry' or 'Jimmy'. I'd say, 'The pitch is not too good today, you know.' If I was talking to a small feller I used to say, 'It's alright for big fellers.' If I was talking to a big feller I said

'It's a bloody good ground for small players.' I used to say that and I don't know if it affected them or not, or whether it used to make any difference.

I used to know all the players who played at Anfield in the opposition by their first name. So I was never embarrassed when they came in. I could call them 'Peter' or 'Jimmy' or 'Tommy'. And I used to go into our dressing room and tell the players: 'I've seen that mob coming in now. Christ Almighty!! They're frightened to death!'

One day, Leeds arrived a bit late. They were held up, and when Don Revie brought the team in I said, 'By God, I'm glad you arrived. We were getting a bit worried. I was frightened to bloody death you wouldn't come.'

Shankly's Greats

Shankly reminisced about some of the great players he admired:

Tommy Lawton was a great player, brilliant in the air and good with his feet, as was Denis Law. Denis was full of enthusiasm for the game and full of awareness, just like Jimmy Greaves. They stuck them in the back of the net and scored the goals they should have scored. It sounds funny saying that but a lot of players score spctacular goals but don't score the ones they should score.

Denis and Jimmy scored thc goals they should have done. They didn't blast them or try to burst the net. All they wanted to do was get the ball over the line. Jimmy knew he could score. He was like Wilf Mannion, Raich Carter, Peter Doherty, Len Shackleton ... blessed with confidence, something they were gifted with. If Jimmy Greaves or Denis Law and some of these other players were through on their own with only the goalkeeper to beat you could get your tea out and drink it ... it was going to be a goal.

If the goalkeeper stayed on his line they'd carry the ball up to him and put it past him. If he came out they'd run past and put it in the net even from a bad angle. If there was no goalkeeper in the net Greaves or Law would have scored even if they were only a foot off the by-line.

It's a lesson for all players. They should be taught what to do in these situations. How many times do you see players through yet missing by trying to 'chip' the keeper or putting them over the bar? Just doing the wrong thing.

Every player should be taught what to do in a given situation. Law and Greaves and Doherty... they knew what to do. If the goalkeeper stayed in they took the ball up to him and said 'thanks very much'. If he came out they sidestepped him, angled themselves and put it into an empty net.

These are the things that these men knew. Law was quicker than the rest of them in the box. Very, very quick. He was lean. He didn't carry any weight. And he had the awareness that Jimmy Greaves had. He'd sidefoot the ball into the net. You didn't stand any chance with him.

Pelé was a great player. He must rank as one of the best of all time. I've said that Tommy Finney was the best I've seen and I'd bracket Pele, Eusebio, Cruyff, Di Stefano and Puskas up there with him.

Not only could Pelé play with skill and ability, he was also as strong as an ox. He was a light-heavy weight of bone and muscle and he could run like a gazelle. Eusebio was in the same category but slightly taller and quicker. Pelé was brilliant and so was that whole Brazil team.

Then there was Ferenc Puskas. I was at Wembley in November 1953 when he captained the Hungarian side that beat England 6–3. I was glad I was there. I remember the markings on the ball. As Puskas was delivering it the ball was spinning like Jack Nicklaus hitting a golf ball. It was reversing itself And it was slowing down as it was approaching its target, Puskas's colleague Hidegkuti, who was another man who could play.

Wilf Mannion once did the same when I was playing against him. He hit a pass that slowed down, ready for his team-mate to control. Puskas had this marvellous ability.

Years later, in 1971, Puskas came to our training ground with Greek club Panathinaikos when they were playing Everton in the European Cup. He was giving the goalkeeper some practice in a training session, watched by all the Greeks in Liverpool, who gave me invitations to have fish and chips with them for the rest of my life!

But Puskas put the ball on the 18-yard line and hit it with his left foot just a foot inside the post. And he did it 12 times in succession. He'd finished playing years before but he lashed the ball just a few inches above the grass into the corner of the net. I wanted to see him doing it. And he did it. I don't know what he'd have done from 12 yards with a penalty!

And I can't forget Bobby Charlton who was one of the greatest players of all time. Fantastic. I saw him playing in a benefit match towards the end of his career and he was the best player on the field. He beat Ray Clemence with a shot from outside the box. Not many can say that.

In 1970, Shankly named his best British team, not taking into account any Liverpool players. This is the side he selected, in the old 2–3–5 formation: Gordon Banks or Frank Swift; George Young, Ray Wilson; Billy Bremner, John Charles, Dave Mackay; Stanley Matthews, Raich Carter, Tom Finney, Peter Doherty or Denis Law, George Best.

Enthused Shankly: 'I'd have Dixie Dean or Tommy Lawton on the bench, giving me the option of taking off Matthews, switching Finney to the wing and bringing on one of the centre forwards! And don't forget, Charles could also play at centre forward. You'd conquer the world with these men!'

Pete on the Carpet

Peter Robinson, Liverpool vice chairman, chief executive and formerly club secretary, had lunch daily with Shankly in the Anfield canteen. And because he was constantly exposed to the Shankly rhetoric he believed its effect would become gradually diluted, especially Bill's regular pronouncements about superiority over Everton. That was until the day Robinson went home and said to his wife:

'Let's get rid of that blue carpet in the living room.'

Just the Ticket

Shankly left Carlisle United to sign for Preston North End in 1933 for a £500 fee. Reflecting on that move, Shankly observed:

'You can hardly *travel* from Carlisle to Preston for that price today.'

Take Five

Tommy Smith underlined Bill Shankly's passion for five-a-sides with a surprising revelation about Liverpool's preparations:

All the time Shanks was at Liverpool we never practised corners, free kicks, penalties, any set pieces at all.

We just played five-a-sides, five-a-sides, five-a-sides. But we just didn't practise anything. I try to explain that to people but nobody will believe me.

The Continental Touch

Journalist James Mossop, then working for the *Sunday Express*, recalled a trophy-winning trip to Germany with Shankly in 1973:

Shankly's preoccupation with the second leg of the UEFA Cup final against Borussia Moenchengladbach consumed all his time although, once his players were on their way to bed on the eve of the match, he did become the first man ever to be allowed into the British Army Officers Club without wearing a tie. He may also have been the first visitor never to take a drink.

Liverpool lost the second leg 2–0, but because of their 3–0 win at Anfield they collected the trophy. The occasion was made for Shankly. As he walked round the field to take his touchline seat before the start he regularly poked his hand through the high perimeter fence to greet Liverpool fans – whether they were from the 3,000 British Servicemen or the 1,000 genuine Scousers.

During the last seconds as Liverpool clung to their lead he was up alongside the same line spreading his hands as though telling his players 'It's all over.'

When, in fact, it was all over there was no crowing from the man. At a hastily arranged Press conference he was extremely kind to the Borussia team and not so kind to the referee from Moscow. 'I feel sorry for the people in Russia,' he said, 'but that fellow should stay there.'

Some managers would have been basking behind cigar smoke and champagne bubbles. He was ready for a cup of tea.

He sat at the front of the coach on a 90-minute ride from Moenchengladbach to Cologne airport comforting a member of the Anfield office staff who had become far more overcome with the strain of the big occasion than any other member of the Liverpool party.

Watching the scramble for duty free goods at the airport shop he rasped: 'Look at that. If you see a queue join it. This reminds me of wartime when people who didn't smoke nevertheless joined the cigarette queues.' Shankly did not queue.

Date of Destiny

The late Horace Yates, sportswriter for the *Liverpool Daily Post*, recalled his first encounter with Bill Shankly:

Everybody with any interest in football has been familiar with the name of Bill Shankly for most of their lives.

Not until December 1959 did our ways take a parallel course. Well do I remember sitting in my office on the night of 1st December. The Liverpool board were meeting.

My telephone rang and it was Mr T.V. Williams, the club chairman, on the line. 'I've a little story for you,' he said. 'The board have just decided to invite Bill Shankly of Huddersfield to become club manager and he has accepted. I am sure you'll find him interesting to talk to.'

What an understatement that was, for the man I consider the finest public relations man in football has been pouring football into my ears ever since.

My reaction to the tip off was to ring the Huddersfield Town ground. Bill was attending a board meeting, but out he came to give me my first interview.

I was captivated from the start. Here was an individual with a built-in news sense, who told you exactly what you wanted to know and in phraseology that needed no adornment.

In subsequent years nobody called on Bill more frequently for interviews and information. I have disturbed him in his busiest and most inconvenient moments and although the air may sometimes have been blue, seldom did he send me away without something to write about.

On occasions we waged wordy warfare to such an extent that any eavesdropper could be forgiven for concluding that here was the end of a lovely friendship.

But Bill did not harbour grudges. Secretly he realised

that he and Pressmen had a job to do and that it was not always possible to see eye to eye.

So often a tentative approach after strained relations was ended by his invitation. 'Come and have a cup of tea.' The disagreement was never mentioned. It was just as though it never happened.

In my first interview with him I recall his saying, 'I am very pleased and proud to become manager of Liverpool, a club of such great potential.

I believe Liverpool have a crowd of followers which rank with the greatest in the game. They deserve success and I hope in my small way to be able to do something towards helping them to achieve it.

I make no promises except that from the moment I take over I shall put everything I have into the job. There is a job to be done, perhaps a big job, but I feel certain we shall see the task through together.

I am not a lazy man. I like to get down to it and set the example which I want following from the top to the bottom. I make few promises but one of them is that everything I do I hope there will be patent commonsense attached to it.'

One Second Division title and three First Division championships plus two FA Cup final wins and a UEFA Cup triumph later, if ever a manager could truthfully claim – 'mission accomplished' – surely it is Bill Shankly.

He has been a manager, a father, confessor, adviser and friend, whose honesty and sincerity shine like a beacon.

Hammering the Hammers

Liverpool were at Upton Park for a game against West Ham in September 1965. Shankly walked into the Liverpool dressing room and said: 'You've got nothing to beat today. I've watched the West Ham players come in. That Bobby

Moore can hardly walk and as for Geoff Hurst...he looks ill to me! Don't be cruel to them. Stop when you've got five!'

It was 4–0 to Liverpool at half-time and 5–0 early in the second half. England winger Peter Thompson ran past the dug-out and asked: 'Shall we put the shutters up now, boss?' Shankly shook his head and yelled:

'NO...humiliate the bastards!!'

(For the record, Liverpool won 5–1 with Roger Hunt scoring a hat trick.)

A Team in His Own Image

Former Manchester United manager Sir Matt Busby was a Liverpool player when he teamed up with Shankly for Scotland during the Second World War. He recalled:

Bill was with Preston then and as a player he had innate power, strength and enthusiasm. He had to be involved in the game for every second of the 90 minutes.

The Liverpool team he built in the 1960s was like that. No side of his ever gave less than 100 per cent. There were no slackers. They swept the opposition aside as they strode forward in search of honours.

Playing alongside Bill as a team-mate and competing with him as a manager gave me immense pleasure at all times.

Hello, Playmate

Shankly after signing man-mountain Ron Yeats: 'With him in defence we could play Arthur Askey in goal.'

A Role for Ray

Shankly had a high regard for Ray Kennedy, the player who arrived on the very day he quit as boss:

Liverpool signed Ray the day I announced my resignation as manager. We'd been trying to buy him for a while. He played up front for Arsenal but the time had come in football, with our experience in Europe, when you bought players to use in other roles.

Before the war clubs didn't ask you if you were a front man, a sweeper or a midfielder. If you had ability they signed you. Ray Kennedy was one such player. He played up front for Arsenal but was an adaptable, natural, stylish player. I visualised him as a wing half of the old type, like Matt Busby was, and left footed as well.

Ray, I felt, had worked hard with John Radford at Highbury where they'd won the League and FA Cup double. They'd done a lot of running, worked hard and borne the brunt. Ray was a little tired and a bit over weight when he came but his success justified the club buying him. The No. 5 on his back is there only to identify him. But he plays in a no man's land, in a world of his own. And he rules that world.

The Same in Any Language

A batch of Italian journalists surrounded Shankly at an airport, all talking excitedly, and simultaneously. Shanks turned to the hard-pressed interpreter and said:

'Just tell them I totally disagree with whatever they're saying.'

By George!

George Scott was a 15-year-old forward when he signed for Bill Shankly's Liverpool in 1960 and as a team-mate of Tommy Smith and Chris Lawler in the reserves. He never made the first team and was sold to Aberdeen...but not before becoming the beneficiary of some classic Shankly rhetoric which he never forgot.

As he left Anfield Shankly told him: 'You're the 12th best player in the world. There's the Liverpool first team then you, son, because you are the leading scorer in the reserves at the greatest club in the world.'

Scott went on to become a successful businessman as head of sales at a Midlands-based medical and surgical wholesaler and observed: 'Shanks changed Liverpool forever by getting the right players in key positions at the heart of the team.

'Then he built on that by ensuring they were not only brilliant individual players but that they all played for each other as a real team. Building a successful sales team is no different.'

Opportunity Knocks

Bill Shankly had this advice for aspiring youngsters:

A number of young boys have come to me and asked how they can get a trial and break into football. I've told them to write and ask the clubs. But I know they're not usually forthcoming. They tend only to take reports from their recognised scouts.

The best advice I can give is to play for a recognised junior club in an organised league, no matter how far down the scale it is. If you play regularly there's always somebody watching you... the opposition, officials of both clubs, the referee and linesmen, parents and a few other spectators.

Now one of those spectators might just be a scout. And I'll tell you this: if you can play somebody will see you. Big clubs have paid scouts and it only needs one of these gifted men to see you and you'll get a chance. You'll get spotted.

Write to the secretary of one of your local leagues, ask to join a club and take it from there. Or go to the grounds where you know local teams play. Put yourself out. They may invite you to train with them right away.

You get nothing staying still. Make your own way. Some men have climbed Mount Everest for God's sake. That's well-nigh impossible . . . but they've done it!

So getting a game with your local football team should be easier than that. And once you get the jersey on blame nobody else but yourself if you fail. When I got a chance with a junior team called Cronberry, as a boy back home working in the pit at Glenbuck, that was all I wanted.

I just wanted the chance to wear the jersey and play. I did the rest. Someone picked me up within eight months and I went to Carlisle as a professional. So once you get the chance take it. It's up to you.

Switching Wings

Bill Shankly's propensity to praise his players to the skies brought a wonderful riposte from his friend Joe Mercer, the former Everton, Arsenal and England wing half who had a brief but successful caretaker stint in charge of England as well as managing Aston Villa, Sheffield United and Manchester City.

'Bill,' said Joe, 'thinks all his geese are swans.'

A Tall Story

Photographer Barry Farrell asked Shankly during the build-up to a Mersey derby against Everton if he would pose for a newspaper picture in Stanley Park, which separates the rival camps of Anfield and Goodison Park. Shankly agreed and Farrell drove him to the park and parked near the boating lake.

'What are you doing now?' inquired Shankly as Farrell opened the car boot and began screwing together some long pieces of wood.

'Well, the idea for the picture is of you walking on water. So I've brought these stilts for you to walk in the lake and give the impression that you are walking across it.'

'I'll throw you in the bloody lake if you think I'm going to do that,' roared Shankly.

Star Salute

Liverpool stars who played under Shankly saluted him like this:

Gerry Byrne: 'Bill Shankly dedicated himself to football. He lived and breathed the game. He was a winner through and through...even our five-a-side games in training were like cup finals. Defeat was a dirty word. I'll never forget one game at Tottenham when Jimmy Greaves took a corner. I thought someone had shouted so I ducked...and the ball went in the net. All the way home on the train Shanks was saying: "I'll put Gerry Byrne in Walton Prison."'

Ian Callaghan: 'Like Sir Matt Busby, Bill Shankly was a personality manager and the force of his character was such that you couldn't help but be affected and motivated by what he said and did. He influenced my life as well as my career. And he had a great knack of saying the right thing to you just when you needed it.'

Ray Clemence: 'His great strength was in his motivational ability. You'd come in sometimes not feeling on top form but he'd get you to go out and play well. He'd always get the best out of you no matter how you felt. When I was at Scunthorpe several clubs were interested in me but I'm sure I wouldn't have been so successful if I hadn't signed for Shanks.'

Peter Cormack: 'I am one of the very few players fortunate enough to have played under two of the great managers... Bill Shankly and Jock Stein. Shankly was outstanding in motivating people. Whenever we had a bad result he could lift us to the highest level for the next match.'

Brian Hall: 'He set out to achieve the almost impossible task of building not only one of the best teams but one of the best clubs in the land. For anyone who can do that I have the most tremendous respect. To achieve it Shanks had to be a very hard taskmaster and I was honoured to be associated with such a great and powerful man.'

Steve Heighway: 'His enthusiasm and personal drive day in day out got through to everyone. It was the reason we always thought we were going to win something. We didn't all like to be driven on but when we won a trophy we realised it was well worth it.'

Roger Hunt: 'Bill Shankly's enthusiasm was his outstanding quality. You could never knock him down. You could lose on the Saturday but he would still come in on the Monday raring to go and he was able to inspire the players with this enthusiasm.'

Emlyn Hughes: 'You read of other players saying how great their managers are at this and that but, for me, Bill Shankly had everything. He was tremendously funny and said some outrageous things at times. But I could never fall out with him, no matter what he said.'

Kevin Keegan: 'Shanks had the courage to throw me in at the deep end when I'd only just arrived at Anfield from Scunthorpe. Not many managers would have done that. He was a humble man in so many ways. I could sit and listen to him, enthralled, for hours ... on football, on living, on honesty and never cheating. He'd make you feel that any mountain could be climbed.'

Chris Lawler: 'There will never be another like him. I knew him from when he first arrived at Anfield. I was a ground-staff boy brushing up and cleaning the first teamers' boots. I believed in him right away. And he had the sheer willpower and enthusiasm to make you strive harder and harder season after season.'

Tommy Lawrence: 'He would never condemn you. Everybody else might have said you'd played badly but he would never say it, even if he really knew it. He made you feel like the best player in the world. After we'd beaten Arsenal in the Cup at Highbury, early in his reign, he stood in the dressing room shouting "Liverpool, Liverpool" then jumped in the bath with us for the first and only time! He was amazing. Unique.'

Alec Lindsay: 'Bill Shankly was the man who took me from Bury to the big-time atmosphere of Liverpool. He pushed his players relentlessly and he was the hardest man I ever met. But he led by example. There'll never be anyone like him for his attitude and terrific enthusiasm for the game. He was unique ... that's for certain.'

Gordon Milne: 'After moving into management myself I could really appreciate what a great job Bill Shankly did. For the majority of players he was good. He got through to about 95 per cent ... a tremendous success rate. So he had to be right.'

Tommy Smith: 'Bill Shankly put Liverpool back on the football map, made a bad ground into a good one and gave a new dimension to the definition of success. It's hard to imagine what would have happened to Liverpool or myself if he'd not become manager. I would like to think I responded to his encouragement and advice and I was honoured to captain such a great club.'

Ian St John: 'Reuben Bennett used to tell the players that they should go down on their knees and thank Shanks for what he had done for them. You don't fully appreciate such things when you are younger but I do now. Anyone who was part of the Shankly legend should feel very lucky and extremely privileged.'

Willie Stevenson: 'He was the most unforgettable character I've ever met or am ever likely to meet. He had many qualities but the one that stood out above all others was his amazing enthusiasm for the game ... he had even more than the players! He created a "family" at Liverpool and even if there was any discontent amongst the players, which every club has from time to time, Shanks kept it within the club.'

Geoff Strong: 'He was a phenomenal man manager. That was his secret. He got out of players possibly what no other man could have got out of them. What more can you want from a manager than that?'

Peter Thompson: 'When I joined Liverpool, Shanks told me he was going to make me into a really great player. He said he was going to give me everything. He let me down on a few things, like heading and tackling! But it was that kind of talk that got the players to play for him.'

Phil Thompson: 'I'll always be grateful to Bill Shankly for giving me my break in the first team. He had the confidence to play me when I was 18 and he was the one to play me in the back four which proved to be my position. As a skinny kid I used to worship Shanks and Liverpool from the Kop. The legend of Shanks is as much a part of Merseyside folklore as the Liver Birds, the Mersey Ferry or Maggie May!'

John Toshack: 'Shanks was the greatest character the game has ever known. He was unique in his relationship with the fans and his love affair with the Kop. He was also the best public relations officer any club ever had, a great manager in all its meanings and the creator of a backroom team that was the foundation for continuing success. I've always remembered one bit of advice he gave me. "Never lose your accent, son," he said.'

Ron Yeats: 'I'm certain I wouldn't have been the player I was without Bill Shankly. Many players owe their careers to him and I'm one of them. I was privileged to become his captain. But before every game he would tell the players that there were 11 captains out on the pitch. So it was easy to be captain given the work rate of the sixties side.'

A Toast From the 'Boot Room'

The late Bob Paisley, who reluctantly succeeded Shankly and

won more trophies than any manager in the history of English football, was at his side for his 15 years at the helm and was the instigator of the world famous 'Boot Room', the latter with the welcome boost of a donation of Guinness from his friend Paul Orr, later to become Lord Mayor of Liverpool. Bob proudly recalled:

> Through all the time Bill and I worked together we missed only two Liverpool first team games between us. Yet, despite all the tension and pressures, we never fell out or had a wrong word. That really pleased me. He established such a warm relationship with the fans that he was a greater hero to them than any player!
>
> His fanaticism for football shone through in the five-a-side games. His passion for football never waned. I'd been appointed club trainer only a few months before Bill arrived in 1959 and I was fascinated to see him bring in new players and how, carefully and shrewdly, he built a team to accept his concept of football. It was simple . . . and simply very successful.

Perhaps the fact that Paisley and Shankly were very different personalities was the secret of their highly productive partnership. 'I never really liked the limelight and if people didn't recognise me that was fine,' added Bob. 'But Bill loved it. He even had steel tips put on his shoes so that people would know he was coming!'

Joe Fagan, who succeeded Paisley as boss in 1983 and became the only manager in English football ever to win a 'treble' (League title, European Cup and Milk Cup in the same season), also claims a special 'double'. Joe recounted:

> I must be one of very few people not only to refuse to join Liverpool as a youngster but to turn down Bill Shankly when he wanted to sign me as a player for Grimsby Town!

Actually, I'd have been delighted to sign but Bill couldn't provide me with a house so I had to say no. But the day he arrived at Anfield he said to me: 'You should have come to Grimsby, Joe. We'd have gone up if you'd come.'

When my two children were burned in an accident Bill was at the hospital before I could get there... comforting and encouraging them. And, of course, talking football! He was a man with humanity.

Ronnie Moran played under Shankly before joining the Anfield backroom staff and declared:

Everybody knows about Bill's unlimited enthusiasm for the game. But I believe it went deeper than that. He had an enthusiasm for life itself. He preached that every job should be done well and that it deserved your best efforts. He said if he'd had to sweep roads for a living he'd have made sure it was done properly.

Tom Saunders, the former headmaster and manager of the England youth and schoolboy teams, recruited by Shankly as Liverpool's youth development officer, remembers some early advice from the great man:

Just after I joined the club Bill said to me: 'Don't build up a youngster too much. Don't tell his parents that he's sure to be a great player because nobody knows.'

That was sound advice and typical of the man, illustrating his honesty. Not for him misleading promises or false claims simply to obtain a young player's signature.

He had a magic and also a practical approach to everyday problems that sometimes made it regrettable that his talents were confined to football.

The Gold Standard

Liverpool chief executive and vice chairman Peter Robinson, who worked as club secretary with Shankly for nine years, believes there was one outstanding quality amongst the many that he possessed. Said Robinson:

Bill's character had so many facets and people quite rightly have spoken of his motivation, enthusiasm, drive, and charisma. But they captured only a part of the man. I would choose another. His honesty.

It shone through everything he did and was perhaps a reason for the things he did. In the strange world of professional football, which is such a competitive environment, double standards are rife. But Bill's amazing honesty gleamed like gold.

Perhaps it was also the reason for his success because a manager who can win the trust of his players and staff can demand that greater effort that produces the great achievements.

Message Understood

Bill Shankly provided an insight into his unique ability to communicate with the public when he declared:

We're professionals at Liverpool. We believe in simplicity. I wouldn't go on television or use words in newspapers that only a few people understand.

Some people use words knowing full well that only 10 per cent of the viewers or readers know what they mean. We don't. We speak the language that everybody understands. Instead of me saying somebody was avaricious I would say he was bloody greedy.

No Sex For Success

Shankly, who once declared, 'It's a bad thing to get married during the football season', believed his players should abstain from sex on the eve of a match.

Ian St John recalls: 'He used to tell us to wear boxing gloves in bed on a Friday night. Or he would say: 'Send the wife to stay with her mother!'

Teddy Bear's Inking

When Shankly stayed at a Preston guest house during his playing days at Deepdale in the 1930s, five year old Margaret Prestwich, daughter of the owners, told him her teddy bear had no buttons. Shankly took out a pen and inked in some buttons, explaining: 'It's the Scottish way.' The youngster was not amused and kicked him in the shins.

'You should sign for Preston!' he declared. But the girl never removed the ink marks and, in 1998, by now Mrs Margaret Gilfoyle, she sent her special bear to be displayed at Anfield's Visitor Centre.

Hard Words and Hand Outs

Philip Stanley Turner, who made wartime apprearances for Everton, joined Carlisle in September 1948 and was there when Shankly was appointed manager at Brunton Park. 'He'd give you a rollicking if you did something wrong but then he'd try to make it up to you. I've seen him have a right go at one of the lads and the following day bring him a box of mushrooms!'

Mr Motivator

Ray Wilson, who played for Shankly at Huddersfield Town before progressing to becoming a world class left back for

England, recalls him as having the ability almost to make black white. 'He could convince you that even if you were 3–0 down at half time you'd still win,' recalled Wilson.

'He'd say: "I've never seen three luckier goals! You're murdering them...I'm amazed they haven't called the police!" It would definitely boost you mentally so that you'd go out and stage a comeback.'

What If...

During the late 1960s Sunderland made an audacious attempt to lure Bill Shankly and club secretary Peter Robinson away from Anfield to take over at Roker Park, the Wearside club's former home.

'It was at a time when Bill wasn't having the best of relationships with the Liverpool board and when the Roker job came up he received an approach about it,' recalled Robinson, later Liverpool's chief executive and vice chairman.

'He asked me that if he decided to go would I go with him. I said I'd think about it. However, things settled down between Bill and the board and nothing else materialised. It's an interesting exercise, though, to wonder what would have happened to the two clubs if Bill had taken it futher.'

Tactics on a Train

Shankly was on a London-bound train from Penrith during the 1950s when he discovered that the great Hungarian side that had toppled England 6–3 at Wembley, the Magical Magyars, were also on board.

He found their compartment, brought a pile of coins out of his pockets and talked tactics with them for the remainder of the journey. Later that year he received a Christmas card signed by Hungary's captain Ferenc Puskas and the rest of the players.

Counted Out

John Toshack recalled Shankly's pre-match message before the 1974 FA Cup semi final replay against Leicester at Villa Park, following a goalless draw at Old Trafford: 'Shanks didn't show up in our dressing room until shortly before kick off. He just stood there, looking at us, with his hands deep in his raincoat pockets.

'Then he said to us: "Imagine that you are being battered by George Foreman [world heavyweight champion at the time] then the lights go out and you have to go through it all again. That's how Leicester feel." That was it. Then he was gone. It was bloody perfect. We went out and won 3–1.'

Spot On

Shankly on the hotly disputed penalty conceded by Alf Young's challenge on George Mutch that gave Bill's Preston side a 1–0 win over Hudderfield in the dying seconds of extra time in the 1938 FA Cup Final:

'Of course it was a penalty! It's a terrible thing when a man has nothing left to do but bring another man down. I was standing next to Alf Young afterwards. Tears were running down his cheeks and I said him: "Aye, and that's not the first one you've given away, either!"'

A Head For the Top

Bob Shankly on his brother Bill's trademark short hair style: 'I cut it for him when he first left our home village of Glenbuck in Ayrshire to join Carlisle in the early 1930s. I did it with the garden clippers to make sure he'd look presentable.'

Spirit of Competition

Shankly was imbued with a highly charged competitive spirit, at whatever level he or his team were involved. He and the Liverpool backroom staff used to have regular matches in the club car park against a team of bin men and he was always as desperate to win those tussles as he would be a major cup final.

To help fuel the competitive fire in his players he arranged for cricket stumps to be used as goalposts in training, knowing it would create endless arguments over whether a goal had been scored. 'If they start having a go at each other over things like that just think what they'll be like in real games against opponents,' Shankly reflected.

Shankly's Football Creed

Ken Jones, columnist on the *Independent*, recalled Shankly's response when asked for his secret of successful football. 'First,' he said 'you need players who can control and pass the ball. Then, you don't let opposing attackers turn. If they do, track them down quickly. Never run the ball out of your own penalty area and always support the man in possession.'

A Man of the People

Television and radio presenter Elton Welsby on Shankly at the 1976 UEFA Cup Final second leg in Bruges: 'I was commentating on the game and Bill was summarising. When we arrived at the stadium he met some Liverpool fans who had hitched a lift to Belgium. He took out his wallet and gave them £60. You should have seen their faces!'

The Real Highway Code

Everton defender and former Goodison captain Mick Lyons had just played in the reserves and, as he was driving home, he was stopped by Shankly, who was also in his car. Shankly began to tell Lyons how to improve his game. As he did so, a traffic jam began to build behind their two stationary vehicles. Lyons was clearly embarrassed by the tailback of impatient drivers on each side of the road. But Shankly told him: 'Och, never mind them, son. This is serious, this is life.'

My Cup Does Not Overflow

After Liverpool won the FA Cup in 1965, for the first time in their history, Shankly was angered at what he considered was a derisory bonus offer by the board. He told the directors: 'I've ended a 73-year wait by this club to win this trophy and this is all you think it's worth.'

www.shankly.com

The creation of the Bill Shankly website (see Chapter 6) has opened up a Pandora's box of Shankly anecdotes, recalled by members of the net-surfing public. Here are a selection from a litany of memories which flooded into it and which capture many facets of the legendary figure:

RUSSELL GREEN [rgreen@cargonewsasia.com.uk] The anecdote about Shankly arriving in the dressing room with his shirt torn and his hair ruffled after his visit to the Kop. I was a young boy sitting on the Pulpit wall on the Kemlyn Road side of the Kop. I remember getting to the ground early and watching the Kop fill up. I remember looking down and seeing a large gap appear in the crowd front and centre of the Kop about half an hour before the game. It was usually somebody relieving themselves or a scuffle. But then through the smoke haze I could make out Shanks, arms folded across his chest. I will never forget the buzz that went around the crowd and the moment when Shanks raised his hands aloft to an almighty roar before heading back into the dressing room. It still sends a tingle down my spine.

BOBBY SOUNDS [bbsounds@lineone.net]
My dad, when he was much younger than today, was a
pretty good footballer. He is very much like Shankly in
many ways in his behaviour. When my dad was playing
semi-professional footie for various clubs he developed a
reputation of being tough, energetic and reasonably
skilful, so much so that he was approached several times
by Everton which, as you can probably understand, was
like being asked to sell your soul to the devil. He flatly
refused. Not long after Bill had started achieving some
notoriety with Liverpool (before I had even started
school) my dad took me to watch Liverpool train at
Melwood, Bill to my surprise and absolute awe, knew
dad . . . He knew him and even knew of the previous
Everton interest. Shanks started to sing my dad's praises
to me, telling me what a good player he would have been
in a Liverpool shirt and also emphasised what an
opportunity the previous manager had lost. Bill gave me
a glass of orange juice, telling me to eat lots of fish, meat,
eggs and veg and to play as much football as possible.
Maybe one day I'd get the call, but this time it would be
a Liverpool rep calling. In adulthood I peaked at five feet
and two inches, but that day and every time I think of
Bill Shankly, I'll never be less than ten feet tall.

IAN THOMSON [tommothson@hotmail.com]
Bill Shankly is a relative of mine. My papa, Mr Alex
Bradford, who was from Logan near Cumnock, was Mr
Shankly's cousin and as children they were very close.
Basically that means that Mr Shankly was my third
cousin!

I was young when Mr Shankly died and now that I am
older and can appreciate how important he was to both
Scottish and British football, I only wish I had made the
effort to meet the man.

Now I have a five-year-old son and I have tried to tell

him how much of an impact Mr Shankly made on the
soccer front. Now my son is a mad Liverpool fan and
last year I took him to Anfield to the museum and the
Stadium Tour. I don't know who was prouder of the Bill
Shankly statue outside the ground, me or my son. He
took great delight in telling the tour guide, as he has his
school teacher and others, that Bill Shankly is his fourth
cousin!

DAVE THRELFALL [Dthrelly@tesco.net]
I was the great man's paper boy during the 1970s for
two years.

My house backed on to Bellefield, some other team's
training ground, and opposite was what is now Shankly
Playing Fields. He was open with the Blue fans as he was
with everyone else. He would always stop and chat with
them, waiting for autographs, at the entrance.

Quite a few mornings he'd be out when I arrived and
he'd say hello and chat a bit. All the stories that are told
about him being a man of the people are completely
true. When he retired he walked a lot and would often
pass my house in Sandforth Road, two doors away from
Everton's Bellefield training ground. He would stop and
chat to the Blues supporters waiting for autographs.

If you said hello to him he would always stop and talk.

MIKE WHALLEY [bigdani@uk.packardbell.org]
It was true about Shanks and five-a-sides, I played with
him as a kid on what's now Shankly Fields in West
Derby, and the Great Man was no spring chicken back
then. But he was the fittest man I'd ever seen at the time!
And obviously just being that close to him was an
honour. Anyhow, the point is there was never a chance,
if Shanks picked you, that you were going to lose that
day, even if it got dark! Brilliant days.

STEVE ASHTON [ashton.family@xtra.co.nz]
Shanks was nothing short of a great man. The things he achieved for Liverpool Football Club and the way in which he achieved them will never be surpassed no matter how many trophies other managers may win. I was only a small boy when he reigned over Liverpool but I can still remember my father taking me to the games to see my heroes, Keegan, Heighway, Tosh and Tommo to name but a few. I never had the chance to speak to the great man but still etched in my mind is the Charity Shield in 1974, for two reasons. Firstly, Keegan being sent off and Shanks as he walked round the perimeter of Wembley coming over to me, as my father held me up, and placing his hand on my head. A moment never to be forgotten.

FRANK BEATTIE [kilmarnockstandard@s-un.co.uk]
I thought you might be interested in this anecdote from Bill's very early days. My mother and her two sisters were brought up in Glenbuck, where their father was the schoolmaster.

They were at the village station one day, as was the lad they called Willie Shankly. It was a big day for him; he was off to Glasgow to play in a football match. Just as the train was pulling in, Bill screamed: 'Ma bits (boots); I've left ma bits at hame'. So he went running up the road to get them. Meanwhile, the train driver was persuaded to hold the train till he came back. Would a driver do that now? No chance.

COLIN WATT [Colin.Watt@cwcom.net]
I know Ali got 'Personality of the Century', but Shanks will always be number one in my book. My father was converted to the red faith (from Glasgow Rangers) in the mid 1960s by the power of this man.

Can I share a story with you: My late grandfather was

a Liverpool fan all his life. Upon his retirement from the docks in the late 1960s, he received his season ticket. He was shocked to find that the club had moved him from his regular seat to one where he wasn't near the people he'd sat with for years, and where he'd get wet when it rained.

My uncle took him to Anfield to try to get his old seat back. He explained he had just retired after working down the docks as man and boy. The people in the ticket office were completely unsympathetic, telling him his seat was no longer available.

On leaving the office, he noticed Shanks walking in. 'Bill, Bill,' shouted my grandfather, and the Great Man came over. My grandfather explained the situation about his retirement, his time down the docks (working every night during the blitz) and a lifetime as a Liverpool fan. Shanks told him not to worry, to hang on and he'd sort it out.

Five minutes later Shanks reappeared with the season ticket for my grandfather's seat, and said 'If you have any bother ever again, ask for me.'

The man will always be number one in my book.

GRAHAM HUDSON [gdhudson@patrons.org.uk]
I have an interesting Shanks 'anecdote' from a time when Nessie opened the 'Shankly Boot Room' at Leeds Road, Huddersfield's old ground. I'm chairman of the Huddersfield Town F.C. Patrons Association but was managing this small room at the time. It was a couple of years before we moved to the McAlpine Stadium.

Nessie was being shown around a room which was being used for some low-key hospitality events and had been decorated in memorabilia including photos, old balls and boots etc. One display was of the Board minutes showing Bill's appointment as manager and his wage. 'Is THAT how much he was on?' Nessie said in horror. So how much he was giving her is unknown!

Her daughter was with her that day. Nessie, what a lovely lady.

SHAUN MANDALE [andersonberth@aol.com]
I hail from Workington and support Liverpool. Bill managed both, I am too young too remember him but I know from my dad that he was the best manager we ever had. God bless him. RIP.

TONY MOOGAN [tmoogan@zdnetonebox.com]
I have been an adoring fan of the great man since the early 1960s. My California licence plate is 'shankly'. It is my pride and joy, having just acquired it recently. When I was sixteen I had a job on a building site on Utting Ave, not far from Anfield. Every morning at about 9am I would watch out for Bill to drive past in his red Viva. This went on for months without me getting the chance to speak to him.

An event happened which made me realise he was the real thing. After an away game in the Midlands in 1964 myself and three mates ended up travelling behind the Liverpool team bus on the M6 motorway. We had draped a flag with the words 'Liverpool the cream of Europe' on the bonnet of the car. One of my mates had just come up with the phrase and when Bill saw this from the team bus he went bananas, dragging the players to the back of the bus, interrupting their nice game of cards. Some of the players looked a bit bewildered and none as enthusiastic as Bill.

This incident made me realise how much enthusiasm he had for football and LFC in particular. I did eventually get to speak to the great man at Melwood, when it was raining cats and dogs, Bill said 'this place is the worst in the world for bad weather'. That's the way it was with Bill, it was either the best or the worst and no inbetweens. LFC and their supporters must be the luckiest people around, to have known and worked with such a man.

GARY LORD [glord48@hotmail.com]
Keep on telling the world about Shankly. This man made Liverpool Football Club.

I remember seeing him standing on the Kop not long after he retired (I was sitting in the Main Stand). He was clearly visible from a distance because the crowd had made space for him, forming a circle around where he was standing. The respect was immense.

His achievements and charisma will always be remembered as long as Liverpool Football Club exists.

JOY BRATHERTON [JBratherto@aol.com]
In December 1973 I travelled from my home in the Midlands to Norwich to watch the match. Arriving there the night before, I settled into my lodgings and it started to snow really heavily. The next morning I went down to the ground to see if the match was on, the turnstile gate was open and on the pitch were three men. I recognised Shanks, Bob Paisley and Joe Fagan. I was only 17 but I wasn't going to miss this chance and walked on to the ground as bold as brass. Shanks welcomed me and thanked me for travelling so far on such an awful day. We spoke for what seemed like an age but it was probably only a few minutes. The moment stays with me today. Which is more than the result of the game does.

On the day I watched his funeral procession pass by all I could think about was that big smile and that warm genuine handshake.

DOUG STACKHOUSE [smokeystak@aol.com]
I grew up watching Carlisle United from 1964–87 then moved to the USA. All I heard growing up was how great

United were when Shanks was in charge. Judging by what he did at Anfield I can see why.

STEPHEN McCLEAN
[steve@paddymac.freeserve.co.uk]
Every day I'd catch a bus from Huyton to school in Widnes. But the attraction of missing it to watch the Reds train at Melwood just a mile or two away sometimes proved a bit too strong. Liverpool were, and still are, everything.

One day, about the third or fourth in a row watching the Reds go through their paces, I asked Shanks for his autograph on the ball that I always took to school for the dinnertime matches. He looked at the uniform and asked why I wasn't in school. I have to say I lied to the Boss and he said: 'You're no use to me or this club if you let yourself down, son. If you want to play here, then you don't cheat and you don't lie.'

I never did it again, but some time later, I did get a trial, put through my own net and nearly died.

Years later, while working for the *Sheffield Star*, the city's evening newspaper, I was at home in Liverpool, Shanks had passed away and the newsdesk rang to ask me to file a story. I told them that all I could hear were church bells. They never ran the piece, they didn't believe it. They never knew.

MARK THOMASON
[Mark_Thomason@triangle-group.com]
My everlasting memory of 'Shanks' was as a young boy attending an amateur boxing night at the Pirrie Labour Club in Liverpool. My father was on the door that night and Shanks was due to do the prize giving.

When Shanks arrived my father jokingly said that he had booked Shanks in for a three round exhibition bout at the end of the night. Shanks quick as a flash, in that Scottish burr replied, 'My fights don't last thre rounds, son.

I suppose you had to be there, but that memory and that Man will live with me for ever.

TOM JONES [tjones@crowntb.freeserve.co.uk]
I was fortunate enough to get a Cup final ticket off Bill in 1974, after a heartfelt plea to the great man from my lovely mum, who died recently. She is up there now, thanking him for the many phone calls we received, sparked off as a result of the thank you letter we sent for the ticket. He actually rang our house on a number of accasions thanking my mum for birthday cards, Christmas cards etc, she would send him.

I will never forget the occasion I answered the phone to him. The Reds had just signed Kenny Dalglish. I asked Shanks what he thought of him, 'GRREEAT player son', was the reply. Not a bad judge, was he!

TONY McCRORIE [tmac@dial.pipex.com]
I saw Shanks many times but met him only once, outside St Andrews (Birmingham City) in the 1960s, when I was about twelve. The quote I always remember was when Shanks was asked what he looked for in a striker and the reply was, 'Apart from the obvious, a man who is not frightened to miss.'

STEVE DARBY [anissa@amaze.net.au]
I have been a professional player and coach for the last twenty years in various parts of the world (USA, Bahrain, Australia, Fiji and currently Malaysia) and I have always tried to instil the Shankly philosophies into my players. I was fortunate enought to go to Anfield Road School and never missed a game in the 1960s. First in the Boys Pen and then in the Kop. Days you cannot forget.

I was about to embark on my first overseas professional coaching job to Bahrain and I was at Melwood watching

Liverpool train, to get ideas. I was early and to my shock I saw Shanks running around Melwood. I plucked up the courage to speak to him as it was like meeting 'God'. I asked hime for advice in my career... his first words were... 'the most important thing to learn is to make tea! So go and make me one!'

He then sat with me for about half an hour and he was just like the image. Unlike many of the football legends I have met in my career he was truly everything he was supposed to be. My current team Johor won the 1998 Malaysian FA Cup and left the dressing room to 'You'll never walk alone'. Grown men are not supposed to have heroes, but if you love football and were brought up in Liverpool in the 1960s you have to have Shanks as a hero. His manner and lifestyle and philosophy of football proves that there are more important things in life than money.

VANGELIS KIOULAFIS [vkioulafis@yahoo.com]
My name is Vangelis Kioulafis and I'm from Athens, Greece. I'm 27 and since the age of seven I have been a Liverpool supporter. I have been twelve times at Anfield and two times at Wembley (1989 FA Cup final, 1992 Charity Shield).

I'm a great fan of Bill Shankly. I think Bill Shankly is the greatest man in the history of football. I will never forget when I have visited Shankly house and met Shankly's widow, Nessie. It was tremendous for me, me and my mates from Greece sitting in Shankly's living room... tremendous.

KEITH EDWARDS [kj.edwards@unsw.edu.au]
As an eight and nine-year-old my dad would take me to work sometimes, and we would go in the Eaton Road café for breakfast. Shanks, who had retired by then, would be sitting in there and would come right over and keep us there for ages, him talking, us listening. About

four years later my dad jumped out of his van in Old Swan. He said it was lashing down, and who ran up to him and made him take the umbrella because of the rain but Bill. 'You have not been in the café for ages,' he said. My dad protested about the umbrella, but Shanks gestured for him to shut up and said, 'Son, you work too hard. I can go home now and dry off, you still have to work all afternoon. Besides, a few years ago you told me the only mistake I have ever made since coming to Liverpool was resigning. So you just resign yourself to the fact that I'm right again and get under the f———g thing.' He spent another twenty minutes getting wet while talking football. My dad said he could see people looking at him thinking why he did not offer Shanks his brolly. At the end of the conversation my dad handed Bill his brolly back and an old lady, walking past at the time told my dad he should be ashamed of himself. Mr Shankly walked away laughing his head off.

I now live in Australia, and the footy team I play for has a trainer/coach who has been at the club for years. He is now a mad Red, 65 years old and everyone knows him by name only, SHANKS. This is a legend that will never die.

JOHN GREGORY [gregory@baytel.net]
I have been connected with football all my life and although I am not a Liverpool fan I can remember being at Anfield just prior to the Shankly era and during it. What a transformation. I knew a bit about Bill from his days at Huddersfield, the five-a-side games went on forever or until his team were victorious, whichever was the sooner. Shanks was the greatest manager of all time. Sure he had success but his appetite for the game, his outstanding personality, his humour, his great knowledge of the game, a voice that just commanded your attention made him the most loved and respected manager of his time, by everyone. He did not have an enemy in the

world and if ever a club and manager were made for each other then Liverpool and Shankly were the ones.

. . . Although I never met him I feel a close friendship with him somehow. I guess it's because I so loved his attitude, not only towards the game but to life itself and above all his great wit. Also, we should never forget how honest he was, a genuine and sincere man, a players' man and a supporters' man also. I am now 67 years of age, a young 67 I believe, and I have both played and followed football for 62 of those years. I would have to say that whenever I think about football which is often, Shanks always comes to my mind and how there will never be another one like him. Rest in peace Bill. We love you and miss you and will never forget you.

GERRY CRUTE [gerrycrute@hotmail.com]
On 12 July 1974 I was at school in Sandfield Park, right next to Bill and Nessie Shankly's house. When the rumour spread that Our Messiah had retired, incredulity, denial, fear, and a whole host of other emotions ran unchecked through the classrooms. At the end of the day, a media frenzy, a group left St Edward's College, walked through the Park and climbed over the wall at the end of Sandforth Close and walked on up to Bill's purple front door. Wearing blazers to match, and summoning every ounce of courage, the bravest of our group knocked at the door.

Nessie answered and was asked, 'Is Bill there, please?' by the twelve-year-olds assembled. The great man came out.

'Have you retired, Bill?'

'Aye, son. I have.'

'Aah, eh, Bill.'

'Aye, son?'

'Aah don't. Please, Bill.'

'Aah, I'm sorry son.'

And the moment ended with Bill signing his autograph on all manner of paper, though not our exercise books or we would all have been in trouble with masters at our rugby playing school who simply wouldn't have understood the significance.

Throughout the next couple of years he was a very, very frequent visitor to our school. He was given permission by the headmaster to use the school facilities which were at the time light years ahead of any other school in the city, and we became almost blasé about seeing Bill as we went to the gym, the baths, the weights room or elsewhere.

One day during a spring half-term holiday along with the rest of the school cross-country squad I turned up at the school at around 9.30, to find a game of football going on in the playground. Some local boys were playing there along with a couple of my teammates. Obviously I joined in and only then noticed a short haired older man, not resembling any of the teachers. When the ball went into play it was obvious that Shanks was playing too. I had died and was playing in heaven, and to make things better Bill was on my side. He spoke, you listened. He coached and you did as he said. And it worked too. I have never played as well, and even when it was my turn to go in goal, I performed out of my skin. A cross came over and I reached as high as I could and somehow managed to trap the ball against the bar, which was the underside of a pillared shed some six feet or so off the ground. One of the other side charged into me. Not prepared to let down my side, most of all Shanks, I struggled to stop the ball from falling over the line. From nowhere Shanks arrived and saved the day. Pushing the boy away he took the ball out of my hands and congratulated me on a good save. He spotted the ball and took the free kick he had awarded himself. As the play developed up the yard he turned back to me and asked if I was OK. I stammered that I was and took a hefty pat of encouragement on my shoulders.

Bill said, 'You're doing well, son,' smiled and looked at me playing football in my athletics kit.

He cocked his head to the side and told me, 'Aye, you've got footballer's legs,' and took off up the yard to put matters to rights elsewhere. I looked down at my legs, which were indeed very well developed as a result of running dozens of mile a week, and playing all sorts of other sports too. The ultimate hero had just paid me the ultimate compliment a fourteen-year-old could receive. Training that day never took place. The master had no chance at all of getting us off the yard and into a run through Sandfield Park and West Derby. No competition. I was in ecstasy (as I am now writing this and remembering how good I felt for months afterwards).

I heard Bill speak in the Mountfield Hall at the University of Liverpool shortly before he died. He said that the worst thing he had ever done was to retire. He said that his mind didn't want to be retired and he felt that he had to keep himself busy or he would shrivel up and die. I can't help thinking that maybe he should have been found a role into which he could have channelled his undoubted gifts, perhaps with children as I had benefited from his undoubted skills that particular day when he made me feel like a king. Maybe we might have enjoyed his presence in this world for longer, and that would have been to everyone's benefit.

God Bless You, Bill. Always remember with extreme fondness. Never alone.

4

Now, Prime Minister

Bill Shankly's voice boomed out over the airwaves in the mid-1970s when he hosted his own Saturday lunchtime chat show on Merseyside commercial radio station, Radio City.

His guests came from all walks of life ... show business, politics, business and, of course, football. My former journalist colleague, Wally Scott, produced the shows and drew many a sharp intake of breath during the studio recordings because of Bill's idiosyncrasies. Wally recalled:

The guests loved coming to talk to Shanks and travelled from all over the country to take part. I remember Denis Waterman coming up from filming *Minder* in London because he wanted to be a guest on the show. Brian Rix was another.

And when we were recording Bill's show with his fellow Scot, Lulu, we had a problem because he wouldn't call her 'Lulu'. She's from Glasgow and Shankly said to her: 'I'm not calling you Lulu. That's not your real name.' He kept calling her by her name Ann Marie. So we had to insert pre-record taped reminders saying 'Bill Shankly is talking to Lulu!'

But the biggest headaches for me came when we had a football guest, which included Joe Mercer, Ian Callaghan and Albert Stubbins. Shanks would get carried away, relive match incidents and get up and leave the microphone to kick an imaginary ball across the studio! I had to keep asking him to get back to the mike! One week we had a guy lined up for Bill's show who had just climbed Everest. I rang Bill and told him and he replied: 'No, I don't want him . . . you can't play football on the top of Everest!' So that was it. I had to find another guest.

For another of his shows I drove Bill to Manchester to record an interview with Bernard Manning. That was very interesting because Manning ended up in tears. Bill could get things out of people nobody else could and when Manning told Shanks about his father he started to cry.

The signature tune for Shankly's show was an up-tempo version of 'Amazing Grace' by Johnny and The Hurricanes. The first show was broadcast on 1 November 1975. The celebrity guest was another man with powerful Merseyside connections . . . the Prime Minister, Harold Wilson, no less. This is exactly how their conversation went . . .

PRIME MINISTER: I was very glad when I heard you were going to do this, and when you wrote to me I wrote, almost by return of post, I think.

SHANKLY: Yes, it was a tremendous quick reply – the leading statesman in the land, in fact the Prime Minister of Great Britain. I mean, for you to find time to come here is unbelievable. I mean, I thought as a football manager I had a hard job, but I can tell you one thing – whereas I had to look after 55,000 you have to look after 55 million.

PRIME MINISTER: Yes, but it's a very similar job, you know. You know what they said about me, when I formed the Cabinet the first time – hardly anyone had ever sat in a Cabinet before – we had been out of office for 13 years and I had to take the penalties, I acted as goalkeeper, I went and took the corner kicks, I dashed down the wing. Now I have got a very experienced Cabinet and I said I am not going to do that. They didn't believe me, I said I'm going to be, what we used to call, a deep-lying centre half – I couldn't say sweeper, because nobody would understand it outside football. And then I think it was the *Liverpool Post* who said that he's doing more than that, in fact he's being a manager, he's not even on the field. To which I said I was very proud for Liverpool to refer to 'The Manager' which means Bill Shankly territory. I know I said this in a speech – I regard it as a compliment – but I went on to say this: 'Where does the manager usually sit? – on the substitutes' bench!' I was reminding my team that I've got people on the substitutes' bench who think they're at least as good as anybody on the field. And I think that's the similarity of the Prime Minister's job and a football manager's job.

SHANKLY: In other words, you delegate the right men for the right job.

PRIME MINISTER: Right – but not only that – like a manager's job, if your team gets relegated, as mine did in 1970, then some people start saying they want a change.

SHANKLY: That's correct. Yes, but you have proven, and I hope you will keep proving, that you are the man.

PRIME MINISTER: I've been there nearly as long as you were at Liverpool.

SHANKLY: Mrs Wilson writes poetry, this is true?

PRIME MINISTER: Yes she does, she always does – since she was a girl – and then a few years ago she was asked to put some in a book. I think, according to her publisher, that it had the biggest sale of any book of poetry since the war.

SHANKLY: Is that a fact?

PRIME MINISTER: Well, it's all genuine stuff that she believes in – she writes about human things – she wrote about Aberfan. She was moved by the Aberfan disaster, when all those school children were killed. I flew down that night, she came soon after. And she also writes about things like the Durham Miners' Gala, and at Durham this year she read them both out.

SHANKLY: Authentic...

PRIME MINISTER: Yes, that's right, things that she feels.

SHANKLY: Actually, I was born in the same county as Scotland's greatest poet, Robert Burns, who was not only a poet but a philosopher, a prophet – everything, you name it. I think that if he had lived until he was as old as Shakespeare or Wordsworth, I think he would possibly have been in the First Division and them in the Second Division.

PRIME MINISTER: I think, well he is in the First Division, isn't he? And I know his poetry less than my wife does, though I've never known it when I've been speaking in Scotland, that somebody on the platform hasn't quoted something – either something familiar or something I didn't know. The Secretary of State for Scotland, who's a great Burns Night speaker, he can recite yards of it at a time – most Scotsmen can, I think...

SHANKLY: He, in actual fact, was one of the early people on socialism.

PRIME MINISTER: He was really, yes.

SHANKLY: Possibly the first one was Jesus Christ, of course, but after that Burns was a real socialist, and one of the instigators of socialism. I think, of course, he was a great character as well, Robert Burns.

PRIME MINISTER: Yes, he was. I haven't read as much about him as I should. As a socialist, if one uses this phrase, and an early one as you say, it was because he felt it. It was because he loved his fellow men. He was not a theoretical socialist. I don't think he would understand anything about the theory of value or any of the scientific socialist writings that I don't bother much with myself, either. But, he just felt a love of his fellow human beings and he wanted to see their lot improved.

SHANKLY: That sums him up. He was born in poverty and he died in poverty.

PRIME MINISTER: And he didn't believe that the Lord

created people to be unequal, but he created one set of people designed to rule the earth and others to be just the hewers of wood and draw the water.

SHANKLY: His books have been translated for the whole of Russia – for most countries in the world – but Russia more than anybody.

PRIME MINISTER: I've found that. I've been to Russia many times and they really, I think, worship the ground he walks on. I think it's been translated into about 160 Russian languages – and I remember, many years ago, they brought out a special postage stamp in his honour, before it was thought of being done in Britain.

SHANKLY: For his anniversary.

PRIME MINISTER: That's right.

SHANKLY: He was, of course, a well-known man with the women.

PRIME MINISTER: Yes, I think he got around a little bit. I think if he had been in one of your football teams, you'd have been on to him about the hours he kept.

SHANKLY: I think I'd have had a detective watching where he went at night time.

PRIME MINISTER: I think, if he had lived today he might be in the Scottish football team.

SHANKLY: It's a well-known fact that in his day, if a man was committed to fornication he was reported to the local minister. And the minister sent for the man and he sat him in front of the congregation on a seat, called the 'cutty stool', and he humiliated him in front of all the congregation. This was a well-known thing. It would appear that Burns was so often there that he had a season ticket.

PRIME MINISTER: Yes, it's what you call a 'sin bin' in football.

SHANKLY: That's correct. But, nevertheless, a fantastic man . . . Huddersfield, Mr Wilson?

PRIME MINISTER: I was born there. I was at school there until I was 16 and then I came to Merseyside.

SHANKLY: Your background was in Huddersfield, which I know well, of course. I was there five years.

PRIME MINISTER: Yes, I know you were manager there.

SHANKLY: I used to play up at Oaks, at the top of the hill there and at the back, the field there was where we started playing five-a-side football on a Sunday afternoon. We started then with five-a-side and finished up with about fifteen-a-side.

PRIME MINISTER: My grandfather and grandmother were married at Oaks – Oaks Chapel. I was there until I was 16. Of course I played football, but never good enough. I used to go and watch Huddersfield Town every week. I played a bit of rugby league, but not professionally of course. Then I came to Merseyside – my father lost his job and got another job on the Wirral and I went to Wirral Grammar School – Wirral County School – as it was then. And I had to play rugby union, and I came to like that as well. But a lot of my formative career was spent on Merseyside as well as in Yorkshire.

SHANKLY: You mention rugby, I think it's a very good thing for character. I think that rugby boys are good boys.

PRIME MINISTER: Soccer is too, it's a good thing for character . . . and bad character sometimes.

SHANKLY: I think that rugby union at school is a good thing for boys.

PRIME MINISTER: Yes, well I played it for two years – I was captain of the school team and a future England international was in the team when we played our first match and got beat, 74–0. Well, it wasn't that bad, we were 37–0 at half time, though we didn't deteriorate.

SHANKLY: You were playing for Everton?

PRIME MINISTER: No, we were playing for the school. You see it was a young school, a new school, only a year old – I was the only boy in the sixth form. Now we asked one of the neighbouring schools to give us their fourth team, and they were suspicious – they gave us their second team and they overwhelmed us.

SHANKLY: That was a form of cheating, wasn't it? You went to Wirral Grammar School and that was strictly rugby, wasn't it?

PRIME MINISTER: Strictly rugby, though at one point the then headmaster, an excellent man, got worried that the boys had nothing to do at lunchtimes. So, as school captain, I said I would organise some healthy sport, and we played football every lunchtime, after lunch. I rather enjoyed playing soccer with ten-foot posts.

SHANKLY: You had every chance of scoring a goal.

PRIME MINISTER: We got the long shots in. I also did a lot of running, I ran for the Wirral Athletic Club. I got a championship and then I ran in the Liverpool and District, where we got the bronze, my team.

SHANKLY: You were cross-country champion of Merseyside schools?

PRIME MINISTER: No, just Wirral. I ran also at a lot of other sports there. I once ran in the Northern Counties Athletic Championship behind the man that set the record that year, and he was the English captain – and I got a good back view of him when we set off, and I never saw anybody's back view for the quarter mile.

SHANKLY: This cross-country, Mr Wilson, this is really a soul destroying job, isn't it?

PRIME MINISTER: I'd never done much, I was a short and middle distancer and then I went out to train at our cross-country headquarters and they asked me to run in the championship because they had a good runner who they wanted to give a chance, and somebody hadn't turned up and I just stuck to him and beat him barefoot.

SHANKLY: This all leads up to the fact that you are the Prime Minister of Great Britain and you've played football and you've played rugby, you were cross-country champion. Now, I've run all distances...

PRIME MINISTER: So have I, I could never decide what my distance was.

SHANKLY: But the cross-country run is really soul destroying.

PRIME MINISTER: Well it is, if you get a bit of a stitch or have the wrong thing to eat or drink beforehand.

SHANKLY: You don't want to give in, you want to go on until you die.

PRIME MINISTER: Well, actually, that's good for politics. I remember when I was up and coming, really, one of the greatest journalists, now dead, said: 'Watch this man, he's a long-distance runner. A long-distance runner who gets there in the end.'

SHANKLY: That's what I said at the beginning of the football season, when they said: 'Who's going to win the League?' I said: 'Listen, this is a marathon, this isn't a short sprint.'

PRIME MINISTER: It's very tight at the moment between the top ones. I heard you actually last season, oh I should think ten or a dozen matches before the end, saying that Derby County were going to win, I heard you on the radio say that.

SHANKLY: We had seen all the teams, Mr Wilson.

PRIME MINISTER: You were quite positive about it, and it was a near thing – but you were right.

SHANKLY: I think they only used the bits they wanted to use. In actual fact my first bet was Liverpool, and Derby County was my failing bet, and they edited it so that it was Derby County.

PRIME MINISTER: Oh, I gave you credit for it you see.

SHANKLY: Well, I did back Derby County, but I had seen all the teams and after I'd seen Derby at Liverpool, I'd then seen all the teams, I'd seen them twice and I felt that they had enough class.

PRIME MINISTER: Your Liverpool team was one of the greatest I've ever seen. It still is, of course.

SHANKLY: Yes, they've got character and they're never beaten, they last the game. The game that we did play was geared to bring everyone into the game and simplify it. Consequently, you didn't have more to do than me.

PRIME MINISTER: Well, my theory about this is the same with politics. I often use the analogy – in fact people say I get boring the way I use analogies in the House of Commons, but it helps you understand it. I say no team is going to win the Cup or the League unless he's got good reserves, and I've paid as much attention to building up my reserves. As I said after being out of office 13 years, I reckon that if my first team went under a bus, my second team could take over, and my third team in some ways shows as much promise as any of them.

SHANKLY: This is true.

PRIME MINISTER: And you've got to give them responsibility young.

SHANKLY: And if we had a well-known player, unable to play through injury, which would be a terrible blow. Some teams, if they lose a key player, that's them gone you know, and the pessimistic will let it get them down. If I had a key player injured, I used to say to the boy apprentice: 'Listen son, you're a better player than him,' and use a little bit of psychology.

PRIME MINISTER: You've got the problem of temporary substitution and the problem of taking people off the substitutes bench, like I do. I mean, for a very long time you had five or six world-class forwards. And your problem was who to leave out. And there was always disappointment whichever one was left out.

SHANKLY: But football is a form of socialism.

PRIME MINISTER: Well I think you have the greatest advantage here, and it's true of certain other parts of the country – of tremendous schools football. I've heard of my own constituents – boys who have gone on to the national championships, schoolboy championships, and from different parts of the country, and different parts of Merseyside. And I've seen those kids playing and you find that those of 10 or 12 are getting watched by the scouts.

SHANKLY: Well I've seen a few 11-year olds and 12-year olds recently and there's a few of them who can play.

PRIME MINISTER: Whether they're born with it or not as long as they work at it.

SHANKLY: If they've got the ability, then a breakthrough is going to come out. And I've got my eyes on them you know. The grit that you showed with your cross-country – this is your character. This is why you rose to be Prime Minister.

PRIME MINISTER: Well, you talk about Robbie Burns, you know, but one of my favourite songs is from Harry Lauder – 'Keep Right On to the End of the Road'. If you've got problems to solve you've got to keep at it. With us – and again I'll take your football analogy – in politics timing is everything. People will nag you, 'Why haven't you done it? Why don't you get on with it?' I was nagged all the summer about the anti-inflation policy. I knew what I wanted, I was confident I would get it. But it had to be the right time so I had to get kicked in the teeth and everything else...because I *seemed* to be complacent and lazy. But there's a time, and you know when that time is to hit that ball, and it's the same thing.

SHANKLY: And only you know that.

PRIME MINISTER: And only you know if you're a professional, and if you're *not*, you'd better make way for somebody else.

SHANKLY: And only a manager of a football club knows what he's got to do and when to do it.

PRIME MINISTER: Exactly, and how he's going to shape them.

SHANKLY: And the man who's willing, he takes the stick if anything goes wrong.

PRIME MINISTER: And how you've got to bring this man on and disappoint another sometimes breaks his heart.

SHANKLY: And he's not going to be told by somebody else when to bring a man on. He brings in his men in the same way you bring your men in – at the right time, and you make your statements at the right time. As you say, it's all timing.

PRIME MINISTER: And footballers, football managers and politicians get it wrong sometimes.

SHANKLY: Oh yes, it's a loud bang when a football manager is wrong. But when you make a large boob, with you then it's a bigger bang, of course.

PRIME MINISTER: Mind you, we have the right to answer back, in Parliament. Our Parliament is the greatest thing in the world. The Americans have got nothing like it. I don't know a lot about the Continentals, but it is democracy. The minister, whatever he's done, he's got to answer for it to a pretty hungry crowd of experts. People who are out to either get him down or support him and you can't touch it, you can't dodge the responsibility.

If you've made a mistake, say so, and I've *always* had Question Time. Macmillan was one of the greatest Prime Ministers. I didn't agree with him on one or two things, neither he with me, but I respected him, and I was told that he used to be almost physically sick worrying about questions twice a week. I know how he felt. And when a Prime Minister *isn't* worried about questions, then democracy's in danger. But I've suddenly changed my psychology.

I used to think of it like cricket, you know, if you are supposed to be a top-class batsman, they mustn't take your wicket, and it makes you a bit offensive, you know. And I suddenly said a fortnight ago: 'I've got it all wrong.'

I treat questions like football now. If they want to score a goal, let them score a goal. I'll go out and try and score two and it's slightly changed my attitude and it's also making Question Time more exciting. I think if you think in sporting analogies, it helps you in other walks of life. Your problem I don't have in the same way, but the jobs are similar in many ways.

I went into the dressing room after the Huddersfield match – they had won, they played very well. I saw the manager talking to them. Although they won, and he said they played marvellously, he told them: 'That marking was wrong. Those little 'uns, you should mark the little ones – let the big ones mark the big ones.' I've often wondered what was said in dressing rooms – it was the first time I'd ever been in one. I was in the Scottish one just after Frankfurt, you know.

SHANKLY: Yes. Ah, yes.

PRIME MINISTER: In the World Cup, I went to see them when I hoped they were going to pile up all the goals they needed. But it must be hard when your team's done badly and they know it, and you know it, to know exactly what to say to them.

SHANKLY: Oh it's a terrible feeling! I mean, you know, what it's like in politics if something goes wrong – I mean it's a terrible feeling if you've had a bad day and you've got beaten.

PRIME MINISTER: And the first minute you go in there what do you say?

SHANKLY: Oh the first minute . . . after it, I mean, you may have something to say . . .

PRIME MINISTER: You can't chew 'em up too badly or you'll break their hearts.

SHANKLY: No, no, no. What you've got to do is you've got to know your cabinet – you know all of these men in your cabinet – you know their strengths and their weaknesses I have got to know all these players and I deal with them the way I think – one needs to be spoken to strongly . . . one needs a little handling – you know all your cabinet and I know all my players.

PRIME MINISTER: You know what they'll take.

SHANKLY: You know what's best for them.

PRIME MINISTER: I'm going on to another thing with your job in mind – you've got certain people. Some are very good at this particular thing or that particular thing. I sometimes alter the system, the machinery of government to make sure that a flyer of this particular kind can really develop on that side, so to speak, just as if you've got – well let's not talk about any local footballers.

But we were chatting the other night about Ray Wilson who went from Huddersfield to Everton. Now if you've got a Ray Wilson there you will develop, I guess, a particular style of play and tactics to make the greatest use of him.

SHANKLY: Great.

PRIME MINISTER: If you've got somebody like Leighton James of Burnley – well I think he's a real, good old fashioned winger of the kind I was brought up to respect and admire and cheer – then in his case, I can imagine Burnley would build their tactics round a man like that whereas without him they'd be doing different tactics.

SHANKLY: Mr Wilson, you're going to be manager of a football team soon!

PRIME MINISTER: I don't think I'd do it very well.

SHANKLY: Your tactics are right!

PRIME MINISTER: I'd rather be an amateur watcher of it.

SHANKLY: You played yourself at what level?

PRIME MINISTER: Oh, I was a goalkeeper in Huddersfield . . . I wasn't very good. I had a year off then because I had typhoid fever and they didn't have the cures for it that they have these days. Then I went on to the wing – but shortly afterwards, as I say, I went to a rugby school and the only thing I could do was run fast and if I got the ball I'd make for the goal line – sometimes successfully, more often not.

SHANKLY: There's another piece of your character coming out. Cross-country . . . the typhoid . . .

PRIME MINISTER: I was camping at a Boy Scouts' camp – we had a local one. We lived in a kind of textile valley and I was up on the moors. We had an arrangement with the farmer who owned it and I got some milk from a local farmer, a milkman, who turned out to be a typhoid carrier. Twelve people got it, six of them died and I nearly did. And I lost nearly a year out of my school.

SHANKLY: You didn't nearly die at all because you weren't going to die.

PRIME MINISTER: Well I didn't know how bad I was actually. They had to starve you out, you see, for many months. But I had a wonderful school master, a maths master. He never had a degree and he was always in a bit of trouble and he was a great socialist. I owe more to him than to almost anybody in this way. I missed so much maths over two terms. He said: 'If you are prepared to stay an hour a day after school, I am, and I'll bring you up to date,' and it was the happiest day I think he ever had in my time. And he was in tears when he announced that I'd finished third in the form in the maths exam . . .

SHANKLY: That's fantastic . . .

PRIME MINISTER: . . . and I'll always owe that to him.

SHANKLY: So the fact that the typhoid retarded you, you gained again.

PRIME MINISTER: It was a challenge. And we had all young masters at Wirral School. It was a new school and apart from the head, there was nobody over 30. And there was a wonderful chap teaching classics and he was a good rugby player and cricket – played for Leicestershire second and he was an example. He was killed at the age of 27 only just after being appointed headmaster – killed in the Lake District climbing – or walking really – and he made an impression on everybody.

SHANKLY: If you look at all the men such as you, who have reached a peak of your career – I mean they all had setbacks, Mr Wilson. Without setbacks you don't know what trouble is do you? You don't know how to fight back.

PRIME MINISTER: I had mine when I was relegated in 1970, you know – when we lost the election – and many people thought we were going to win. I wasn't so sure and I had to set out and build it all up again. I had to keep the team together first and not let them get disheartened. But that was a harder task than actually running the government before. Harder to be leader of a national party in opposition than if you've got the responsibility of government.

SHANKLY: How does it feel when you get beat in a big match?

PRIME MINISTER: And then you get relegated.

SHANKLY: In actual fact, vote-wise there are more socialists than anybody else.

PRIME MINISTER: There are a lot of estimates...

SHANKLY: How come, Mr Wilson, that a man can vote and then change his mind in the next election?

PRIME MINISTER: Sometimes they vote for personalities as well as policies. I read somewhere that basically, there are committed Labour people, more than Conservatives and of course more young people are coming on that way, but they change from time to time. They get fed up with the government as supporters get fed up with the team and I think that's what's happened. I'll tell you though, I was listening to the World Cup that Sunday night – and the Sunday before I was winning two–nil with about 20 minutes to go when I heard England had lost 3–2. I thought there'd be an effect and do you know a lot of voters said: 'I can't stand anything after this...' You know, it affected them. I think it had some effect on the election – not decisive, of course.

SHANKLY: In Mexico.

PRIME MINISTER: In Mexico, yes, and I think that the mistake was to take Charlton off. It was a signal to the Germans. All they had to do was pile into the attack. As long as Bobby was there they'd got to cover their own goal and they weren't going to get the equaliser or the winning goal. That's only a matter of opinion.

SHANKLY: Me, who was a manager at one time – you, as Prime Minister. We're used to having to make that decision. The manager made it, but things went wrong. If he hadn't taken Charlton off they might have lost just the same.

PRIME MINISTER: We might have lost.

SHANKLY: So he, in his wisdom, thought he was right. So you would have done the same thing and so would I.

PRIME MINISTER: Maybe, maybe. You've got to follow your judgement.

SHANKLY: Sure you have. If you can't make decisions you're nothing.

PRIME MINISTER: You've got to make decisions. You'll get attacked and misrepresented, sometimes praised. Sometimes you make a big mistake and you don't get attacked for it. They may not know it – but you know you've made the mistake.

SHANKLY: You've been 35 years on Merseyside?

PRIME MINISTER: I came here in 1932, to live here and go to school. Then I was elected for Ormskirk in 1940 which included a lot of Liverpool – 37,000 people within the Liverpool boundary – in West Derby, Dovecot and Croxteth and then there were boundary changes and I went to the new division of Huyton, still keeping Kirkby. But now, of course, Huyton has lost Kirby, and all the time it's been growing. It's an entirely different place. It was a farm village when I came.

SHANKLY: Not long ago we went into the Common Market. I don't know really anything about the Common Market. Candidly my whole life has been about football.

PRIME MINISTER: Well, it's been going on since 1962, and we always said it's good for us – if we're not going to be crippled by it, and if it doesn't break up the Commonwealth. This is what the Labour Party said in Opposition and then when we were in Government we applied. But De Gaulle vetoed it, as he had vetoed Harold Macmillan. Then the Conservatives took us in, under Mr Heath. But, I didn't think he had the country behind him. We said we would negotiate and if we didn't get the right terms we would recommend coming out. Then we had a referendum and the country decisively voted. Now nobody's in any doubt. We're a *democratic* country, people fought hard against what I was saying in the referendum, but loyally accepted it. I think that's the kind of country we are. We've got big problems to solve. We've got to strengthen our own economy to make us better partners as well as survive and prosper there. I still have strong criticisms of the European countries, *but* mainly their football style again.

SHANKLY: Whether we are in the Common Market or not, we still have to work hard. It won't make any difference really.

PRIME MINISTER: There's an argument for being in and an argument for being out, but we came out strongly in the end for staying in. It's a big league is this one, you can't go in as cripples – you've *got* to build up your economic strength. People who say 'We're done for' are totally wrong. There's more ingenuity and hard work in this country than people realise. We're showing through our exports now how well we're doing in a world of depression.

SHANKLY: Ever since I can remember there've been rumours that we're finished. It's pessimism. There's always a shortage of optimism and people willing to get their jackets off. I was born and brought up in the pits and I was in the pits when I was 14.

PRIME MINISTER: Which coalfield were you in?

SHANKLY: The Ayrshire coalfield.

PRIME MINISTER: I used to know them very well. I used to know every miners' leader in Ayrshire when I was younger.

SHANKLY: We were in William Beard and Company.

PRIME MINISTER: Beard and Dolmillington.

SHANKLY: That's right.

PRIME MINISTER: The managing director's name- I'm going back 30 years – was A.K. McKosh.

SHANKLY: That's the man. I was in that area. Even then there was nothing but pessimism. It was a mining area. If you couldn't play football you were out. You had no job.

PRIME MINISTER: We are now developing new sources of mining in Scotland in areas that were nearly closed. We're putting in a lot of money now to develop new seams, because there's new methods now for mining.

SHANKLY: The area I was in was only scratched.

PRIME MINISTER: We're going out to sea. The North Sea has got coal as well as oil – and there are new ways of getting them.

SHANKLY: Under the sea at Fife and all.

PRIME MINISTER: I like going to coal mining areas, I like getting out of London. I've got nothing against London, there are some wonderful people there. But if you are going to have any job to do with politics or running this country you've got to get out and meet people where they are – not just in London. I know there are demonstrators – I don't worry about them. This afternoon I was surprised, even in Liverpool where a couple of times a month there would be crowds outside. They weren't demonstrating either – when I was opening a community health centre. But I like to be out of London on a Friday and go around the country and meet people – real people. Get away from the hot-house atmosphere of politics.

SHANKLY: As you say, I think that the House of Commons is a hot-house. I mean being in it all week it must be a tremendous feeling to get out of it, to get away.

PRIME MINISTER: Yes, it's a great job to do but everybody who's there will do it better if they refresh themselves . . .

SHANKLY: Yes, you can be too close to it for too long – you can't see the wood for trees.

PRIME MINISTER: That's right. You need a breath of fresh air.

SHANKLY: Fresh? When you come to Liverpool?

PRIME MINISTER: I've been here three times in the last month, and I shall be coming up five times in the next couple of months. You know I once paid you that tribute at a football dinner. I said you were the fairest-minded man I've ever met when you said there were two good teams in football on Merseyside. No I did say, if you remember, I criticised you a bit for that . . . for not mentioning Tranmere Rovers. You then agreed with me – you did a lot to help Tranmere Rovers from Liverpool.

SHANKLY: I did last season for a little while . . .

PRIME MINISTER: Before that. When you were manager.

SHANKLY: Oh yes. We were trying to help ourselves as well.

PRIME MINISTER: That makes sense, doesn't it?

SHANKLY: But we did try to help them, there is no doubt about that, and we've helped many people. And if you can't help people then it's a bad day.

PRIME MINISTER: Yes.

SHANKLY: Yes. I've played football all my life and I've been in the game 43 years now. I try to keep fit. I mean I've got an easier task than you, of course, but have you lost a little weight . . . ? I think you have. You look well.

PRIME MINISTER: I have lost about a stone.

SHANKLY: So how do you keep fit?

PRIME MINISTER: Not in the ways I would like to. I would like a lot more exercise. When I was at Downing Street before, I used to play golf every weekend when I could, you know, and I played a bit of golf. And then I got a gammy knee a couple of years ago. And now I've taken it up again this year. My problem is there's so much, things are moving at such a pace all the time, internationally and nationally, that I haven't had the exercise. I take the dog for a walk – he likes that. But I haven't had time to play golf since I came back from my holidays.

SHANKLY: So in actual fact . . .

PRIME MINISTER: . . . the answer is 'not enough'.

SHANKLY: Mr Wilson. Not enough but I think that possibly dieting – if you're not getting too much exercise but I think you should have a . . .

PRIME MINISTER: The real truth is you know, it's not

dieting. Although the doctor thought I was mad, I started drinking a lot of beer – I like it – it makes me eat less. Now I think I'm a bad guinea pig because most people put weight on with beer. But it works with me. I wouldn't recommend it to any of our footballers!

SHANKLY: If you drink more beer and you eat less, then I mean, you're losing weight... then it must be working. Because you look fit now. And you must have shed a few pounds.

PRIME MINISTER: I'm much fitter. I'm lower now than I have been for 15 years.

SHANKLY: Is it possible that you could get a routine, that you could go and have a walk – two or three miles?

PRIME MINISTER: I can't get the time. I do when I try to – to arrange golf, it means arranging a partner, some friend to come out and then suddenly you find you can't do it and it's not fair to him. But that dog's waiting all the time! And if I get the chance of an hour – he's now found the way to the local pub from Chequers!

SHANKLY: That's your dog, Paddy?

PRIME MINISTER: Yes. A great big soft, daft Labrador.

SHANKLY: Is there any way at home, Mr Wilson, you can get away from the people who are surrounding you all the time and have a walk?

PRIME MINISTER: Yes. Yes. Yes.

SHANKLY: You can do that? Do you do that daily or nightly?

PRIME MINISTER: I wouldn't have time but if I did have time, well, I mean, I'd have to have security protection because a lot of strange people are around these days. But they're good fun, my security people. We've played golf together, my detectives and I, we go boating together. Long holidays is my answer. I take a long holiday because I never know when I'll be brought back. Sometimes I've been brought back for a week in the middle of the summer holidays, so I go for three weeks' holiday as I get hardly any Saturdays or Sundays off. If I'm not brought back by a crisis – and I wasn't this summer – then it's a long holiday and I enjoy it.

SHANKLY: You go to the Scilly Isles.

PRIME MINISTER: Always. Yes. Walking, walking, swimming, boating.

SHANKLY: Wonderful.

PRIME MINISTER: A bit of fishing.

SHANKLY: But this is the whole thing. If you keep fit it's got to be regular.

PRIME MINISTER: It should be.

SHANKLY: It's got to be a little often. And the way to eat and keep fit and not put weight on is to do it often.

PRIME MINISTER: But there is a bigger thing than this and that's sleep. I can always sleep. Last week when I was tired I slept for 10 hours... and nine hours the next day.

SHANKLY: Mr Wilson, if you can sleep that well, you have a long life.

PRIME MINISTER: And the answer is 'never worry'. If you worry in the night – you say, 'If this problem can be solved I'll do it better at nine o'clock than three o'clock.' I've taught a lot of people how to sleep. Funny! We're talking about beer and now they've brought a glass in from the outside studio. They must have seen me getting thirsty.

SHANKLY: To eat, the proper way to eat is a little – often. Why have a great big meal and then have a long...?

PRIME MINISTER: I don't go in for big meals very much.

SHANKLY: Well in America and some places they have big plates and it's over and above what you need.

PRIME MINISTER: I'm eating a lot less than I was, now.

SHANKLY: Well if you have a little pick...

PRIME MINISTER: I don't eat too often.

SHANKLY: But you have said now that beer for you doesn't put weight on. And your dog – is it out of condition, because some dogs do if they're lying about?

PRIME MINISTER: He gets a little bit of weight. On holiday he walks, I walk him and he walks me, we both walk hard and we're swimming two or three hours a day – he's a beautiful swimmer. I swim a bit at Chequers. In Mr Heath's time some generous people built a swimming bath there, that's a good way of being exercised quickly.

SHANKLY: That's good for you too. Not only that – the exercise you get – but the water refreshes you.

PRIME MINISTER: Yes. I'm not a good swimmer. But I learned to swim on Merseyside at Port Sunlight swimming baths, which is where we used to go from Wirral Grammar School.

SHANKLY: But the water refreshes you...?

PRIME MINISTER: Oh it does. Nothing like sea water. Cold sea water.

SHANKLY: Do you go into the sauna bath?

PRIME MINISTER: No, I've never done that.

SHANKLY: Well, steam baths are good too. Sauna baths are good if you don't have too much of it and then you come out and get into the swimming pool.

PRIME MINISTER: You lose all your weight in the hot bath and then you get thirsty and put it back.

SHANKLY: Well, no I think it refreshes you.

PRIME MINISTER: Does it?

SHANKLY: I think so.

PRIME MINISTER: I like a swimming pool but in Scilly the water is very cold, very pure and invigorating and it's good for me.

SHANKLY: We've come back to a question that's appertaining to football. What's England's chances in the World Cup? First and foremost, of course, they've got to qualify and I would say to you, really, what chances have they got in the European Nations Cup?

PRIME MINISTER: Isn't it time for me to take over the interview? What it should be... well I don't know, I'll simply say that the only time we've ever won the World Cup was when we had a Labour Government – at least we've got that condition fulfilled. I think we were very unlucky in

Mexico – it could have gone much better – we were unlucky. But, I don't know. They're building up a new team. I think in the end they had to break up that very great team of 1966, perhaps clung, tried to keep the team together too long but there's a lot of experiment going on, a lot of brand new lads.

SHANKLY: The next is in the Argentine, which makes it more difficult and possibly advantageous to the Latins, you know.

PRIME MINISTER: The only thing the high altitude in Mexico was good to...

SHANKLY: Mr Wilson, the game should never have been played in Mexico.

PRIME MINISTER: No, no. Any more than the Olympics should. But I think we've a better chance now than I would have thought possibly two or three years ago when we saw that disaster of not getting into the, not qualifying...

SHANKLY: Not qualifying was a killer. Scotland qualified and they were a little unlucky.

PRIME MINISTER: Well, as I say, I saw them in Frankfurt.

SHANKLY: I think that Don Revie now... he's searching out what he can do for the best.

PRIME MINISTER: He's experimenting.

SHANKLY: Well, we were talking about getting the best players and utilising them and possibly it'll take them longer than people think.

PRIME MINISTER: What were you naturally?

SHANKLY: Right-footed. Oh yes.

PRIME MINISTER: But you could do both?

SHANKLY: I was a reasonable kicker of a ball with my left foot but I was naturally right-footed.

PRIME MINISTER: What was your favourite position?

SHANKLY: I played what then was called right half – I was a midfield player. Or I'd be a sweeper-up. We were talking about judgement of course which we had to have. What do you regard as your biggest mistake, if you did have a big mistake?

PRIME MINISTER: Oh well, that's my secret! I have had a number, including some that the commentators in the Opposition have got on to. I think one or two that I would say particularly here. I think, on Rhodesia for example in the 1960s, I thought they really were willing to negotiate and get a solution and I went on. We had meetings on HMS *Fearless* and HMS *Tiger*. I went there and I think I put a lot of energy into it but it was wasted. Now the situation's changed I hope it's going to be alright. But I think I underrated, for example, the economic situation in the 1960s, I didn't realise how virulent could be an attack on sterling, sometimes from people just talking and gossiping without really knowing the facts. I was trying to build up the industrial strength and didn't allow enough, I think, for the fact that we could be knocked sideways by a run on sterling. We've learned a lot from those days – I think those are the kind of mistakes I would . . .

SHANKLY: Well, I wouldn't call that a mistake . . .

PRIME MINISTER: And I think like you. I sometimes put the odd person in the team that afterwards I thought had been a mistake.

SHANKLY: Well, wouldn't call them mistakes . . . I'd call them happenings.

PRIME MINISTER: Not many. You say in football – you don't have mistakes, you have happenings. I like the happenings to lead to a win not a loss.

SHANKLY: What made you become a socialist?

PRIME MINISTER: Really very similar to the reason I think anyone you were brought up with would say. I was brought up in an area, the textile valleys of West Riding, where unemployment, the depression was so great and where my own father was out of work for a year or two. But we didn't have it hard. We didn't have it bad – but a lot of the kids, kids in my patrol in the Scouts, my football team at school, their parents were out of work. Lads in what we now call the 11-plus couldn't go on to secondary schools because of that. I think that's what really started it but a lot of it was, as I say, a partly philosophical influence and mostly from the religious teachers.

SHANKLY: Well I think you are what you are, you're born what you are and I think a man is a socialist at heart.

PRIME MINISTER: I think that's true to a large extent. Though my father voted Labour in 1906, he also worked for Winston Churchill in the 1908 election as his sub-agent. I was brought up on that legend. Perhaps in my mind the Tories never had a chance because I was a little indoctrinated the other way by my family.

SHANKLY: Well I think you are a natural born socialist, and I think that the politics in me is me.

PRIME MINISTER: That's right. It's part of your whole make-up.

SHANKLY: It's part of my make-up. The same as religion is part of my make-up.

PRIME MINISTER: Quite right, absolutely right.

SHANKLY: And football's my religion.

PRIME MINISTER: And do not say that if a person is religious he's got to be a socialist. All I say is if he is a religious person, in my view, he should not feel that his politics and his religion are cohtradictory. He must feel that what he is doing in politics represents his conception of what religion tells him.

SHANKLY: Oh yes, without doubt ... Now who is the best player you ever did see?

PRIME MINISTER: That's difficult ... Alec Jackson of Huddersfield. In three years between 1928 and 1930 they were in the Cup final twice and in the semi final with two replays in the first year.

SHANKLY: And the second team won the Central League three successive seasons?

PRIME MINISTER: They did.

SHANKLY: You mentioned Alec Jackson. The man had great confidence. He was so brilliant.

PRIME MINISTER: He was, and it was a tragedy when he was killed. I'm not saying there is nobody as good today. That sounds like a very old fogey. But I am saying that if I were to start picking out one or two today, I'd be unfair to a lot of others. I think there are people as good as he was today, many would say better. We haven't seen them competing against each other.

SHANKLY: Yes, well I was lucky enough and fortunate enough to play in a team where a fellow called Tom Finney played with me, and of all the players I've seen, I would pick Tommy Finney. Tommy had everything.

PRIME MINISTER: Wasn't there a story, though, that when he replaced Matthews on the wing for a match the centre forward, Stan Mortenson, said: 'It's not the same! Matthews always had the lace placed correctly!'

SHANKLY: Great players both.

PRIME MINISTER: You've brought a lot of them on yourself, haven't you?

SHANKLY: Well we've a team here...they complement other...they play as a team.

PRIME MINISTER: You signed two players from Scunthorpe.

SHANKLY: Clemence for £18,000 and Keegan for £35,000.

PRIME MINISTER: At a time when the ruling rate was a couple of hundred thousand for a first class player.

SHANKLY: Clemence has been a brilliant player.

PRIME MINISTER: I've seen him play some good games.

SHANKLY: Mr Wilson, you and I are sitting here – both from socialist backgrounds. That's not to say that we have no time for anybody else, because, I mean, the whole world's with us. I've got friends in all walks of life. And I don't let politics or religion bother me, I'll tell you that now. That's a fact. But you were honoured with the OBE and so was I, so that's one each.

PRIME MINISTER: We got one each.

SHANKLY: Who's going to get the next goal?

PRIME MINISTER: Well, actually in some ways I think I'm pulling rank...mine was given to me by Winston Churchill! In your case it was a *lesser* Prime Minister who recommended you!

SHANKLY: Very good! A wonderful answer. Wonderful talking to you.

PRIME MINISTER: Well thank you very much – I've enjoyed it!

Shankly and Wilson also came together in the Granada TV studios in April 1981 in an interview by Shelley Rohde. When the subject came round to football this is how the conversation went:

ROHDE: What have you got out of football all these years ?

SHANKLY: Everything I've got I owe to football. You only get out of the game what you out into it, Shelley. So I put in all my heart and soul, to the extent that my family suffered.

ROHDE: Do you regret that at all?

SHANKLY: I regret it very much. Somebody said: 'Football's a matter of life and death to you'. I said: 'Listen, it's more important than that.' And my family's suffered. They've been neglected.

ROHDE: How would you do it now, if you had your time again?

SHANKLY: I don't know, really. If I had the same thoughts, I'd possibly do the same thing again.

ROHDE: So what are the qualities of a good footballer?

SHANKLY: Ability...and dedication to the game. And giving people their money's worth. The players have got an obligation to the public to do that.

ROHDE: You sound as if it's more of an entertainment.

SHANKLY: Well, entertainment comes second for me. Entertainment you can laugh at. I don't laugh at football.

WILSON: It's a religion, too, isn't it?

SHANKLY: I think so, yes.

WILSON: A way of life.

SHANKLY: That's a good expression, Sir Harold. It is a way of life. And it's so serious that it's unbelievable. And I wonder what all the rest of the world does.

The cover of the match programme for Bill Shankly's first game as Liverpool manager when Cardiff City were the Anfield visitors on 19 December, 1959.

5

Shankly's Chosen Few

It seems incredible in this football age, when top clubs regularly call on more than 30 players for first team duty each season, that a mere 71 donned a Liverpool jersey during Bill Shankly's managerial reign from December 1959 to July 1974.

This rather exclusive band provided what will surely prove a permanent entry in football's record books: the lifting of the 42-game League championship in 1966 using only 14 players of which Bobby Graham made just a single appearance and Alf Arrowsmith five, two of them as a substitute.

Aston Villa matched that feat as title winners in 1981 but the Anfield creed of quality before quantity, laid down by Shankly, shone through again when Liverpool used only 15 players in becoming champions in 1979 (under Bob Paisley) and 1984 (under Joe Fagan), both in 42-match programmes.

Thus, Liverpool can claim three of the five smallest championship squads in English football history with Sunderland completing the select nap hand by also using 15 players in 1893, but in a fixture list of only 30 games.

This Anfield trend reached its zenith under Fagan in that 1983–84 season when they became the first English club to win a treble by annexing the European Cup and the League Cup, along with the title, and fielded just 16 players in their 67 games. Of those players, Gary Gillespie appeared only once.

Over a 40-year span Liverpool called on fewer players than any other top-flight club, fielded 52 during the 1960s, an identical total in the 1970s, 54 in the 1980s and 74 in the 1990s.

The select 71 which did duty for Shankly in all competitive first team games over a period of almost 15 years include 11 who made just a single senior appearance, which makes the low total even more remarkable. The complete list, with an asterisk against those who appeared only once, is in alphabetical order:

Alan A'Court, Alan Arnell, Steve Arnold*, Alf Arrowsmith, Alan Banks, Phil Boersma, Derek Brownbill*, Gerry Byrne, Ian Callaghan, Bobby Campbell, Phil Chisnall, Ray Clemence, Peter Cormack, Alun Evans, Roy Evans, Chris Fagan*, Phil Ferns, Jim Furnell, Bobby Graham, Brian Hall, Jimmy Harrower, Tony Hateley, Steve Heighway, Dave Hickson, Alan Hignett*, Emlyn Hughes, Roger Hunt, Alan Jones, Kevin Keegan, Chris Lawler, Frankie Lane, Tommy Lawrence, Tommy Leishman, Kevin Lewis, Billy Liddell, Alec Lindsay, Doug Livermore, Larry Lloyd, Tom Lowry*, Jimmy Melia, John McLaughlin, Gordon Milne, Bill Molyneux*, John Molyneux, Ronnie Moran, Fred Morris (he made 48 appearances but only one under Shankly), John Morrissey, John Ogston*, Steve Peplow, Ian Ross, Dave Rylands*, John Sealey*, Bert Slater, Tommy Smith, Ian St John, Willie Stevenson, Trevor Storton, Geoff Strong, Bobby Thomson, Peter Thompson, Phil Thompson, Max Thompson, John Toshack, Peter Wall, Alan Waddle, Gordon Wallace, Johnny Wheeler, Jack Whitham, Dick White, Dave Wilson*, Ron Yeats.

The Shankly era came long before the dawn of the controversial rotation selection system, first launched on English football by Ruud Gullit at Chelsea and, to a lesser extent, by Sir Alex Ferguson at Manchester United. Now, one of Shankly's successors, the current Liverpool manager Gerard Houllier, is a convinced advocate of rotation.

Its proponents say that the modern game is more demanding and more taxing than yesteryear, that football in the twenty-first century is faster and takes a greater mental and physical toll which makes it imperative to rotate players who have to cover more miles per match than their predecessors.

Opponents of rotation claim that players just want to play, that the mental jolt of being left out of the side, however strong the case made out for their exclusion for reasons other than injury, outweighs any physical advantage that may accrue.

They also point out that the standard of playing surfaces today, protected from the ravages of ice and snow by undersoil heating, are far superior to those on which players had to plough through mud and constantly combat heavy pitches, which was considerably draining on stamina.

Liverpool's appearance figures, from Shankly's arrival until the end of the 1990s, are not down to coincidence. They relate to the philosophy and the climate in which such consistency and freedom from injury could flourish. That flowed from Shankly, who believed passionately in the right preparation for his players. He was a fitness fanatic who created a training and coaching regime in which injuries were anathema.

Asked once what his team was for the following day's match he replied instantly and with characteristic hyperbole: 'Same as last season.' Conversely, if a player was injured he was said by a scornful Shankly to have joined 'the bastards' club!'

Shankly believed that nobody should get hurt and deep in the psyche of a man who worshipped at the shrine of physical fitness, there was, I suspect, a fear of injuries.

How fortuitous, therefore, that his right-hand man Bob Paisley, himself destined to become a managerial legend, was not a only a physiotherapist of massive renown but was armed with a cunning psychology to prevent potential confrontations between Shankly and any player whose fitness was in question.

'Bob had Shanks sussed out,' recalled Shankly's first great centre forward, Ian St John. 'If you wanted to play and Bob felt you were fit to play he'd say: "Tell Shanks you're unfit." When the boss came in he'd ask: "How are you, son?" You'd say: "I don't think I'm fit, boss."

'To which Shanks would invariably reply: "Jesus Christ, son. I've played with worse than that. So has Bob. We used to play in that condition, didn't we Bob?" The upshot was that you'd agree to play and Bob would give you a wink, knowing his ploy had worked again.'

'On the other hand, if you were struggling with a knock or Bob felt you needed a rest you'd go the other way. You'd go to Shanks and say: "I feel OK boss, I think I'm all right to play." Sure enough, he'd come back and say something like: "No, son, you're not right. You were carrying the injury in training."'

Goalkeeper Tommy Lawrence provided another example of life with Shankly. 'I got injured in a Monday match at Wolverhampton early in the 1963–64 season. The muscle had gone in my leg. It was really bad. Shanks wouldn't speak to me after the game but the following morning he asked me how I was. I just said it wasn't too bad because you didn't like saying you were unfit.

'Bob told me to say I was fit and on the Friday, the day before our next game, Shanks got me out. He said: "Right. Come on, run round the pitch." I could hardly walk but after I'd made it round the pitch Shanks asked me how I felt. I said: "I'm fit."

'Well, he nearly exploded! "F——— fit! You're a cripple! A bleedin' cripple! Get out o' ma sight!" As far as Shanks was concerned before he asked me to run round the pitch I could have raced a dozen greyhounds with my kecks down. But as soon as I said I was fit that was me finished! I missed our next two games.

'I remember Shanks sending Alfie Arrowsmith to Coventry when he got injured. He wouldn't speak to him for about three months when he had a bad leg. If you were unfit you were out, you were away, you were nobody then.'

Roger Hunt, one of England's 1966 World Cup heroes, believes there was a positive effect from Shankly's injury phobia:

He thought you shouldn't get injured and, when you considered it, it was good thinking, really, because you felt guilty if you were injured.

I once overheard him talking to Tony Book outside the dressing room when he used to stand in the corridor on match days. Tony had come with Manchester City but he had an Achilles tendon injury and wasn't playing. I heard Shanks saying to him: 'Don't rush that, son. Don't rush it at all.'

Now, if that had been one of us with an injury he'd have said we were malingering. It was a very good thing for Shanks and us that Bob was there because Shanks respected his opinion. Bob knew so much about injuries and treatment. Reuben Bennett was also around the dressing room, too, and you could speak to him as well.

When Bob had hung up his boots as a player he studied physiotherapy and really went into it. He did a good job and was far more knowledgeable than we gave him credit for at the time.

One day, Shanks told us a new muscle machine he'd ordered had arrived from Germany. He got the instruction books out and started reading them. As far as we were concerned the main thing was to make sure you weren't one of the guinea pigs.

As it turned out it was Jimmy Melia who got pulled in to be the first one on the machine, which was set up in the treatment room. You put pads on your legs and when you got to a certain level of pain you knocked it off.

Bob was doing the three or four dials and he asked Jimmy if he could feel anything. 'No', said Jimmy 'turn it up a bit more.' So Bob turned it up. 'I still can't feel anything... a bit more, Bob', said Jimmy. Bob turned it to maximum but then looked round at the electric plug.

At that moment Shanks shouted: 'The ruddy thing's not even switched on,' and gave the mains plug a kick. Boof! Up went Melia! Everyone collapsed in laughter.

Mind you, Albert Shelley, who was the first team trainer, wouldn't go near any of the machines. He was very suspicious of them. 'No, we'll have the old lamp in,' he'd say. Or sometimes he'd give you a rub down.

Shankly's arrival at Anfield had a profound impact on Ian Callaghan, who was then a young amateur wondering what life held for him and if he had a future in football.

The upshot was that he launched a distinguished career that was to bring him European Cup, FA Cup, UEFA Cup and League championship medals, the Footballer of the Year Award in 1974, an MBE and the glorious distinction of making more appearances for Liverpool, 856 in total, than any player in the club's history, a record that will surely stand for ever. Callaghan recalled:

I was on the club's books when Shanks became manager and, typically, he stole the show the first time I met him. I was a 17-year-old apprentice central heating engineer who played in Liverpool's 'A' team and trained twice a week as an amateur at the club's Melwood training ground.

It was March 1960, just three months after Shanks had come from Huddersfield, and our family lived in a tenement block in the Toxteth district of Liverpool, which was hardly the most affluent area.

Shanks wanted me to sign professional and he came to our flat to talk to my parents. His arrival caused a mini sensation. In those days cars were just not seen in Toxteth so you can imagine the stir it caused when Bill Shankly drew up and got out of his Ford Corsair!

We weren't well off and my mum and dad, naturally, were concerned that I should have a steady job. But Shanks convinced them almost instantly that I should sign for Liverpool as a full-time professional. He had that gift and he had a tremendous presence. His charisma was unique.

He told my parents that he would look after me, give me the proper food and get me steaks to build me up because I was very small and a weakling in those days. I discovered, at that moment, as my parents did, that when Bill Shankly said something you believed him.

After meeting him my parents were quite happy for me to be a footballer. So I packed my job in and signed professional for Liverpool. The following month, on 16 April 1960, I made my first team debut. Not only that, but I replaced my boyhood hero, the great Billy Liddell, a magnificent Scottish international, a legend of the Kop and one of the finest players in football history.

It was a home game in the old Second Division against Bristol Rovers. We won 4–0 and, thanks to Shanks, my career was underway. If Bill Shankly said you were going to climb Everest you would believe him. That was part of his management genius.

Whatever the situation he gave you hope and confidence. You never doubted him and you never had any reason to doubt him. He was a leader . . . and you followed him. His powers of motivation were incredible. He could convince you black was white!

From that day when he came to our flat Shanks was a second father figure to me. He did look after me, just as he had promised my parents. I never even had to ask for a pay rise. He did it automatically.

You were always in awe of Shanks but he made you laugh every day. He loved to make people laugh. We used to report to Anfield in the morning before going by coach to our training ground, Melwood, a couple of miles away in the West Derby district of the city.

Shanks would make the journey by car with Bob Paisley and Reuben Bennett. They both told me that on the way Shanks would come out with a few remarks on topical subjects and see how they were received by Bob and Reuben.

If they laughed Shanks would come out with the same line either at team meetings or to the press, whom he would meet after the training session. But if Bob and Reuben didn't laugh in the car Shanks would think up something new. So he actually rehearsed his ad libs! But he had the timing of a great comedian.

Everyone who knew Shanks had the utmost respect for him. It was impossible not to. He was a very clever man. When he arrived at Anfield the place was almost falling down and the transformation of the club into what it is today is due to the magnificent job he did. He took it by the scruff of the neck.

In the process Shanks built an incredible relationship with supporters, more than any manager before or since. He was a man of the people for the people and, as the inscription on his Anfield statue says, he made them happy.

They will still be talking about him a century from now because there's never been anyone like him and there never will be. Cliché it might be, but he was a one-off. They broke the mould when they made Bill Shankly. It was a privilege to know him and an honour to play for him.

The deep affection and bond that developed between Shankly and the public was matched by his power over people. Shankly's first great captain, Ron Yeats, will never forget the aftermath of Liverpool's first ever FA Cup win, achieved with a 2–1 extra time Wembley victory over Leeds on 1 May 1965.

Some 24 hours later Yeats witnessed something extraordinary, an experience that has lived with him. 'When we brought the Cup back to Liverpool on the Sunday evening I've never seen a turn-out of so many people,' he recalled.

'There must have been a quarter of a million, maybe more. It was an amazing sight. They were hanging off buildings, lamp posts, anywhere they could get a vantage point. I wish we'd been on a crowd bonus that night!

'But when we got to the town hall and Shanks stepped forward to speak it was unbelievable. He just put up his hand and 250,000 people fell silent. Then he talked. After each statement he would pause and a huge roar would go up. Then they listened as he talked again. He had the same kind of power over a crowd as you see in the newsreels of Hitler.'

Yet away from the madding crowd, in his small Anfield office, Shankly never forgot individuals. He would personally reply to letters from the public, writing his response on his Empire Corona portable typewriter.

A number of such letters are on display at the Liverpool FC Museum and Visitor Centre, where you can also experience the feel and the atmosphere of the home dressing room before the game that Shankly – and many pundits and punters – rated as the greatest in Anfield history, the 3–1 defeat of world club champions Internazionale of Milan in the 1965 European Cup semi final.

It is a popular exhibit in which I was heavily involved. In the spring of 1997 my friend Brian Hall, one of Shankly's 71 chosen players and who is now Liverpool's public relations executive, asked me to turn back the clock some 32 years.

He told me that the museum centre was to feature a re-creation of the dressing room as it was on that magical night when Inter arrived on 4 May 1965, which came only three days after the club's first FA Cup triumph.

'In the dressing room exhibit we will have life-size models of five players from that Liverpool team,' said Brian. 'We'd like you to write a script for the recording of a conversation between them that might have taken place in the dressing room before they went out to play Inter in that unforgettable match.'

There were to be life-size models of Shankly and Bob Paisley with Shankly's voice cut into the chat between the players. The chosen quintet of former Anfield stars comprised Tommy Lawrence, nicknamed by Joe Mercer as the first 'sweeper keeper' in English football, Ron Yeats, Ian Callaghan, Roger Hunt and Ian St John.

The recordings were done by Mal Jefferson, of Southport-based Mastersound. And he chose Liverpool's current away dressing room as the venue because its acoustics were closer to those of the old home dressing room, which had long since disappeared as part of stadium renovations.

Mal spent a great deal of time making separate recordings of ambience and background noises, including water running into baths, toilets flushing, the sound of studs on the floor as players walked across the dressing room, a ball being bounced against a wall, papers rustling, teapots clanking and the door opening and closing.

He also recorded separate tracks of extraneous sounds such as the 'clip clop' of police horses as they passed the dressing room window outside the ground and, of course, the songs and chants of the Kop, who surpassed themselves that night.

Former players and staff were consulted and asked about the old dressing room so that the layout, colours, paintwork, windows, flooring, coat hooks, benches and other fine detail were painstakingly incorporated.

Writing the script was a welcome challenge and I assembled a memory-jogging list for the five former players.

The FA Cup win loomed large in the material, as did injured
Gerry Byrne and Gordon Milne parading the newly won
trophy around Anfield prior to the kick-off against the
illustrious Italian club.

There was a great deal of enjoyable banter and laughter at
the recording sessions but I was impressed at how quickly the
famous five put their thoughts into fast reverse over a 32-year
span and talked as if they were preparing all over again to run
out and face Helenio Herrera's mighty side, who were
humbled by Shankly's men in an electric atmosphere.

Memories flooded back, including a recollection from Ian
Callaghan which revealed that even the great Shankly
suffered from nerves. 'As we got ready in the dressing room
Shanks would comb his hair about 24 times,' said Ian.
'Actually he didn't comb his hair – he just used to hold the
comb still and move his head from side to side. He'd also
drink several glasses of water.'

The recordings were monitored by Brian Hall and his staff
who then selected the clips they wanted which Mal Jefferson
completed with background effects, including the Kop's
marvellously irreverent rendition of 'Santa Lucia', and
assembled on a continuous audio loop which plays at the
museum display to bring football history to life.

It is also a fascinating study in football history to reflect on
the financial rewards the game offered at the dawn of the
Shankly era. His starting wage after arriving from
Huddersfield was £50 a week and he also refused a contract,
preferring to let his team and results do the talking.

Shankly's starting salary was more than twice as much as
his top paid players in an era just before the maximum wage
was abolished, as revealed in the pay chart from August
1960, the beginning of Shankly's first full season in charge.

Today's bountiful football contracts have made
Premiership footballers the *nouveau riche*. When Shankly
took charge at Liverpool many of his players travelled to
Anfield each day by bus. Now a player could easily own the

LIVERPOOL FOOTBALL CLUB & ATHLETIC GROUNDS CO. LTD
Anfield Road
Liverpool 4

Gentlemen, Officials, Players and Trainers Wages   WEEK ENDING 17 AUGUST 1960

We shall be glad if you will credit the following accounts with the amounts listed in column six and debit our general account with £517:13:2

Name	1 Wages			2 Bonus			3 Less Income Tax			4 Less House rental			5 Less Insurance			6 Nett Amount			Bonus Matches
	£	s	d	£	s	d	£	s	d	£	s	d	£	s	d	£	s	d	
Acourt, A.	23	0	0	4	0	0	5	12	0					9	11	20	18	1	Nantes
Arnell, A.J.	18	0	0				2	11	0	1	17	6		9	11	12	15	7	
Banks, A.	13	0	0				2	0	0					9	11	10	10	1	
Byrne, G.	23	0	0	4	0	0	5	14	0					9	11	20	16	1	Nantes
Callaghan, I.R.	23	0	0	2	0	0	5	17	0					9	11	18	13	1	Nantes
Campbell, R.	15	0	0				1	17	0					9	11	19	13	1	
Carlin, W.	13	0	0				2	12	0					9	11	9	18	1	
Davies, R.	12	0	0				1	8	0					9	11	10	2	1	
Ferns, P.	1	0	0					2	0				–	–		1	2	0	
Green, F.A.	15	0	0				2	5	0					9	11	12	5	1	
Harrower, J.	18	0	0					13	0	1	15	4		9	11	14	16	9	
Hickson, D.	23	0	0	4	0	0	5	5	0	2	1	0		9	11	19	4	1	Nantes
Hunt, R.	23	0	0	4	0	0	4	10	0					9	11	22	8	1	Nantes
Jones, A.F.	16	0	0				1	13	0					9	11	13	17	1	
Lawrence, T.	13	0	0				1	14	0					9	11	10	16	1	
Leishman, T.	23	0	0	4	0	0	6	15	0					9	11	19	15	1	Nantes
Lewis, K.	23	0	0	4	0	0	5	14	0	1	17	6		9	11	18	18	7	Nantes
Liddell, W.	20	0	0				1	7	0	2	0	2		9	11	16	2	11	
Melia, J.	23	0	0	4	0	0	2	12	0					9	11	23	18	1	Nantes
Molyneux, J.A.	20	0	0				4	1	0					9	11	15	9	1	
Moran, R.	23	0	0	4	0	0	5	3	0					9	11	21	7	1	Nantes
Morrissey, J.J.	17	0	0					15	0					9	11	15	15	1	
Nicholson, J.F.	17	0	0				2	2	0					9	11	14	3	1	
Parry, J.E.	14	13	0				2	3	0					9	11	11	17	1	
Reid, S.M.	–	–	–				–	–	–				–	–		–	–	–	
Slater, B.	23	0	0	4	0	0	5	14	0	1	12	8		9	11	19	3	5	Nantes
Twist, F.	5	0	0					13					–	–		4	7	0	
Wheeler, J.E.	23	0	0	4	0	0	5	0	0					9	11	21	10	1	Nantes
White, D.	23	0	0	4	0	0	5	18	0	1	15	1		9	11	18	17	0	Nantes
Training Staff																			
Shelley, F.A.	13	0	0				1	4	0					9	11	11	6	1	
Fagan, J.	16	0	0				–	–	–	1	13	2		9	11	13	16	11	Nantes
Paisley, R.	17	0	0	4	0	0								9	11	19	6	3	Nantes
Bennett, R.	19	0	0				1	13	0					9	11	16	17	1	
Bush, W.T.	17	0	0				1	14	0					9	11	14	16	1	

bus company and be ferried around in a chauffeur-driven limousine such has been the scale of the financial revolution.

Ian St John has some fascinating memories about Anfield earnings even after the abolition of the maximum wage in 1961 and the headline-grabbing elevation of Fulham's Johnny Haynes to the princely sum of £100 a week.

'Shanks and Matt Busby at Manchester United were quite close and I think they got their heads together after the wage ceiling had been lifted,' he said. 'They both had an old-fashioned attitiude towards pay and wages and players at Liverpool and United had a hard battle to get decent salaries.

'I was on a basic of £35 a week and we sent in a deputation of Gordon Milne, big Ron Yeats and Ian Callaghan to ask for an extra tenner a week. They came out with a fiver. So I was on £40 a week until I left Liverpool.'

But the smile on St John's face reflects something on which I am sure all of Shankly's chosen men, whatever their earnings, would agree . . . that they shared something beyond price, namely the honour and privilege of playing for the most charismatic manager the British game has known.

6

A Legend Down the Line

It is powerful testimony to the legend of Bill Shankly, a son of the early years of the twentieth century, that his name lives on in the information super highway of the twenty-first in the form of a website dedicated to his deeds.

Although Shankly died almost two decades before the dawn of the new millennium he is assured of immortality. Far from receding into history his reputation and deeds have been polished and burnished by the passing of time and the website he inspired – http://www.shankly.com – was described by Liverpool FC's own match day magazine as 'an online shrine' to his memory.

It was created by Lanark-based Derek Dohren, a life-long Liverpool supporter born within the sound of the Kop. He explained:

As an IT professional I desperately needed to create a site of my own and Bill Shankly, a man I have long admired since my earliest days on the Kop in the 1960s, was the obvious subject matter.

Thus 'Bill Shankly – the Greatest', as it appeared to the world for the first time in July 1997, began life as no more than a small collection of pages covering most of the well-worn facts and statistics: his playing and managerial records, the ubiquitous quotes, a nod of acknowledgement to Glenbuck and a few column inches of biographical notes.

'But it was the start of something big. With gathering pace the site took on a life of its own, with new material added week after week. I began receiving anecdotes from ordinary people, whose lives had been made all the better for meeting the great man, however briefly.

'Extraordinary stories came in from all over the world, from his former newspaper delivery boy, from fans who stood on the Kop with him, from a man who once bumped into him in a café and from a Greek lad he had invited into his house for a cup of tea and a sandwich.

'The stories captured the warmth, humour, passion and humility of the man whose generosity of spirit made him a legend the world over. Also, in researching his earlier life, I came to realise that the austerity of his childhood, events at Carlise, the war, his time at places like Workington and Grimsby, all helped to make him what he was.

'The Shanks legend is a bit like Buddy Holly or Elvis in that it seems to crystallise every year. But the danger is that the Shankly legend just gets reduced to the "life and death" quote and his name is threatened with turning into some cheesy pop image.

'In fact, he was a humble man, in tune with working people, who found his spiritual home in Liverpool. He had a charismatic quality that raised him above others and made him a born leader.

'Of course, in terms of trophies lifted, matches won, points gained, goals scored and goals conceded Shankly doesn't quite cut it as the best manager of all time.

'He's not even Liverpool's most successful manager. That honour goes, quite clearly, to his successor, the brilliant Bob Paisley. But that's not what shankly.com is all about. The real heart of the website is to be found in the feedback pages, amongst the anecdotes and memories.

'People are reading the site from some really bizarre places. From China, the Faroe Islands, Venezuela, Egypt,

Moldova, Botswana. The name of Shankly is global and that's the best tribute of all to his greatness. To millions of people Shankly WAS the greatest. He connected with them. He was one of them. He gave them a pride and a feeling of worth through his football teams.

'He was special and he made them feel special, too. Not that Shanks was perfect – far from it. After all, it's a perilously thin line that separates passion and commitment from self-centred obsession. But that was the line he walked and walked pretty impressively most of the time.

'It seems to suit the soundbite world we live in to reduce the Bill Shankly legend to nothing more than a couple of over-used and misunderstood quotes. The fight to free Shanks from the awful clichéd caricature must go on. It's an honour to be involved in the battle.

More traditional tributes to Shankly are dotted around Britain. In his Scottish birthplace of Glenbuck, the South Ayrshire pit village consigned to the history books by opencast mining operations, stands a memorial to the old community's most famous son, the greatest in its long history of producing professional footballers.

Further south at Deepdale, home of Preston North End, his former club named their new 6,000-seat North Stand the Bill Shankly Kop, which has a giant portrait of the celebrated Scot crafted into the stand's seating. The man himself would have been delighted that not only does the Kop house the impressive National Football Museum it is also alongside the award-winning Tom Finney Stand, which salutes Preston's club president, the England forward who was hailed by Shankly as a player without peer.

When the Bill Shankly Kop was officially opened in August 1998 the Preston chairman Bryan Gray observed: 'Bill Shankly was one of football's great men. Although he is best known for his time as manager of Liverpool he spent virtually all of his playing career at Deepdale, during which time he won many honours.'

On Merseyside, situated proudly at the Kop stand entrance, is a permanent reminder of Shankly's influence on the Liverpool club, the city and the nation in the form of a 7ft 6in bronze statue of the Anfield legend.

It serves to emphasise not only Shankly's unique place in the annals of the game he graced, both as a player and manager, but also his impact as a social phenomenon in a north-west port city whose golden era had passed and for which hardship, deprivation and unemployment were the new order. Shankly called himself a socialist with a small 's' – 'The first socialist was Jesus Christ', he would say. But Shankly was also a Pied Piper. People followed him. Now they remember him with a discernible warmth.

In April 1997 I stood in a glen in what was then left of old Glenbuck...a few crumbling walls and mainly deserted houses. But as the wind whistled, the hillsides were imbued with the spirit of Bill Shankly. Around 2,000 people attended a moving ceremony witnessed by locals, Liverpool supporters, former players and members of Shankly's family. Accompanied by the skirl of a bagpipe band, Shankly's niece Barbara Alexander officially pulled the drapes from the stone plaque which bears the inscription:

> Seldom in history can a village the size of Glenbuck have produced so many who reached the pinnacle in their chosen sport. This monument is dedicated in their glory and to the memory of one man in particular...Bill Shankly.
>
> The legend, the genius, the man...born here 2nd September 1913, died 29th September 1981. From Anfield with love...thanks Shanks.

The mining community, whose population was never more than 1,200, incredibly spawned 55 professional footballers who played in the top flight in England and Scotland.

Alec Tait, who won an FA Cup winners medal with Tottenham in 1901 when they beat Sheffield United 3–1 in a Burnden Park replay, was the first of them. He was so proud that he persuaded Spurs to let him take the trophy across the border where it was displayed in a Glenbuck shop window.

One of the village's last residents, 92-year-old Agnes Boland, recalled: 'There was poverty but the people had a lovely outlook. They would not walk around thinking they were poor. The men were miners, gardeners and fishermen and, whenever they could, they played football until the daylight went. And the women were all so handy making the things they couldn't afford.'

John Shankly, nephew of Bill, whose four brothers also became professional players, observed: 'If you wanted to get out of the pits it had to be through football. It was the only recreation they had in the wee villages in those days.'

Scottish Coal, whose open quarrying sounded the death knell for Glenbuck, helped fund the Shankly memorial and the former Liverpool manager's towering centre half and first great captain, Ron Yeats, spoke at its unveiling. Accompanied by two other one-time Anfield players, Willie Stevenson and Brian Hall, Yeats told the people braving the elements on the hillside: 'It didn't matter how big you were, Shanks made you feel 10 feet tall. If he hadn't come to Liverpool when he did we would not see the club as it is now and we would not have won the trophies we have done.'

I had the pleasure and privilege of being invited to address a memorial day civic reception at nearby Muirkirk after the ceremony. It was an experience I will always cherish, not least for a spontaneous presentation to Bill Shankly's great-nephew, three-year-old wheelchair-bound Clark Shankly.

Jack Moran, the 67-year-old who spent a week on a charity walk from Anfield to attend the Glenbuck memorial unveiling and whose son John helped organise a football match between a Merseyside eleven and a team of youngsters representing the long defunct Glenbuck Cherrypickers, had the guests in tears. He draped the Liverpool scarf he had worn during his marathon walk around the neck of Clark with the wish that it should stay in the Shankly family.

Guests at the reception also heard celebrated country singer Lee Brennan perform his tribute song 'The Shanks'.

Bill's widow Nessie was unwell and unable to travel to Scotland from her Liverpool home but sent a message expressing her delight at the unveiling of the memorial and its associated events.

Eight months later, in December 1997, homage was paid to Bill Shankly at Liverpool, the club he resuscitated after arriving in 1959, when the wraps were taken off his Carlsberg-commissioned statue in front of the Anfield Visitor Centre, at the opposite end of the ground from the imposing Shankly Gates. Nessie Shankly, accompanied by Bob Paisley's widow, Jessie, attended the ceremony along with former Liverpool players of many generations, including members of the 1947 title-winning team and the sixties and seventies sides as well as current players.

The statue, designed and crafted by Liverpool-born sculptor Tom Murphy who also created statues of John Lennon and Dixie Dean, weighs three-quarters of a ton and captures Shankly with arms outstretched triumphantly in a celebratory gesture. The four-sided plinth was fashioned from Scottish granite with a black granite shoulder, to recall Shankly's days working at the Glenbuck pit as a surface coal grader, and it stands on a red granite disc. The plinth bears the simple dedication: 'Shankly – He Made The People Happy'.

Murphy, whose other works include a statue of Diana, Princess of Wales for the Liverpool Women's Hospital, spent six months on the Shankly statue studying videos and photographs and being advised by Nessie, former Liverpool players and Shankly's tailor Dennis Newton 'to ensure that every button and pleat was correct'.

'That pose was chosen because it was so much HIS pose,'

said Murphy. 'Everyone remembers him standing in front of the Kop crowd like that. 'l wanted to capture the energy of his character and his tremendous presence. I wanted to make it look like a living thing.'

Nessie asked Ron Yeats to perform the opening ceremony by snipping the cord to remove the curtains. He declined to make a public speech but said later:

It was a great honour to be asked to cut the ribbon. Bill was like a second father to me and I have always had nothing but admiration for Nessie, too. There is not enough time in the world to talk about the contribution Bill made to Liverpool Football Club.

It is all very well for managers to take over clubs when they are doing well, when all the structures for success are already there. But when Bill came here the whole thing was falling apart – the team and the stands.

He took this place by the throat and made it great. He was a people's man and he will never be forgotten in Liverpool. He was a great man in football and a lovely man outside football. The other quality Bill had was honesty. If anyone was ever dishonest with him they didn't last long.

Carlsberg spokesman Niall O'Keefe said: 'Bill Shankly was probably the greatest manager in the world and is a legend beyond Merseyside. To many he put Liverpool and English football on the map and laid the foundations for the success of the club today. This statue is our gift to the club and its fans.'

Willie Stevenson, who had been present in Glenbuck, was in attendance at Anfield too, and said: 'Above all, I remember Bill Shankly for his sense of humour. He was a very fair man and nowhere near as hard as people like to make him out to be. He didn't suffer fools but I consider myself fortunate to have played under him. All he wanted was dedication and every man to play for his team-mates.'

Roy Evans, one of Shankly's Anfield managerial successors following Paisley, Fagan, Dalglish and Souness and preceding current boss Gerard Houllier, with whom he spent a short period in a joint-management role, has his own, powerful memories.

'Shanks signed me for Liverpool as a schoolboy,' he recalled. 'Like millions of others I'll never forget him. His name will live as long as football is played.' After his departure from Liverpool in November 1998, ending a 35-year association with Anfield, Evans carried out a special mission steeped in Shankly nostalgia.

He attended an auction on behalf of the Gola company at Christie's South Kensington auction rooms with the aim of securing the last pair of boots Shankly wore during training sessions when he was Liverpool manager. The 1974 boots still bore the initials 'W.S.'

Evans landed the prized boots with a bid of £5,980, more than double the pre-sale estimate, and they were put on display at manufacturers Gola's headquarters at Rawtenstall, Greater Manchester. 'The bidding was far more nerve-wracking than any football match,' Evans admitted.

'I had a man next to me, kicking me, telling me when to bid and when to stop. Shanks meant much to me and to the fans and I was honoured to have taken part. There's a good chance I once cleaned his boots in my early Liverpool days as an apprentice, which was why Gola asked me. I'm sure Shanks would have been delighted with the outcome.'

Football's world body FIFA officially recognised Shankly and his achievements in February 1999 when he was inducted into their International Football Hall of Champions, the award collected on the Shankly family's behalf by Ron Yeats at a glittering ceremony in Barcelona.

Shankly became only the third manager to be granted entry on to the prestigious FIFA scroll following the inaugural induction of Manchester United inspiration Sir

Matt Busby and Dutch legend Rinus Michels. He joined a galaxy of star players including Bobby Moore, Franz Beckenbauer, Sir Bobby Charlton, Johan Cruyff, Alfredo Di Stefano, Eusebio, Sir Stanley Matthews, Pelé, Michel Platini, Ferenc Puskas, Lev Yashin, Just Fontaine, Garrincha, Gerd Muller and Dino Zoff.

A FIFA citation said: 'In accordance with the philosophy of the IFHOC to be elected into this prestigious institution is a recognition of excellence in football, based on achievements and a consistent contribution to the positive image of the game.'

As the old century drew to a close, and the new millennium beckoned, an Anfield afternoon in December 1999 captured the remarkable emotion Shankly's memory still evokes. It was the fortieth anniversary of his landmark arrival as Liverpool manager and players from Shankly's 1965 and 1974 FA Cup-winning sides paraded on the pitch prior to the kick off of the Premiership match against Coventry.

They included Kevin Keegan, Emlyn Hughes, Ian St John, Gordon Milne, Ian Callaghan, Tommy Smith, Brian Hall, Peter Thompson, Roy Evans and Ronnie Moran and tears flowed unashamedly as a moving rendition of Shankly's favourite 'Amazing Grace' was played by a lone Scottish piper and the Kop held aloft a mural depicting a Scottish flag between Liverpool's Eternal Flame.

Keegan, who was England manager at the time, declared: 'It's good to be back home and to have the chance to pay tribute to Bill. He changed my life and I miss him. Liverpool's rise was due to Bill. A lot of people were involved in building this club but everyone would agree that it was down to him.'

Houllier, guardian of the management chalice handed down from Shankly through the generations and the man charged with re-igniting Anfield fortunes, has no doubt about the Scot's elevated place in football's pantheon. 'His greatest legacy to this club was the pride he restored,' said

Houllier, who watched Shankly's team from the Anfield
terraces during his spell on Merseyside as a school teacher.
'Shankly brought belief to the players and made Anfield a
fortress. He had everlasting values of pride and belief that we
must live up to. In the history of football you have around 15
managers or coaches who have influenced their country's or
their club's football and who left a heritage. Bill Shankly is
among them.

'A historian draws inspiration from the great men in
history, what they did and what they brought. A manager
likes to read, listen to and see things about his club. This is
particularly so for me at Liverpool because I'm working at
the club where my heart is.'

Shankly would echo that. He put his heart into Liverpool
and his spirit will forever envelop the club and his name ring
down the ages.

7

The Statistics

Shankly's Record as a Player

Cronberry juniors
Scottish Junior League 1930-32
Carlisle United Division Three North
Joined July 1932
Debut 31 December 1932 v Rochdale
Made 16 appearances

Preston North End
Division Two Joined
July 1933
Debut 9 December 1933 v Hull City (won 5-0)
First League goal v Liverpool, 2 February 1938
Made 297 appearances
Final game v Sunderland 19 March 1949
Scored 13 league goals (8 penalties)

Honours
1933-34 Runners-up Division Two
1936-37 FA Cup Runners-up
1937-38 FA Cup Winners

International Record for Scotland:
1938 v England
1939 v England
1939 v Wales
1939 v Northern Ireland
1939 v Hungary

Wartime internationals:
1940 v England
1941 v England (two apps)
1942 v England (three apps)
1943 v England

Shankly's Record as a Manager

Carlisle United. Joined March 1949
First game in charge, 9 April

Season	P	W	D	L	Pos
1948-49	7	1	4	2	15th Div 3 North
1949-50	42	16	15	11	9th Div 3 North
1950-51	46	25	12	9	3rd. Div 3 North

Grimsby Town. Joined July 1951

Season	P	W	D	L	Pos
1951-52	46	29	8	9	2nd Div 3 North
1952-53	46	22	9	15	5th Div 3 North
1953-54	26	11	4	11	17th Div 3 North

Shankly resigned on 2 January 1954.

Workington. Joined 6 January 1954

Season	P	W	D	L	Pos
1953-54	20	8	6	6	18th Div 3 North
1954-55	46	18	14	14	8th Div 3 North
1955-56	19	9	3	7	

Shankly resigned as manager on 15 November 1955

Huddersfield. Joined 10 December 1955
Became manager 5 November 1956

Season	P	W	D	L	Pos
1956-57	26	11	4	11	12th Div 2
1957-58	42	14	16	12	9th Div 2
1958-59	42	16	8	16	14th Div 2
1959-60	19	8	5	6	6th Div 2

Shankly resigned on 1 December 1959

Liverpool. Joined December 1959
First game 19 December

Shankly's Record at Liverpool

Season	Lge Pos	FA Cup	Lge Cup	Euro	Charity Shield
1959-60	3 (Div 2)	4	–	dnq	
1960-61	3 (Div 2)	4	3	dnq	
1961-62	1 (Div 2)	5	dne	dnq	
1962-63	8	Sf	dne	dnq	
1963-64	Champions	Qf	dne	dnq	
1964-65	7	Winners	dne	EC Sf	Jt winners
1965-66	Champions	R3	dne	CWC F	Jt winners
1966-67	5	R5	dne	EC R2	winners
1967-68	3	Qf	R2	FC R2	
1968-69	2	R5	R4	FC R1	
1969-70	5	Qf	R3	FC R2	
1970-71	5	F	R3	FC Sf	
1971-72	3	R4	R4	CWC R2	Losers
1972-73	Champions	R4	Qf	UEFA Winners	
1973-74	2	Winners	Qf	EC R2	

(Shankly also led out the Liverpool team for the 1974 Charity Shield win over Leeds.)

EC European Cup. CWC European Cup-Winners' Cup. FC Inter-Cities Fairs Cup. UEFA UEFA Cup. F Finalists. Sf Semi-finalists. Qf Quarter-finalists. dne did not enter. dnq did not qualify

Season-by-season League breakdown

Season	P	W	D	L	Pos
1959-60	21	11	5	5	3rd Div 2
1960-61	42	21	10	11	3rd Div 2
1961-62	42	27	8	7	1st Div 2
1962-63	42	17	10	15	8th Div 1
1963-64	42	26	5	11	1st Div 1
1964-65	42	17	10	15	7th Div 1
1965-66	42	26	9	7	1st Div 1
1966-67	42	19	13	10	5th Div 1
1967-68	42	22	11	9	3rd Div 1
1968-69	42	25	11	6	2nd Div 1
1969-70	42	20	11	11	5th Div 1
1970-71	42	17	17	8	5th Div 1
1971-72	42	24	9	9	3rd Div 1
1972-73	42	25	10	7	1st Div 1
1973-74	42	22	13	7	2nd Div 1

Shankly's Honours List

1961-62: Division Two champions
1962-63: FA Cup semi finalists
1963-64: League champions
1964-65: FA Cup winners, European Cup semi finalists, Charity Shield jt. winners
1965-66: League champions, European Cup Winners Cup runners up, Charity Shield jt. winners
1966-67: Charity Shield winners
1968-69: League runners-up
1970-71: FA Cup runners-up, European Fairs Cup semi finalists
1972-73: League champions, UEFA Cup winners, Manager of the Year
1973-74: FA Cup winners, League runners-up, OBE in Queen's Birthday Honours List
1978:   PFA Merit Award

Shankly's games as Liverpool manager

	P	**W**	**D**	**L**
Div. 1	504	260	129	115
Div. 2	105	59	23	23
FA Cup	75	40	22	13
L/Cup	30	13	9	8
Europe	65	34	13	18
C/Shield	5	2	2	1
Total	784	408	198	178

Shankly's managerial record in Mersey derbies

1962-63: Everton 2 Liverpool 2, Liverpool 0 Everton 0
1963-64: Liverpool 2 Everton 1, Everton 3 Liverpool 1
1964-65: Liverpool 0 Everton 4, Everton 2 Liverpool 1
1965-66: Liverpool 5 Everton 0, Everton 0 Liverpool 0 ,
1966-67: Everton 3 Liverpool 1, Liverpool 0 Everton 0
          Everton 0 Liverpool 1 (FA Charity Shield)
          Everton 1 Liverpool 0 (FA Cup 5)
1967-68: Liverpool 1 Everton 0, Everton 1 Liverpool 0
1968-69: Everton 0 Liverpool 0, Liverpool 1 Everton 1
1969-70: Everton 0 Liverpool 3, Liverpool 0 Everton 2
1970-71: Liverpool 3 Everton 2, Everton 0 Liverpool 0
          Liverpool 2 Everton 1 (FA Cup semi final)
1971-72: Everton 1 Liverpool 0, Liverpool 4 Everton 0
1972-73: Liverpool 1 Everton 0, Everton 0 Liverpool 2
1973-74: Everton 0 Liverpool 1, Liverpool 0 Everton 0
TOTAL: Played 27, won 11, drawn 8, lost 8

Liverpool match by match through the
Shankly years

Season 1959-60 (December to April)

Football League Division 2

Date	Venue	Opponents	Score H.T.	F.T.
1959				
19th December	H	Cardiff City	0.2	0.4
26th December	A	Charlton Athletic	0.1	0.3
28th December	H	Charlton Athletic	0.0.	2.0
1960				
2nd January	A	Hull City	1.0	1.0
16th January	H	Sheffield United	2.0	3.0
23rd January	A	Middlesbrough	3.1	3.3
13th February	A	Plymouth Argyle	1.1	1.1
20th February	H	Swansea Town	2.0	4.1
27th February	A	Brighton & Hove Albion	1.0	2.1
5th March	H	Stoke City	3.0	5.1
12th March	A	Portsmouth	1.0	1.2
19th March	H	Huddersfield Town	2.0	2.2
30th March	A	Aston Villa	3.0	4.4
2nd April	H	Lincoln City	1.2	1.3
6th April	H	Derby County	0.1	4.1
9th April	A	Leyton Orient	0.2	0.2
16th April	H	Bristol Rovers	1.0	4.0
18th April	H	Rotherham United	1.0	3.0
19th April	A	Rotherham United	0.2	2.2
23rd April	A	Ipswich Town	1.0	1.0
30th April	H	Sunderland	1.0	3.0
FA Cup				
9th January	H	Leyton Orient	1.0	2.1
1st February	H	Manchester United	1.2	1.3

Season 1960-61

Football League Division 2

Date	Venue	Opponents	Score H.T.	F.T.
20th August	H	Leeds United	2.0	2.0
24th August	A	Southampton	1.3	1.4
27th August	A	Middlesbrough	0.1	1.1
31st August	H	Southampton	0.1	0.1
3rd September	H	Brighton	2.0	2.0
7th September	H	Luton Town	2.1	2.2
10th September	A	Ipswich Town	0.1	0.1
14th September	A	Luton Town	1.1	1.2
17th September	H	Scunthorpe	2.1	3.2
24th September	A	Leyton Orient	2.1	3.1
1st October	H	Derby County	0.0	1.0
8th October	A	Lincoln City	0.0	2.1
15th October	H	Portsmouth	1.3	3.3
22nd October	A	Huddersfield Town	1.2	4.2
29th October	H	Sunderland	0.0	1.1
5th November	A	Plymouth Argyle	2.0	4.0
12th November	H	Norwich City	1.1	2.1
19th November	A	Charlton Athletic	1.0	3.1
26th November	H	Sheffield United	1.1	4.2
10th December	H	Swansea Town	2.0	4.0
17th December	A	Leeds United	0.1	2.2
26th December	H	Rotherham United	2.0	2.1
27th December	A	Rotherham United	0.0	0.1
31st December	H	Middlesbrough	2.2	3.4
14th January	H	Brighton & Hove Albion	1.0	1.3
21st January	H	Ipswich Town	0.1	1.1
4th Februry	A	Scunthorpe United	1.1	3.2
11th February	H	Leyton Orient	3.0	5.0
18th February	A	Derby County	3.1	4.1
25th February	H	Lincoln City	2.0	2.0
4th March	A	Portsmouth	2.1	2.2
11th March	H	Huddersfield Town	1.1	3.1
18th March	A	Swansea Town	0.1	0.2
24th March	H	Plymouth Argyle	1.1	1.1
31st March	H	Bristol Rovers	1.0	3.0
1st April	A	Sheffield United	0.0	1.1
4th April	A	Bristol Rovers	1.1	3.4
8th April	H	Charlton Athletic	1.0	2.1
15th April	A	Norwich City	0.1	1.2

22nd April	H	Stoke City	1.0	3.0
29th April	A	Sunderland	0.1	1.1
3rd May	A	Stoke City	1.1	1.3

LEAGUE CUP

19th October	H	Luton Town	1.0	1.1
24th October	A	Luton Town	1.0	5 2
16th November	H	Southampton	0.1	1.2

FA CUP

7th January	H	Coventry city	2.0	3 2
28th January	H	Sunderland	0.2	0 2

Season 1961-62

Football League Division 2

Date	Venue	Opponents	Score	
			H.T.	F.T.
19th August	A	Bristol Rovers	1.0	2.0
23rd August	H	Sunderland	0.0	3.0
26th August	H	Leeds United	1.0	5.0
30th August	A	Sunderland	0.0	4.1
2nd September	A	Norwich City	0.1	2.1
9th September	H	Scunthorpe United	2.1	2.1
16th September	A	Brighton	0.0	0.0
20th September	A	Newcastle	2.0	2.1
23rd September	H	Bury	2.0	5.0
30th September	A	Charlton Athletic	1.0	4.0
4th October	H	Newcastle	1.0	2.0
7th October	A	Middlesbrough	0.0	0.2
14th October	H	Walsall	1.1	6.1
21st October	A	Derby County	0.1	0.2
28th October	H	Leyton Orient	1.2	3.3
4th November	A	Preston North End	1.0	3.1
11th November	H	Luton Town	1.0	1.1
18th November	A	Huddersfield	2.1	2.1
25h November	H	Swansea	0.0	5 0
2nd December	A	Southampton	0.1	0 2
9th December	H	Plymouth Argyle	1.1	2.1
16th December	H	Bristol Rovers	1.0	2.0
23rd December	A	Leeds United	0.0	0.1
26th December	A	Rotherham United	0.0	0.1
13th January	H	Norwich City	2.1	5.4
20th January	A	Scunthorpe	1.1	1.1

3rd February	H	Brighton	0.1	3.1
10th February	A	Bury	2.0	3.0
24th February	H	Middlesbrough	2.1	5.1
3rd March	A	Walsall	0.0	1.1
10th March	H	Derby County	2.1	4.1
17th March	A	Leyton Orient	0.1	2.2
24th March	H	Preston North End	3.0	4.1
28th March	H	Rotherham United	0.0	4.1
31st March	A	Luton Town	0.1	0.1
7th April	H	Huddersfield Town	0.1	1.1
21st April	H	Southampton	2.0	2.0
23rd April	H	Stoke City	1.1	2.1
24th April	A	Stoke City	0.0	0.0
28th April	A	Plymouth Argyle	1.1	3.2
30th April	H	Charlton Athletic	0.0	2.1
4th May	A	Swansea	2.1	2.4

FA CUP

6th January	H	Chelsea	4.1	4.3
27th January	A	Oldham Athletic	0.0	2.1
17th February	H	Preston North End	0.0	0.0
21st February	A	Preston North End	0.0	0.0
27th February	N*	Preston North End	0.0	0.1

*at Old Trafford

Season 1962-63

Football League Division 1

Date	Venue	Opponents	Score	
			H.T.	F.T.
18th August	H	Blackpool	0.0	1.2
22nd August	A	Manchester City	1.1	2.2
25th August	A	Blackburn Rovers	0.0	0.0
29th August	H	Manchester City	1.1	4.1
1st September	H	Sheffield United	1.0	2.0
3rd September	A	West Ham	0.1	0.1
8th September	A	Nottingham Forest	0.1	1.3
12th September	H	West Ham	1.0	2.1
15th September	H	Ipswich Town	1.0	1.1
22nd September	A	Everton	1.1	2.2
29th September	A	Wolves	1.1	23
6th October	H	Bolton Wanderers	1.0	1.0
13th October	A	Leicester	0.2	0.3
27th October	A	West Bromwich A.	0.1	0.1

				3rd
November	H	Burnley	0.1	1.2
10th November	A	Manchester United	0.1	3.3
14th November	H	Arsenal	0.0	2.1
17th November	H	Leyton Orient	3.0	5.0
24th November	A	Birmingham City	0.0	2.0
1st December	H	Fulham	0.0	2.1
8th December	A	Sheffeld Wednesday	1.0	2.0
15th December	A	Blackpool	1.1	2.1
22nd December	H	Blackburn Rovers	1.1	3.1
13th February	H	Aston Villa	3.0	4.0
16th February	H	Wolves	1.0	4.0
2nd March	H	Leicester	0.1	0.2
5th Marth	A	Ipswich Town	2.1	2.2
9th March	A	Arsenal	2.1	2.2
20th March	H	West Bromwich A.	0.0	2.2
23rd March	A	Burnley	1.0	3.1
8th April	H	Everton	0.0	0.0
12th April	H	Tottenham	0.2	5.2
13th April	H	Manchester United	0.0	1.0
l5th April	A	Tottenham	1.3	2.7
18th April	H	Nottingham Forest	0.2	0.2
20th April	A	Fulham	0.0	0.0
29th April	H	Sheffield Wednesday	0.1	0 2
2nd May	A	Leyton Orient	1.2	1.2
8th May	H	Birmingham City	1.0	5.1
11th May	A	Sheffield United	0.0	0.0
13th May	A	Bolton Wanderers	0.0	0.1
18th May	A	Aston Villa	0.0	0.2

FA CUP

9th January	A	Wrexham	1.0	3.0
26th January	A	Burnley	1.0	1.1
20th February	H	Burnley	1.1	2.1†
16th March	A	Arsenal	1.0	2.1
30th March	H	West Ham	0.0	1.0
27th April	N*	Leicester	0.1	0.1

*at Hillsborough   † after extra time

Season 1963-64

Football League Division 1

Date	Venue	Opponents	Score	
			H.T.	F.T.
24th August	A	Blackburn Rovers	0.1	2.1
28th August	H	Nottingham Forest	0.1	1.2
31st August	H	Blackpool	0.2	1.2
3rd September	A	Nottingham Forest	0.0	0.0
7th September	A	Chelsea	1.1	3.1
9th September	A	Wolves	1.1	3.1
14th September	H	West Ham	0.2	12
16th September	H	Wolves	2.0	6.0
21st September	A	Sheffield United	0.1	0.3
28th September	H	Everton	1.0	2.1
5th October	H	Aston Villa	2.2	5.2
9th October	H	Sheffield Wednesday	1.1	3.1
19th October	H	West Bromwich A.	1.0	1.0
26th October	A	Ipswich Town	2.1	2.1
2nd November	H	Leicester	0.1	0.1
9th November	A	Bolton Wanderers	1.1	2.1
16th November	H	Fulham	0.0	2.0
23rd November	A	Manchester United	0.0	1.0
30th November	H	Burnley	0.0	2.0
7th December	A	Arsenal	0.0	1.1
14th December	H	Blackburn Rovers	0.1	1.2
21st December	A	Blackpool	0.0	1.0
26th December	H	Stoke City	1.1	6.1
11th January	H	Chelsea	0.1	2.1
18th January	A	West Ham	0.1	0.1
1st February	H	Sheffield United	4.0	6.1
8th February	A	Everton	0.2	1.3
19th February	A	Aston Villa	2.2	2.2
22nd February	H	Birmingham City	1.0	2.1
4th March	A	Sheffield Wednesday	0.1	2.2
7th March	H	Ipswich Town	1.0	6.0
14th March	A	Fulham	0.0	0.1
21st March	H	Bolton Wanderers	2.0	2.0
27th March	A	Tottenham	1.0	3.1
28th March	A	Leicester	1.0	2 0
30th March	H	Tottenham	2.1	3.1
4th April	H	Manchester United	2.0	3.0
14th April	A	Burnley	1.0	3.0

18th April	H	Arsenal	2.0	5.0
22nd April	A	Birmingham City	0.3	1.3
25th April	A	West Bromwich A.	2.0	2.2
29th April	A	Stoke City	0.0	1.3

FA CUP

4th January	H	Derby County	2.0	5.0
25th January	H	Port Vale	0.0	0.0
27th January	A	Port Vale	1.0	2.1†
15th February	A	Arsenal	1.0	1.0
29th March	H	Swansea	0.2	1.2

† after extra time

Season 1964-65

Football League Division 1

Date	Venue	Opponents	Score	
			H.T.	F.T.
22nd August	H	Arsenal	1.0	3.2
26th August	A	Leeds United	1.2	2.4
29th August	A	Blackburn Rovers	2.0	2.3
2nd September	H	Leeds United	0.1	2.1
5th September	H	Blackpool	0.1	2.2
9th September	A	Leicester	0.1	0.2
12th September	A	Sheffield Wednesday	0.1	0.1
14th September	H	Everton	0.3	0.4
26th September	H	Aston Villa	2.1	5.1
7th October	H	Sheffield United	1.1	3.1
10th October	A	Birmingham City	0.0	0.0
13th October	H	Leicester	0.1	0.1
17th October	H	West Ham	2.1	2.2
24th October	A	West Bromwich A.	0.2	0.3
31st October	H	Manchester United	0.1	0.2
7th November	A	Fulham	0.1	1.1
14th November	H	Nottingham Forest	1.0	2.0
21st November	A	Stoke City	1.1	1.1
28th November	H	Tottenham	1.0	1.1
5th December	A	Burnley	1.0	5.1
12th December	A	Arsenal	0.0	0.0
19th December	H	Blackburn Rovers	2.1	3 2
26th December	A	Sunderland	2.0	3.2
28th December	H	Sunderland	0.0	0.0
2nd January	A	Blackpool	0.2	3.2

16th January	H	Sheffield Wednesday	1.1	4.2
6th February	A	Aston Villa	1.0	1.0
13th February	H	Wolves	0.1	2.1
24th February	H	Birmingham City	1.1	4.3
27th February	A	West Ham	1.0	1.2
13th March	A	Sheffield United	0.2	0.3
20th March	H	Fulham	1.2	3.2
1st April	A	Nottingham Forest	1.1	2.2
3rd April	H	Stoke City	0.1	3.2
6th April	H	West Bromwich A.	0.1	0.3
9th April	A	Tottenham	0.1	0.3
12th April	A	Everton	0.2	1.2
16th April	A	Chelsea	0.2	0.4
17th April	H	Burnley	0.0	1.1
19th April	H	Chelsea	2.0	2.0
24th April	A	Manchester United	0.1	0.3
26th April	A	Wolves	2.0	3.1

FA CUP

9th January	A	West Bromwich A.	1.0	2.1
30th January	H	Stockport County	0.1	1.1
3rd February	A	Stockport County	1.0	2.0
20th February	A	Bolton Wanderers	0.0	1.0
6th March	A	Leicester	0.0	0.0
10th March	H	Leicester	0.0	1.0
27th March	N*	Chelsea	0.0	2.0
1st May	N**	Leeds United	0.0	2.1 ET

CHARITY SHIELD

15th August	H	West Ham	1.1	2.2

EUROPEAN CUP

17th August	A	Reykjavik	0.0	5.0
14th September	H	Reykjavik	2.1	6.1
25th November	H	Anderlecht	2.0	3.0
16th December	A	Anderlecht	0.0	1.0
10th February	A	Cologne	0.0	0.0
17th February	H	Cologne	0.0	0.0
24th February	N	Cologne***	2.1	2.2 ET†
4th May	H	Inter Milan	2.1	3.1
12th May	A	Inter Milan	0.0	0.3

* Villa Park   ** Wembley   *** In Rotterdam   † won on spin of disk

Season 1966-67

Football League Division 1

Date	Venue	Opponents	Score	
			H.T.	F.T.
21st August	A	Leicester	1.0	3.1
28th August	H	Sheffield United	0.0	0.1
1st September	A	Sheffield United	0.0	0.0
4th September	A	Blackpool	1.2	3.2
6th September	A	West Ham	4.0	5.1
11th September	H	Fulham	1.0	2.1
15th September	H	West Ham	0.1	1.1
18th September	A	Tottenham	0.1	1.2
25th September	H	Everton	1.0	5.0
2nd October	H	Aston Villa	1.0	3.1
9th October	A	Manchester United	0.1	0.2
16th October	H	Newcastle	2.0	2.0
23rd October	A	West Bromwich A.	0.1	0.3
30th October	H	Nottingham Forest	0.0	4.0
6th November	A	Sheffield Wednesday	0.0	2.0
13th November	H	Northampton Town	3.0	5.0
17th November	H	Blackburn Rovers	3.0	5.2
20th November	A	Stoke City	0.0	0.0
27th November	H	Burnley	1.0	2.1
4th December	A	Chelsea	0.0	1.0
11th December	H	Arsenal	1.1	4.2
18th December	A	Newcastle	0.0	0.0
27th December	H	Leeds United	0.1	0.1
28th December	A	Leeds United	1.0	1.0
1st January	H	Manchester United	1.1	2.1
8th January	A	Arsenal	0.0	1.0
15th January	H	West Bromwich A.	2.2	2.2
29th January	H	Leicester	0.0	1.0
5th February	A	Blackburn Rovers	2.1	4.1
12th February	H	Sunderland	0.0	4.0
19th February	H	Blackpool	2.1	4.1
26th February	A	Fulham	0.1	0.2
12th March	H	Tottenham	0.0	1.0
19th March	A	Everton	0.0	0.0
26th March	A	Aston Villa	1.0	3.0
6th April	H	Sheffield Wednesday	1.0	1.0
9th April	A	Northampton Town	0.0	0.0

11th April	A	Sunderland	2.2	2.2
16th April	H	Stoke City	1.0	2.0
23rd April	A	Burnley	0.1	0.2
30th April	H	Chelsea	0.0	2.1
10th May	A	Nottingham Forest	0.0	1.1

CHARITY SHIELD

14th August	A	Manchester United	1.1	2.2

FA CUP

22nd January	H	Chelsea	1.1	1.2

EUROPEAN CUP WINNERS CUP

29th September	A	Juventus	0.0	0.1
13th October	H	Juventus	2.0	2.0
1st December	H	Liege	1.0	3.1
15th December	A	Liege	0.1	2.1
1st January	A	Honved	0.0	0.0
8th March	H	Honved	1.0	2.0
14th April	A	Celtic	0.0	0.1
19th April	H	Celtic	0.0	2.0
5th May	N*	Borussia Dortmund	0.0	1.2

* at Hampden Park, Glasgow

Season 1965-66

Football League Division 1

Date	Venue	Opponents	Score	
			H.T.	F.T.
20th August	H	Leicester	2.2	3.2
24th August	A	Manchester City	1.1	1.2
27th August	A	Everton	0.1	1.3
30th August	H	Manchester City	2.0	3.2
3rd September	A	West Ham	0.1	11
5th September	A	Blackpool	1.1	21
10th September	H	Sheffield Wednesday	1.1	1.1
17th September	A	Southampton	1.0	2.1
24th September	H	Sunderland	1.1	2 2
1st October	A	Aston Villa	1.1	3.2
8th October	H	Fulham	2.2	2.2
15th October	A	Nottingham Forest	1.1	1.1
29th October	A	Stoke City	0.1	0.2
5th November	H	Nottingham Forest	1.0	4.0

9th November	H	Burnley	1.0	2.0
12th November	A	Newcastle	1.0	2.0
19th November	H	Leeds	1.0	5.0
26th November	A	West Bromwich A	0.1	1.2
3rd December	H	Sheffield United	0.0	1.0
10th December	A	Manchester United	2.2	2.2
24th December	A	Chelsea	2.0	2.1
26th December	H	Chelsea	0.0	2.1
31st December	H	Everton	0.0	0.0
7th January	H	West Ham	2.0	2.0
14th January	A	Sheffield Wednesday	1.0	1.0
18th January	A	Leicester	0.0	1.2
21st January	H	Southampton	2.1	2.1
4th February	A	Sunderland	2.1	2.2
11th February	H	Aston Villa	1.0	1.0
25th February	A	Fulham	0.1	2.2
4th March	H	Stoke City	1.0	2.1
18th March	A	Burnley	0.0	0.1
25tm March	H	Manchester United	0.0	0.0
27th March	H	Arsenal	0.0	0.0
28th March	A	Arsenal	0.0	1.1
1st April	A	Tottenham	1.0	1.2
7th April	H	Newcastle	0.0	3.1
22nd April	H	West Bromwich	0.0	0.1
28th April	A	Sheffield United	0.0	1.0
3rd May	A	Leeds United	1.0	1.2
6th May	H	Tottenham	0.0	0.0
13th May	H	Blackpool	1.3	1.3

CHARITY SHIELD

13th August	A	Everton	0.0	1.0

EUROPEAN CUP

28th September	H	Petrolul Ploestl	0.0	2.0
12th October	A	Petrolul Ploestl	0.1	1.3
19th October	N*	Petrolul Ploestl	2.0	2.0
7th December	A	Ajax	0.4	1.5
14th December	H	Ajax	0.0	2.2

FA CUP

28th January	A	Watford	0.0	0.0
1st February	H	Watford	2.0	3.1

18th February	H	Aston Villa	0.0	1.0
11th March	A	Everton	0.1	0.1

* at Brussels

Season 1967-68

Football League Division 1

Date	Venue	Opponents	Score	
			H.T.	F.T.
19th August	A	Manchester City	0.0	0.0
22nd August	H	Arsenal	1.0	2.0
26th August	H	Newcastle	3.0	6.0
28th August	A	Arsenal	0.1	0.2
2nd September	A	West Bromwich A.	1.0	2.0
5th September	A	Nottingham Forest	0.0	1.0
9th September	H	Chelsea	1.0	3.1
16th September	A	Southampton	0.1	0.1
23rd September	H	Everton	0.0	1.0
30th September	H	Stoke City	1.1	2.1
7th October	A	Leicester	1.0	1.2
14th October	H	West Ham	2.0	3.1
24th October	A	Burnley	0.1	1.1
28th October	H	Sheffield Wednesday	1.0	1.0
4th November	A	Tottenham	0.1	1.1
11th November	H	Manchester United	0.2	1.2
18th November	A	Sunderland	1.1	1.1
25th November	H	Wolves	1.0	2.1
2nd December	A	Fulham	0.0	1.1
9th December	H	Leeds	2.0	2.0
16th December	H	Manchester City	0.0	1.1
23rd December	A	Newcastle	1.1	1.1
26th December	A	Coventry	1.1	1.1
30th December	H	Coventry	1.0	1.0
6th January	H	West Bromwich A	1.1	4.1
20th January	H	Southampton	0.0	2.0
3rd February	A	Everton	0.1	0.1
12th February	A	Chelsea	0.1	1.3
24th February	H	Leicester	0.1	3.1
2nd March	A	Wolves	0.1	1.1
16th March	H	Burnley	1.1	3.2
23rd March	A	Sheffield Wednesday	1.0	2.1
6th April	A	Manchester United	2.1	2.1
12th April	H	Sheffield United	1.1	1.2
13th April	H	Sunderland	1.1	2.1

15th April	A	Sheffield United	1.1	1.1
20th April	A	West Ham	0.1	0.1
27th April	H	Fulham	2.1	4.1
29th April	H	Tottenham	1.1	1.1
4th May	A	Leeds	0.1	2.1
11th May	H	Nottingham Forest	3.1	6.1
15th May	A	Stoke City	0.0	1.2

LEAGUE CUP

13th September	H	Bolton Wanderers	0.1	1.1
27th September	A	Bolton Wanderers	1.1	2.3

FAIRS CUP

19th September	A	Malmo	1.0	2.0
4th October	H	Malmo	2.0	2.1
7th November	H	Munich 1860	3.0	8.0
14th November	A	Munich 1860	1.1	1.2
28th November	A	Ferencvaros	0.1	0.1
9th January	H	Ferencvaros	0.1	0.1

FA CUP

27th January	A	Bournemouth	0.0	0.0
30th January	H	Bournemouth	2.0	4.1
17th February	A	Walsall	0.0	0.0
19th February	H	Walsall	3.0	5.2
9th March	A	Tottenham	0.0	1.1
12th March	H	Tottenham	1.0	2.1
30th March	A	West Bromwich A.	0.0	0.0
8th April	H	West Bromwich A.	1.0	1.1
18th April	N*	West Bromwich A.	1.1	1.2

* at Maine Road

Season 1968-69

Football League Division 1

Date	Venue	Opponents	Score	
			H.T.	F.T.
10th August	H	Manchester City	1.1	2.1
14th August	A	Southampton	0.1	0.2
17th August	A	Arsenal	0.1	1.1
20th August	H	Stoke City	0.1	2.1
24th August	H	Sunderland	3.0	4.1

27th August	A	Everton	0.0	0.0
31st August	A	Leeds United	0.1	0.1
7th September	H	Queens Park Rangers	1.0	2.0
14th September	A	Ipswich Town	0.0	2.0
21st September	H	Leicester	4.0	4.0
28th September	A	Wolves	3.0	6.0
5th October	A	Burnley	2.0	4.0
8th October	H	Everton	0.0	1.1
12th October	H	Manchester United	1.0	2.0
19th October	A	Tottenham	1.1	1.2
26th October	H	Newcastle	1.1	2.1
2nd November	A	West Bromwich A	0.0	0.0
9th November	H	Chelsea	2.1	2.1
16th November	A	Sheffield Wednesday	1.0	2.1
23rd November	H	Coventry City	1.0	2.0
30th November	A	Nottingham Forest	1.0	1.0
3rd December	H	Southampton	1.0	1.0
7th December	H	West Ham	1.0	2.0
14th December	A	Manchester United	0.0	0.1
21st December	H	Tottenham	0.0	1.0
26th December	H	Burnley	1.1	1.1
11th January	H	West Bromwich A.	0.0	1.0
18th January	A	Chelsea	0.0	2.1
1st February	H	Sheffield Wednesday	0.0	1.0
15th February	H	Nottingham Forest	0.1	0.2
22nd February	A	West Ham	0.1	1.1
15th March	A	Sunderland	1.0	2.0
29th March	A	Queens Park Rangers	1.0	2.1
31st March	H	Arsenal	0.1	1.1
5th April	H	Wolves	1.0	1.0
7th April	A	Stoke City	0.0	0.0
12th April	A	Leicester	1.0	2.1
19th April	H	Ipswich Town	2.0	4.0
26th April	A	Coventry City	0.0	0.0
28th April	H	Leeds United	0.0	0.0
12th May	A	Manchester City	0.0	0.1
17th May	A	Newcastle	0.1	1.1

LEAGUE CUP

4th September	H	Sheffield United	0.0	4.0
28th September	H	Swansea	0.0	2.0
15th October	A	Arsenal	0.1	1.2

FA CUP

4th January	H	Doncaster Rovers	0.0	2.0
25th January	H	Burnley	2.1	2.1
1st March	A	Leicester	0.0	0.0
3rd March	H	Leciester	0.1	0.1

FAIRS CUP

18th September	A	Bilbao	0.2	1.2
2nd October	H	Bilbao	0.1	2.1†

† Bilbao won on toss of disk after extra time.

Season 1969-70

Football League Division 1

Date	Venue	Opponents	Score	
			H.T.	F.T.
9th August	H	Chelsea	1.0	4.1
12th August	H	Manchester City	1.0	3.2
16th August	A	Tottenham	2.0	2.0
20th August	A	Manchester City	1.0	2.0
23rd August	H	Burnley	1.0	3.3
27th August	A	Crystal Palace	1.0	3.1
30th August	A	Sheffield Wednesday	1.1	1.1
6th September	H	Coventry City	1.1	2.1
9th September	H	Sunderland	2.0	2.0
13th September	A	Manchester United	0.0	0.1
20th September	H	Stoke City	2.1	3.1
27th September	A	West Bromwich A.	1.1	2.2
4th October	H	Nottingham Forest	0.1	1.1
7th October	H	Tottenham	0.0	0.0
11th October	A	Newcastle	0.0	0.1
18th October	A	Ipswich	1.1	2.2
25th October	H	Southampton	1.0	4.1
1st November	A	Derby County	0.2	0.4
8th November	H	Wolves	0.0	0.0
15th November	H	West Ham	1.0	2.0
22nd November	A	Leeds United	1.1	1.1
29th November	H	Arsenal	0.1	0.1
6th December	A	Everton	0.0	3.0
13th December	H	Manchester United	1.1	1.4
26th December	A	Burnley	3.0	5.1
10th January	A	Stoke City	1.0	2.0

17th January	H	West Bromwich A.	0.0	1.1
31st January	A	Nottingham Forest	0.1	0.1
16th February	H	Newcastle	0.0	0.0
28th February	H	Derby County	0.1	0.2
3rd March	A	Coventry City	1.1	3.2
7th March	H	Leeds United	0.0	0.0
11th March	A	Southampton	1.0	1.0
14th March	A	Arsenal	0.1	1.2
16th March	H	Sheffield Wednesday	0.0	3.0
21st March	H	Everton	0.1	0.2
24th March	H	Ipswich Town	2.0	2.0
28th March	A	West Ham	0.1	0.1
30th March	A	Wolves	1.0	1.0
3rd April	H	Crystal Palace	1.0	3.0
14th April	A	Sunderland	0.0	1.0
18th April	A	Chelsea	1.1	1.2

LEAGUE CUP

3rd September	A	Watford	1.0	2.1
24th September	A	Manchester City	1.1	2.3

FAIRS CUP

16th September	H	Dundalk	5.0	10.0
30th September	A	Dundalk	2.0	4.0
12th November	A	Setubal	0.0	0.1
26th November	H	Setubal	0.1	3.2

FA CUP

7th January	A	Coventry City	1.1	1.1
12th January	H	Coventry City	1.0	3.0
24th January	H	Wrexham	0.1	3.1
7th February	H	Leicester	0.0	0.0
11th February	A	Leicester	0.0	2.0
21st February	A	Watford	0.0	0.1

Season 1970-71

Football League Division 1

Date	Venue	Opponents	Score	
			H.T.	F.T.
15th August	A	Burnley	1.1	2.1
17th August	A	Blackpool	0.0	0.0

22nd August	H	Huddersfield	2.0	4 0
25th August	H	Crystal Plalce	1.0	1.1
29th August	A	West Bromwich A.	1.0	1.1
5th September	H	Manchester United	1.1	1.1
12th Septmber	A	Newcastle	0.0	0.0
19th September	H	Nottingham Forest	2.0	3.0
26th September	A	Southampton	0.0	0.1
3rd October	H	Chelsea	1.0	1.0
10th October	A	Tottenham	0.0	0.1
17th October	H	Burnley	1.0	2.0
24th October	A	Ipswich Town	0.1	0.1
31st October	H	Wolves	0.0	2.0
7th November	A	Derby County	0.0	0.0
14th November	H	Coventry City	0.0	0.0
21st November	H	Everton	0.0	3.2
28th November	A	Arsenal	0.0	0.2
5th December	H	Leeds United	0.0	1.1
12th December	A	West Ham	2.1	2.1
19th December	A	Huddersfield Town	0.0	0.0
26th December	H	Stoke City	0.0	0.0
9th January	H	Blackpool	1.1	2.2
12th January	H	Manchester City	0.0	0.0
16th January	A	Crystal Palace	0.0	0.1
30th January	H	Arsenal	1.0	2.0
6th February	A	Leeds United	1.0	1.0
16th February	H	West Ham	0.0	1.0
20th February	A	Everton	0.0	0.0
27th February	A	Wolves	0.1	0.1
13th March	A	Coventry City	0.1	0.1
20th March	H	Derby County	1.0	2.0
29th March	H	Ipswich Town	1.0	2.1
2nd April	H	West Bromwich A.	0.0	1.1
6th April	H	Newcastle	1.1	1.1
10th April	A	Stoke City	1.0	1.0
12th April	A	Chelsea	0.1	0.1
17th April	H	Tottenham	0.0	0.0
19th April	A	Manchester United	1.0	2.0
24th April	A	Nottingham Forest	0.0	1.0
26th April	A	Manchester City	2.1	2.2
1st May	H	Southampton	1.0	1.0

LEAGUE CUP

8th September	A	Mansfield Town	0.0	0.0
22nd September	H	Mansfield Town	1.1	3.2†
5th October	A	Swindon Town	0.0	0.2

FAIRS CUP

18th September	H	Ferencvaros	1.0	1.0
29th September	A	Ferencvaros	0.0	1.1
21st October	H	Dinamo Bucharest	0.0	3.0
4th November	A	Dinamo Bucharest	0.1	1.1
9th December	A	Hibernian	0.0	1.0
22nd December	H	Hibernian	1.0	2.0
10th March	H	Bayern Munich	1.0	3.0
24th March	A	Bayern Munich	0.0	1.1
14th April	H	Leeds United	0.0	0.1
28th April	A	Leeds United	0.0	0.0

FA CUP

2nd January	H	Aldershot	1.0	1.0
23rd January	H	Swansea	0.0	3.0
13th February	H	Southampton	1.0	1.0
6th March	H	Tottenham	0.0	0.0
16th March	A	Tottenham	1.0	1.0
27th March	N	Everton	0.1	2.1
8th May	N	Arsenal‡	0.0	1.2

* at Old Trafford   † after extra time   ‡ at Wembley – after extra time

Season 1971-72

Football League Division 1

Date	Venue	Opponents	Score	
			H.T.	F.T.
14th August	H	Nottingham Forest	2.1	3.1
17th August	H	Wolves	2.1	3.2
21st August	A	Newcastle	1.2	2.3
24th August	A	Cystal Palace	0.0	1.0
28th August	H	Leicester	2.2	3.2
1st September	A	Manchester City	0.0	0.1
4th September	A	Tottenham	0.1	0.2
11th September	H	Southampton	1.0	1.0
18th September	A	Leeds United	0.0	0.1
25th September	H	Manchester United	2.0	2.2

2nd October	A	Stoke City	0.0	0.0
9th October	H	Chelsea	0.0	0.0
16th October	A	Nottingham Forest	1.1	3.2
23rd October	H	Huddersfield Town	0.0	2.0
30th October	A	Sheffield United	0.1	1.1
6th November	H	Arsenal	1.1	3.2
13th November	A	Everton	0.0	0.1
20th November	A	Coventry City	0.0	2.0
27th November	H	West Ham	0.0	1.0
4th December	A	Ipswich Town	0.0	0.0
11th December	H	Derby County	2.1	3.2
18th December	H	Tottenham	0.0	0.0
27th December	A	West Bromwich A.	0.1	0.1
1st January	H	Leeds United	0.0	0.2
8th January	A	Leicester	0.1	0.1
22nd January	A	Wolves	0.0	0.0
29th January	H	Crystal Palace	1.0	4.1
12th February	A	Huddersfield Town	0.0	1.0
19th February	H	Sheffield United	1.0	2.0
26th February	H	Manchester City	1.0	3.0
4th March	H	Everton	1.0	4.0
11th March	A	Chelsea	0.0	0.0
18th March	H	Newcastle	3.0	5.0
25th March	A	Southampton	0.0	1.0
28th March	H	Stoke City	1.1	2.1
1st April	H	West Bromwich A.	1.0	2.0
3rd April	A	Manchester United	0.0	3.0
8th April	H	Coventry City	1.0	3.1
15th April	A	West Ham	1.0	2.0
22nd April	H	Ipswich Town	1.0	2.0
1st May	A	Derby County	0.0	0.1
8th May	A	Arsenal	0.0	0.0

LEAGUE CUP

7th September	H	Hull City	2.0	3.0
5th October	H	Southampton	0.0	1.0
27th October	A	West Ham	1.1	1.2

EUROPEAN CUP WINNERS CUP

14th September	A	Servette	0.1	1.2
27th September	H	Servette	1.0	2.0
20th October	H	Bayern Munich	0.0	0.0
3rd November	A	Bayern Munich	1.2	1.3

FA CUP

Date	Venue	Opponents		
15th January	A	Oxford United	0.0	3.0
5th February	H	Leeds United	0.0	0.0
9th February	A	Leeds United	0.1	0.2

Season 1972-73

Football League Division 1

Date	Venue	Opponents	Score	
			H.T.	F.T.
12th August	H	Manchester City	1.0	2.0
15th August	H	Manchester United	2.0	2.0
19th August	A	Crystal Palace	0.1	1.1
23rd August	A	Chelsea	2.1	2.1
26th August	H	West Ham	1.2	3.2
30th August	A	Leicester	2.2	2.3
2nd September	A	Derby County	1.0	1.2
9th September	H	Wolves	1.0	4.2
16th September	A	Arsenal	0.0	0.0
23rd September	H	Sheffield United	3.0	5.0
30th September	A	Leeds United	1.1	2.1
7th October	H	Everton	0.0	1.0
14th October	A	Southampton	1.0	1.1
21st October	H	Stoke City	0.1	2.1
28th October	A	Norwich City	1.0	1.1
4th November	H	Chelsea	1.0	3.1
11th November	A	Manchester United	0.1	0.2
18th November	H	Newcastle	2.1	3.2
25th November	A	Tottenham	2.0	2.1
2nd December	H	Birmingham City	2.3	4.3
9th December	A	West Bromwich A.	1.0	1.1
16th December	A	Ipswich Town	1.0	1.1
23rd December	H	Coventry City	2.0	2.0
26th December	A	Sheffield United	1.0	3.0
30th December	H	Crystal Palace	0.0	1.0
6th January	A	West Ham	0.0	1.0
20th January	H	Derby County	1.1	1.1
27th January	A	Wolves	1.1	1.2
10th February	H	Arsenal	0.0	0.2
17th February	A	Manchester City	0.1	1.1
24th February	H	Ipswich Town	0.0	2.1
3rd March	A	Everton	0.0	2.0
10th March	H	Southampton	2.1	3.2

17th March	A	Stoke City	0.0	1.0
24th March	H	Norwich City	0.0	3.1
31st March	H	Tottenham	0.1	1.1
7th April	A	Birmingham City	0.1	1.2
14th April	H	West Bromwich A.	1.0	1.0
17th April	A	Coventry City	1.0	2.1
21st April	A	Newcastle	1.1	1.2
23rd April	H	Leeds United	0.0	2.0
28th April	H	Leicester City	0.0	0.0

LEAGUE CUP

5th September	A	Carlisle United	1.0	1.1
19th September	H	Carlisle United	2.0	5.1
3rd October	A	West Bromwich A.	0.0	1.1
10th October	H	West Bromwich A.	0.0	2.1†
31st October	H	Leeds United	1.1	2.2
22nd November	A	Leeds United	0.0	1.0
4th December	H	Tottenham	0.0	1.1
6th December	A	Tottenham	0.3	1.3

FA CUP

13th January	A	Burnley	0.0	0.0
16th January	H	Burnley	1.0	3.0
3rd February	H	Manchester City	0.0	0.0
7th February	A	Manchester City	0.1	0.2

UEFA CUP

12th September	H	Eintracht Frankfurt	1.0	2.0
26th September	A	Eintracht Frankfurt	0.0	0.0
24th October	H	AEK Athens	2.0	3.0
7th November	A	AEK Athens	2.1	3.1
29th November	A	Dynamo Berlin	0.0	0.0
13th December	H	Dynamo Berlin	2.1	3.1
7th March	H	Dynamo Dresden	1.0	2.0
21st March	A	Dynamo Dresden	0.0	1.0
10th April	H	Tottenham	1.0	1.0
25th April	A	Tottenham	0.0	1.2
9th May	H	Borussia Moenchengladbach		*
10th May	H	Borussia Moenchengladbach	2.0	3.0
23rd May	A	Borussia Moenchengladbach	0.2	0.1

* 27 mins. Abandoned   † after extra time

Season 1973-74

Football League Division 1

Date	Venue	Opponents	Score	
			H.T.	F.T.
25th August	H	Stoke City	1.0	1.0
28th August	A	Coventry	0.0	0.1
1st September	A	Leicester City	0.0	1.1
4th September	A	Derby County	1.0	2.0
8th September	H	Chelsea	1.0	1.0
12th September	A	Derby County	1.2	1.3
15th September	A	Birmingham City	0.0	1.1
22nd September	A	Tottenham	1.1	3.2
29th September	A	Manchester United	0.0	0.0
6th October	H	Newcastle	1.0	2.1
13th October	A	Southampton	0.1	0.1
20th October	A	Leeds United	0.1	0.1
27th October	H	Sheffield United	1.0	1.0
3rd November	A	Arsenal	0.0	2.0
10th November	H	Wolves	1.0	1.0
17th November	H	Ipswich Town	3.1	4.2
24th November	A	Queens Park Rangers	1.0	2.2
1st December	H	West Ham	1.0	1.0
8th December	A	Everton	0.0	1.0
15th December	A	Norwich	1.1	1.1
22nd December	H	Manchester United	1.0	2.0
26th December	A	Burnley	0.1	1.2
29th December	A	Chelsea	1.0	1.0
1st January	H	Leicester	0.1	1.1
12th January	H	Birmingham City	2.1	3.2
19th January	A	Stoke City	0.0	1.1
2nd February	H	Norwich City	0.0	1.0
5th February	H	Coventry City	1.0	2.1
23rd February	A	Newcastle	0.0	0.0
26th February	H	Southampton	0.0	1.0
2nd March	H	Burnley	0.0	1.0
16th March	H	Leeds United	0.0	1.0
23rd March	A	Wolves	1.0	1.0
6th April	H	Queens Park Rangers	2.0	2.1
8th April	A	Sheffield United	0.0	0.1
12th April	A	Manchester City	1.0	1.1
13th April	A	Ipswich Town	0.1	1.1

16th April	H	Manchester City	4.0	4.0
20th April	H	Everton	0.0	0.0
27th April	A	West Ham	0.1	2.2
2nd May	H	Arsenal	0.0	0.1
8th May	A	Tottenham	0.0	1.1

EUROPEAN CUP

19th September	A	Jeunesse Esche	1.0	1.1
3rd October	H	Jeunesse Esche	0.0	2.0
24th October	A	Red Star Belgrade	0.1	1.2
6th November	H	Red Star Belgrade	0.0	1.2

LEAGUE CUP

8th October	A	West Ham	1.1	2.2
27th October	H	West Ham	1.0	1.0
21st November	A	Sunderland	1.0	2.0
27th November	A	Hull City	0.0	0.0
4th December	H	Hull City	2.0	3.1
19th December	A	Wolves	0.0	0.1

FA CUP

5th January	H	Doncaster Rovers	1.2	2.2
8th January	A	Doncaster Rovers	1.0	2.0
26th January	H	Carlisle United	0.0	0.0
29th January	A	Carlisle United	0.0	2.0
16th February	H	Ipswich Town	1.0	2.0
9th March	A	Bristol City	0.0	1.0
30th March	N*	Leicester	0.0	0.0
3rd April	N**	Leicester	0.0	3.1
4th May	N***	Newcastle	0.0	3.0

1974 CHARITY SHIELD

| | N*** | Leeds United | 1.0 | 1.1† |

N* at Old Trafford   N** at Villa Park   *** at Wembley   † Liverpool won on penalties